Neal Whitten's
Let's Talk!

More No-Nonsense Advice for Project Success

Neal Whitten's
Let's Talk!

More No-Nonsense Advice for Project Success

Neal Whitten, PMP

MANAGEMENTCONCEPTS

MANAGEMENTCONCEPTS
8230 Leesburg Pike, Suite 800
Vienna, VA 22182
(703) 790-9595
Fax: (703) 790-1371
www.managementconcepts.com

Printed in the United States of America

Library of Congress Cataloging-in-Publication Data

Whitten, Neal.
  Neal Whitten's let's talk! : more no-nonsense advice for project success / Neal Whitten.
        p. cm.
  Intended to complement: Neal Whitten's no-nonsense advice for successful projects / Neal Whitten. c2005.
    Includes index.
    ISBN 978-1-56726-199-8
  1. Project management. 2. Project management—Examinations, questions, etc.
I. Whitten, Neal. Neal Whitten's no-nonsense advice for successful projects / Neal Whitten. II. Title. III. Title: Lets talk! : more no-nonsense advice for project success.
IV. Title: More no-nonsense advice for project success. V. Title: No-nonsense advice for project success.

HD69.P75W493 2007
658.4'04—dc22

                                                                    2006103509

10   9   8   7   6   5   4   3   2   1

About the Author

Neal Whitten is a popular speaker, mentor, trainer, consultant, and author in the areas of project management and employee development. He has more than 35 years of front-line project management, software engineering, and human resource experience.

In his 23 years at IBM, Neal held both project leader and management positions. He managed the development of numerous software products, including operating systems, business and telecommunications applications, and special-purpose programs and tools. For three years, he also managed and was responsible for providing independent assessments on dozens of software projects for an assurance group. Neal is president of The Neal Whitten Group, which he founded shortly after leaving IBM in 1993.

Neal is the author of six books, including: *Neal Whitten's No-Nonsense Advice for Successful Projects* (Management Concepts), *The Enter*Prize *Organization: Organizing Software Projects for Accountability and Success* (Project Management Institute); *Managing Software Development Projects: Formula for Success, Second Edition* (John Wiley & Sons); and *Becoming an Indispensable Employee in a Disposable World* (Prentice Hall).

Neal is a frequent presenter and keynote speaker at conferences, seminars, workshops, and special events. He has developed and instructed dozens of project management, software development, and personal development classes, and presented to thousands of people from across hundreds of companies, institutions, and public organizations. He has written more than 80 articles for professional magazines and is a contributing editor of PMI's *PM Network*® magazine.

The services of The Neal Whitten Group include trouble-shooting projects, performing project reviews, training organizations in the practical application of project management principles, and training all members of a project in the adoption of an effective, productive work culture. Popular workshops include *No-Nonsense Advice for Successful Projects,*

Leadership, Accountability . . . and YOU, Project Review Mentoring Workshop, and *Role Clarification Workshop.*

Neal is a member of PMI and has been a certified Project Management Professional (PMP) since 1992. He can be reached through his website: *www.nealwhittengroup.com.*

To Bill and Bobbie Bancroft

(Thank you for being there!)

I also dedicate this book to all of you who "pass it on." *It* can be the gift of sharing a smile, offering a compliment, opening a door, giving up your seat, permitting the car ahead to merge, helping a lost soul in time of need, or any of countless other deeds of heartwarming humanity—be they small or large. At the end of the day, we all want to be noticed, feel appreciated, feel that someone cares—feel that proverbial hand on our shoulder. I honor all of you who have taken a moment to honor another. I encourage you to *pass it along* when someone performs a good deed for you or, even better, initiate the good deed. This inspiration can be contagious and just might be the catalyst to inspire another in the face of despair. *Together, we can all make a big, big difference in the small world that we share!*

. . . and to Barbara!

Table of Contents

Preface

Success does not just happen—it is made to happen. It's born of behaviors and choices that lead to good performance. When we understand what is expected of us in the workplace, our performance rises to the occasion.

How would you like to ask a recognized project management (PM) authority questions regarding *best practices in behaviors* and other project and organizational issues? Now you can! This book answers more than 700 insightful, personal, and sometimes sensitive questions on a broad range of topics. You are sure to find questions reflecting issues you routinely face on your projects and in your organization. It's like having a private chat with your own personal mentor.

The issues that these Q&As address include:

- Accountability, dependencies, and commitments
- Leadership styles, attributes, and behaviors
- Sharing power
- Interpersonal communications
- Resolving conflict through escalation
- Mentoring
- Ethics and integrity
- Awards and recognition
- Personal development, jobs, and careers
- Promoting change in your organization
- Methodologies and processes
- Project culture
- Quality.

The lessons these Q&As teach can have a profound impact on a person, project, or organization in key areas such as leadership, professional maturity, personal initiative, productivity, employee morale, costs, schedule commitments, and customer satisfaction—just to name a few.

Following on the heels of *Neal Whitten's No-Nonsense Advice for Successful Projects*, this book offers more of the no-nonsense advice that has helped countless leaders and projects. Designed and written for *all project stakeholders* (anyone associated with a project) as well as *all employees* in an organization or company, this book is for anyone who aspires to become a consistently effective leader, project member, or employee and therefore more valuable to their project, organization, and company. It is my hope that *Neal Whitten's Let's Talk! More No-Nonsense Advice for Project Success* will make the difference for you between demonstrating consistently successful behaviors and exhibiting weak and ineffective behaviors.

No theories here—this stuff works! Now go make a *bigger* difference!

Best behaviors,

Neal

Acknowledgments

I began my career at IBM. While there, I was most fortunate to come across many people who were inspirational, exceptional coaches or simply believed in me. Though not an exhaustive list, they include Dennis Andrews, Don Barovich, Stan Bernstein, Has Day, Neil Eastman, Don Estridge, Tom Greaves, Bob Manente, Pat McCarty, Joe Stearns, Jim Turner, and Phil Zeiss. It is amazing what an outstretched hand can mean along one's journey. *Thank you!*

I have benefited greatly from all those who have gone before me as well as those who are now immersed in the practice of their crafts—from those just entering the broad field of project management to those who are seasoned veterans. Like many in any field, I have savored successes and sometimes suffered setbacks, all the while learning, growing, improving, and achieving. Of the bright spots I have experienced, I primarily owe those opportunities and moments to the many practitioners and supporters around me. I am most grateful for their influence in helping me be far better than would otherwise have been possible. No one becomes proficient at their craft without help.

Regarding this book, I especially would like to thank the following people for their dedicated, candid, and significant feedback and support through their reviews of the manuscript: Bill Arcudi, Kristen Schaffer, Don Norton, Don Matter, and Paul Sapenaro and his gifted team: R. J. Coberly, Michelle Flynn, George Kather, and Robin Woods.

I also would like to thank the following people for their respective comments, suggestions, and support as the manuscript evolved into the book: Kevin Addesso, Ed Ahearn, Patti Bunker, Mance Irvin, Scott Moody, and Marti Owensby.

And finally I am grateful to the highly professional staff at Management Concepts for their continued invaluable support and guidance during manuscript development, editing, and production. I would especially like to acknowledge the special contributions of Editorial Director Myra Strauss and her team of Jill Sulam, Lois Anne Smith of Page Grafx, and Kathy Clancy.

Thank you all!

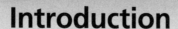

Introduction

I am very fortunate to work with thousands of people each year—year after year. I make contacts through mentoring, consulting, and speaking; by leading training seminars and workshops; by performing project reviews and project management troubleshooting; and by writing many articles and books. These opportunities help me monitor the pulse of the people behind the projects, organizations, and companies. Throughout this journey, I have noted a common set of issues that are critical to the consistent success of these projects and organizations. Many of the topics and issues were addressed in my previous project management book, *Neal Whitten's No-Nonsense Advice for Successful Projects*.

This book also addresses these critical topics, focusing even more on behaviors and their importance to the individual's success. The individual's success, in turn, contributes to the success of projects and organizations. People want to emulate behaviors that will help them successfully turn their professional dreams into reality. This book, *Neal Whitten's Let's Talk! More No-Nonsense Advice for Project Success,* reveals *best behavioral practices*.

The presentation style and formatting of *Neal Whitten's No-Nonsense Advice for Successful Projects* was well received. Among other features, I included Q&As at the end of each chapter. I received considerable positive feedback regarding the value of the Q&As and how effectively they focused on specific issues. Because of this feedback, I have chosen to write this entire book in a Q&A format. This format:

- Lets you quickly find the most relevant topics, issues, and questions
- Offers smaller and more focused nuggets of information to enhance retention
- Makes the book especially useful as a reference tool in which specific lessons can easily be found and marked
- Gives you, the reader, a feeling of having a personal mentor by your side, guiding you through your workday.

From this point forward, I will communicate using the Q&A format.

**Key strengths
of this book**

Q_{i.1} What are the key strengths of this book?

A_{i.1} This book has two key strengths:

1. It answers hundreds of common questions about real project management issues. These questions have been asked by thousands of people who are on the front lines in their projects and organizations—people just like you who are striving to do their best work, make positive contributions to their companies, and enhance their careers.

2. The questions are answered by a leading project management authority and mentor who has more than 35 years of experience—including many successes and some setbacks. The best teachers are often those who have made mistakes along the way, but who have learned from those experiences and become stronger and more effective, in part because of those errors.

**Process to
select Q&As**

Q_{i.2} How did you decide which Q&As to include?

A_{i.2} After selecting topics and issues with widespread interest and importance, I listed the most common questions that I routinely encounter on those topics. I could easily have included many, many more Q&As; however, I attempted to settle on those that can help the reader answer different but related questions. For example, once you have learned how best to deal with a difficult project team member, much of what you've learned also helps you deal with difficult contractors, vendors, and other project stakeholders and employees.

**Audience for
this book**

Q_{i.3} Who is the audience for this book?

A_{i.3} The book is targeted to *all project stakeholders* (anyone associated with a project) as well as *all employees* in an organization or company. I focus first on projects and have included specific chapters targeting the following stakeholders: the project manager, resource manager, project sponsor, business analyst, project analyst, client, contractors, and vendors. Most of the book's Q&As, however, are relevant to any member of a project or any employee in an organization. This book is for anyone who aspires to become a consistently effective leader, project member, or employee—and therefore more valuable to their project, organization, and company.

Qi.4   **In reading a question, how will I know from whose perspective the question is being asked? For example, is it being asked by a project manager, resource manager, employee, or other individual?**

Ai.4   If the question is being asked by a specific stakeholder—such as a project manager or business analyst—that person will be identified. For example, a question may begin, "As a project manager, how should I deal with . . . ." If no specific stakeholder is identified, then the question likely applies to any project member or employee.

Qi.5   **Can senior managers and executives benefit from the book?**

Ai.5   Big time! The book defines *best-practice behaviors* that senior managers and executives want their employees to adopt to create the most effective enterprise. It also defines a productive culture that senior managers and executives must create and nurture to help employees perform at their best.

Qi.6   **Is the book exclusively about professional behaviors?**

Ai.6   No. It also addresses some project process-related topics that can have a profound impact on a project or organization. Such topics include the Project Management Institute (PMI) and the Project Management Body of Knowledge (*PMBOK® Guide*); project management orga-

Professional behaviors . . . plus more

nization (PMO); project planning, schedules, and budgets; project tracking; scope and change control; and quality and post-project reviews.

Similarity to Neal Whitten's No-Nonsense Advice for Successful Projects

Q_{i.7} You stated that this book is, in many ways, a continuation of your last book, *Neal Whitten's No-Nonsense Advice for Successful Projects* (hereafter referred to as the "first book"). Is there any duplication of information in these books?

A_{i.7} This book has a small amount of similar information, as both books address topics essential to effective project management. Moreover, based on reader feedback from the first book, I have provided additional information on some of the topics addressed in that book.

For example, both books have separate chapters for the project manager, resource manager, and project sponsor. The first book focuses more on the roles and responsibilities of these positions. This book focuses more on the behaviors that people in these power positions must exhibit, model, and deal with, as well as the issues they must work through. In several cases, where appropriate, this book refers the reader to the first book.

Another example: The first book's "Foster Interpersonal Communications" chapter is similar to this book's "Interpersonal Communications" chapter, which addresses many more communications-related issues.

Q_{i.8} Do I need the first book to effectively use this book?

A_{i.8} No. This book is meant to stand alone. A few reviewers of this manuscript said that reading the first book *first* provided a great foundation for some areas of *this* book and helped them appreciate it all the more. But most of the reviewers said it did not matter; to them, this book's value was fully apparent, and it was effective as a standalone publication.

The first book details the common topics and issues that repeatedly emerge as critical to the consistent success of people, projects, and organizations. In many ways, the books complement one another: Their value as a pair is greater than their summed individual values.

Q_{i.9} Do your answers to these questions apply to all organizations and companies or just to some?

Applicability of Q&As to you, your projects, and your organization

A_{i.9} For the most part, I have defined a successful business culture that can be adopted by all companies and governmental, educational, and institutional enterprises. But any enterprise can modify the solutions I offer according to its individual preferences and needs.

My experience is that most enterprises can and will want to adopt the majority of my cultural model. Why? Because it creates an environment that encourages the best from its people—it sets them up for success. The culture of a project, organization, or company must be deliberate and well defined to the employees; otherwise, they will not reach their potential for peak performance.

Q_{i.10} Are you saying that I may not agree with all of your answers?

A_{i.10} Most readers will find most of my answers compelling and will likely readily endorse them—even though they may have to give them some thought first. Some of my answers, however, may go against conventional wisdom and may require even more thought before they are adopted—if they ever are.

My role is not to give you the absolute answers (if that is even possible), but to give you ideas—building blocks—from which you can derive your own answers. My job is to "plant seeds" in you; your job is to grow the seeds in which you have the most interest or for which you have the greatest need.

It is not my intent to get us—you and me—to agree on everything. It doesn't matter that we may not always agree; however, it does matter—to me—that I can help you learn to think for yourself. I want you to walk away from this book feeling that you have been helped—and that you are more self-reliant, independent-thinking, and deliberate than ever before.

Organization of book

Q_{i.11} How is the book organized?

A_{i.11} There are five parts to the book; the first three parts are divided into 33 chapters.

Part One: Project Stakeholders

This part has a separate chapter for each of the eight key types of stakeholders common to most projects. Groups with dedicated chapters include Project Manager, Boss/Resource Manager, Project Sponsor, Business Analyst, Project Analyst, Client, Contractors, and Vendors.

Part Two: The People Side

This part tends to be more personal in nature and provides advice for individual project members and employees. Fifteen unique topics are covered, each in its own chapter: Accountability, Dependencies and Commitments; Leadership Styles, Attributes, and Behaviors; Sharing Power; Interpersonal Communications; Resolving Conflict through Escalations; Meetings; Celebrations; Overtime Work; Mentoring; Ethics and Integrity; Telecommuting/Working from Home; Awards and Recognition; Personal Development, Job, and Career; Promoting Change in Your Organization; and Mergers and Acquisitions.

Part Three: The Project Side

Part Three focuses mostly on project processes and procedures. I address ten unique topics: Project Management Institute (PMI) and *A Guide to the Project Management*

Body of Knowledge (PMBOK® Guide); Methodologies and Processes; Project Management Organization (PMO); Project Culture; Project Plans, Schedules, and Budgets; Project Tracking; Scope Change Control; Quality; Post-Project Reviews; and Surveys of Client Satisfaction.

PART FOUR: INTRODUCING THESE TOPICS AND DISCUSSIONS IN YOUR ORGANIZATION

This part suggests how you can integrate these topics and discussions into your project, department, or organization—and create and nurture the successful business culture you seek to establish.

PART FIVE: CLOSING THOUGHTS

I leave you with something to think about.

Qi.12 Any last comments before I delve into the book?

Ai.12 Yes. The book was designed and written for you. If you have any comments about the book's content or formatting, please send them to me via my Web site, www.nealwhittengroup.com. I cannot promise to respond to each comment due to the volume of correspondence I receive; however, I will read each and every comment. Thank you for your interest and support. Happy reading!

One last comment—mine and yours . . . .

Project Stakeholders

Part One has eight chapters—one chapter for each of eight key groups of project stakeholders. These groups were chosen because of their universality across most projects and because I routinely field many questions about them. A sampling of the issues addressed in each chapter is listed below.

CHAPTER 1: THE PROJECT MANAGER

Taking on too many "monkeys"; understanding scope of accountability; behaving as an "absolute" dictator; working with insufficiently skilled project members; dealing with competing projects; developing project members; being both a project manager and a resource manager; dealing with difficult resource managers; taking on an excessive workload; and taking on a troubled project.

CHAPTER 2: THE BOSS/RESOURCE MANAGER

Focusing on employee strengths versus weaknesses; dumping employees on project managers; assigning jobs to employees; making commitments for employees; accountability for commitments made by employees; managing commitments based on priority; determining the closeness of your relationship with employees; dealing with poorly performing employees; frequency of performance evaluations; coaching, counseling, and tracking employees; your role in downsizing employees; employees tooting their own horns; and employees seeking help from their bosses.

CHAPTER 3: THE PROJECT SPONSOR

Finding a project sponsor; defining the relationship between the project manager and the project sponsor; disagreeing with the project sponsor; involvement of the project sponsor with the project; and what to do if a client/project sponsor relationship is disruptive to the project manager.

CHAPTER 4: THE BUSINESS ANALYST

Ensuring an effective requirements document; understanding the client's business-related processes; meeting minimum requirements; producing results that conform to requirements; the power of the business analyst; creating a healthy contentious environment; disagreeing with the project manager; fostering a good relationship with the project manager; and being the client's advocate.

CHAPTER 5: THE PROJECT ANALYST

Enabling the project manager to be more effective; providing primary interface to project management tools; assisting in the preparation of project plans; constructing an overall project plan; role in project tracking meetings; expanding the project manager's reach; and backing up the project manager.

CHAPTER 6: THE CLIENT

Client not providing enough dedicated people; working with internal versus external clients; confiding in client about company-sensitive information; saying "no" to a client; honoring a client's request that undermines a project's outcome; what to do if the client is displeased with the project manager's performance; and whether the client must always come first.

CHAPTER 7: CONTRACTORS

Hiring contractors in lead positions; contractor as the project manager or resource manager; treatment of contractors; begrudging contractors; uncooperative contractors; and cost-effectiveness of contractors.

CHAPTER 8: VENDORS

The project manager's accountability over the vendor's performance; low vendor quality; resolving disagreements with a vendor; what to do if a vendor removes project-critical personnel; overseeing vendor performance; and the criticality of the project manager's leadership.

CHAPTER 1

The Project Manager

66 Shallow men believe in luck.
Strong men believe in cause and effect. 99

—Ralph Waldo Emerson, American author,
poet, and philosopher

Q_{1.1} Can you briefly describe the project manager's job?

A_{1.1} The project manager (PM) directs the planning and execution of a project and is held personally accountable for the success of the project. The PM is a *nurturer* of projects.

Q_{1.2} What are the primary duties of a project manager?

A_{1.2} The project manager:

- Is fully accountable for the project
- Applies lessons learned from past projects
- Ensures that project roles and responsibilities are well defined
- Leads the project planning activities
- Leads the project tracking and problem-management activities
- Promotes project management best practices
- Manages daily to the project's top three priorities
- Ensures the proper level of client involvement
- Encourages and supports escalations
- Communicates project status to project stakeholders
- Enforces effective change control
- Promotes good working relationships
- Makes things happen.

Primary duties of the project manager

This list of the project manager's most significant duties is taken from *Neal Whitten's No-Nonsense Advice for Successful Projects*, Chapter 14, "Duties of the Effective Project Manager."

Taking on too many "monkeys"

Q1.3 As a project manager, I feel that I probably take on too many tasks that members of my team should be assigned. Any advice on how to deal with this?

A1.3 As a general rule, the project member who has the dependency should be assigned the action item. However, if the problem affects more than one project member, then the project manager should strive to find someone to own and lead the effort and effectively work it to closure. There may be times (albeit infrequently) when it is okay for the PM to take on such a "monkey"—for example, if the problem is urgent, the project member is clearly overloaded, or the PM is the right person to deal with the issue because of his skills, position of influence and power, or availability.

PM as critical path

Q1.4 Why do you say "albeit infrequently" when referring to moments in which a project manager should take on a "monkey"? Wouldn't you agree that it is noble for the project manager to take on some of the work of project members so that they are free to perform other work?

A1.4 No, not in most cases. By doing project members' work for them, you may inadvertently deny them a chance to learn and practice commitment, accountability, and leadership skills. But the biggest downside is that you, as the PM, can become the major critical path on the project. A project plan shows one critical path, the one that is typically referred to, but there can be another critical path that can do greater harm to the execution of a project plan. That critical path is the *availability* of the PM to help discover potential problems and fix them. A PM who is busy doing others' work cannot perform his or her own duties, which include tracking progress, seeking out potential problems, and being available to help remove or mitigate obstacles for others. The most effective project managers remain relatively available to help other stakeholders be successful within their own domains of responsibility.

Q_{1.5} **Can you give an example of a project manager taking on too much work, becoming a project's critical path, and, therefore, not being available to perform many of his duties?**

A_{1.5} I was asked to mentor a project manager I'll call Vihar for a day. I observed his behavior in meetings and working with others one on one. His project had about a dozen core members. I began the day by watching Vihar run his weekly project tracking meeting. After the meeting, I told him that I counted 50 open action items, 40 of which were assigned to him. I said that it is unusual for a PM to own so many action items; doing so puts the PM at risk of becoming the critical path on the project. I asked why he owned so many action items.

By the end of the day, I understood why. Vihar was easily intimidated, and many project members resisted taking on new action items, even though those action items were in their domains of responsibility. When project members refused to take ownership of action items, he took them on himself. Vihar's behavior limited his availability to manage across the project, which severely handicapped his effectiveness.

As stated earlier, the PM should avoid becoming the project's critical path, but instead should be available to "grease the skids" and help other project members who find themselves as the critical path or have the potential to become so.

Q_{1.6} As a project manager, am I accountable for the performance of the project members who have been assigned to work on my project?

PM's accountability for all project members' performance

A_{1.6} Yes, but you are also accountable for the performance of *all* people who fall within your domain of responsibility—people you need to perform work so that your project and team are successful. Your *domain of responsibility* includes all responsibilities and commitments that fall within the scope of your assignment. This means that your domain of responsibility does not just include your core project members; it includes anyone on whom you depend, whether it be for only two hours, two hours per week, or full time. Moreover, your domain of responsibility includes the performance of vendors, contractors, client personnel, part-timers, college co-ops or interns, and anyone and everyone who has a role to play in making your project successful.

Q_{1.7} Are you saying that I am accountable for the performance of certain people, even if I am not their resource manager (boss)?

A_{1.7} Yes, but only as their performance relates to your project.

Q_{1.8} But that isn't fair. How can I possibly get them to work well with me if I do not control the direction of their careers or their performance evaluations, salary increases, and job opportunities?

A_{1.8} Your job includes creating a work culture and environment that is properly structured, productive, constructive, efficient, and effective and that ultimately sets the project members up for success. This includes ensuring that each project member is fully aware of and committed to your expectations. In my experience, at least 95 percent of your project members will work satisfactorily with you as long as they understand what you expect from them. (By the way, they should also know that you will be providing feedback on their performance to their own resource managers.)

Q_{1.9} Ninety-five percent seems like an unusually high number, but I'll accept it if you say so. How do I work with the other five percent?

A_{1.9} Almost all project members want to do the right thing. They want to do their share of project duties, and they want to be on a winning team. Those who do not can be difficult to work with. You initially work with them in the same way you would work with the cooperative 95 percent. Make sure they understand what you expect from them. If they choose not to cooperate, be sure that you have reasonably tried to fix any problems. If that doesn't work, ask their resource managers to help ensure they meet their commitments. If resource managers will not cooperate with you (which is not likely), then continue the escalations up the "food chain" until the issues are resolved.

Q_{1.10} As the project manager, I believe that everyone must agree with me and do what I say. Am I correct to expect this?

PM as absolute dictator

A_{1.10} Not entirely. Your team, collectively, likely knows more than you do about many things. Your job is to tap into team members' intellectual capital, and you should welcome ideas that are counter to yours. But once you have settled on what you think is the best course of action, you must do your best to sell your team on it. If project members still disagree with you, you must nevertheless move ahead with what you believe to be the best business decision.

Q_{1.11} As a project manager, what do I do if a resource manager assigns someone to my project who lacks the required skills to perform satisfactorily?

Insufficiently skilled project member

A_{1.11} If you know immediately that the person assigned will not perform satisfactorily, then discuss the problem with the resource manager. If the RM does not help resolve the issue, escalate higher.

But if you only suspect that the individual might not perform satisfactorily, meet with him and his RM. Explain your concerns, and ask the RM to assign a buddy or mentor to the person to help him be successful. Most RMs will welcome the idea of having someone work with the person. On the off chance that the RM is not helpful, respectfully tell the RM that if the project begins to suffer because of the project member's weak performance, then you will expect the RM to take swift action to remedy the situation—or you will escalate the issue higher. (Q&A 2.19, Chapter 2, "The Resource Manager," discusses this problem from the RM's perspective.)

Deferring vacation of project member

Q1.12   What if the project manager needs a project member to defer his or her vacation so that the project is delivered to the client on time? Does the project manager have the authority to make this decision?

A1.12   Typically, no. However, the project member's RM does have this authority. The PM has the duty to complete the project on time, within cost, and with the expected quality. If problems arise that might impede the project's success, the PM must clearly identify the problems and creatively work to solve them. If the PM believes deferring a project member's vacation is the correct business decision, then the PM first speaks to the project member. The RM may also participate in this discussion. If the project member and RM will not cooperate, then the issue must be escalated.

Q1.13   What if no one, including the project sponsor, insists that the vacation be deferred? What does the project manager then do?

A1.13   The worst-case scenario is that the project will be completed late. But as long as the correct people were involved in the decision to not defer the vacation—most notably the project sponsor and client—and affected parties are aware of any harm that the project member's absence might cause, then the PM does the best she can under the circumstances.

Q1.14 If the client was not consulted, who has the duty to inform the client that the delivery will be late?

A1.14 If the project sponsor made the final call on whether to allow the project member to take vacation as scheduled, he must talk to the client. However, the client should have been included in the decision process in the first place.

Q1.15 Who is mostly at fault—the project member or the project manager—if the project is delivered late because the project member took vacation as planned?

A1.15 Accountability for the late delivery is shared by the PM, the RM, and the project member. The PM is ultimately accountable for the project and, therefore, the performance of all project members. In most cases, the PM should have anticipated the problem by observing the progress being made on the activities within the project member's domain of responsibility. Moreover, the PM should have identified the project member's vacation in the project plan.

Meanwhile, the RM should have worked closely with her employee to ensure that the employee would fulfill his commitments before leaving for vacation—and created a workaround if the employee failed to do the necessary work. Of course, the project member should have anticipated any potential problems early on and created a plan to mitigate them.

Q1.16 I am a project manager. What if a project member is neglecting my project because her resource manager has directed her to work on another project or assignment?

Competing projects

A1.16 It is common for project members to work on more than one project at a time. As a PM, you are focused on your own project. If your project is suffering, then you must work with the project member to resolve the issue. The project member must work with her boss in resolving the issue. If this doesn't work, approach the project member's boss for help. Unless you are directed by a higher authority (e.g., a boss or project sponsor) to do otherwise, you should behave as if your project is the most important project in the organization and company to protect your domain of responsibility.

Q1.17 What if the project member's boss says that my project is a lower priority?

A1.17 If the project member's boss is not your boss or a boss within your immediate management chain, continue to escalate until the issue is resolved. If you lose the escalations, then consider reevaluating the project schedules so that they remain realistic and achievable.

Skill development of project members

Q1.18 As a project manager, am I responsible for developing the skills of the project members assigned to my project?

A1.18 Your project members' resource managers are responsible for ensuring that their employees have the basic skills to perform their jobs. But it is your responsibility to ensure that your project members are adequately trained to perform tasks specific to your project—such as project planning, status reporting, the escalation process, and project communications.

Even though resource managers must make sure their employees get proper and timely job training, you must stay abreast of project members' training to be sure that it will help them fulfill their project duties.

PMs writing performance reviews

Q1.19 As a project manager, should I write performance reviews for the project members that have been assigned to work on my project?

A_{1.19} No, not if you mean actually writing the performance review. Resource managers have that responsibility and should be trained in fair administration of the performance evaluation process.

Q_{1.20} **What should I do if a resource manager requests my feedback on his employee's performance?**

A_{1.20} You should take the time to accommodate the request, provided your delivery is verbal, not written. The RM should consider your response and apply it appropriately to fairly evaluate the employee's performance based on her job level. The higher the employee's job level, the more she is expected to achieve for the business.

By the way, you should *want* to work with RMs in developing your project members. This symbiotic relationship can help improve your project members' performance while they are assigned to your project.

Q_{1.21} **But how can a resource manager fairly review his employee's performance when I, as the project manager, might know more about the performance of the employee than the resource manager?**

A_{1.21} When an RM assigns an employee to your project, that RM must continue to work as closely as is appropriate with the employee. In order for the RM to assist the employee in meeting project commitments, as well as continue to help the employee develop her potential, the RM must meet regularly with the employee. These meetings are typically held weekly, but the frequency can vary depending on the skill level of the employee. Even so, the PM will be familiar with aspects of the employee's performance that the RM may not or could not be. Therefore, the RM is expected to gather performance feedback from various sources, including you as the PM.

Q_{1.22} **Why are you opposed to project managers actually writing the project member's performance review?**

A₁.₂₂ Here are two of the more important reasons:

- The PM's primary role is the nurturing of projects; the RM's primary role is the nurturing of people. The time the PM spends in conducting performance reviews is time not spent nurturing the project.
- PMs typically do not receive adequate training in appropriately evaluating employee performance.

Would you like to guess the typical RM's *least* favorite duty? *Writing and administering performance reviews!* If RMs feel this way, think how PMs feel about doing RMs' job for them.

Q₁.₂₃ **I can't quite let this go. Have you had clients whose project managers have written performance reviews, or partial performance reviews, for their project members— and all involved parties did not mind? And if so, are you okay with it if all parties involved agree to it?**

A₁.₂₃ Yes to your first question. Many of my clients have their PMs write some information that either is filtered by the RM or that becomes a part of, or even the complete, formal evaluation for a project member. In other cases, PMs are asked to complete a short form intended to take minimal time. Whatever the PM writes should be fact-based and not overly subjective. RMs may request that the form be completed anywhere from quarterly to annually, or when a project has completed. Many RMs prefer written assessments because they may save the RM from having to meet with the PM to discuss an employee's performance. Plus, it is *written* history for the record.

I also think it is all right for PMs to write partial performance reviews for project members if all involved parties think that this is okay. As I said in the book's Introduction (Q&A i.10), my job is to "plant seeds" in you; your job is to grow the seeds in which you have the most interest or for which you have the greatest need.

It is not my intent to get us to agree on everything, but I do want to encourage you to think about your behaviors and actions and be open to considering other views and solutions. So yes, I am okay with it, but I personally would not recommend PMs *write* evaluations for reasons already stated.

Q_{1.24} Do you think that one person can effectively be both a project manager and a resource manager at the same time?

One person
being both
PM and RM

A_{1.24} This is a bad idea in most cases, for two major reasons:

1. ***The PM and RM roles require two very different skill sets.*** The PM must have strong project-management-related skills, and the RM strong people-development skills. It is much harder to fully develop one of these skill sets if you are required to focus on both. Developing either is a full-time commitment.

2. ***The PM and RM roles have two very different focuses.*** One zeroes in on projects, the other on people. In most organizations, projects will carry more weight than will employee development. This means that a person who is both a PM and an RM often must sacrifice nurturing and developing employees so that projects receive the appropriate attention. As a result, morale may drop and employee attrition rise. Holding both roles simultaneously can result in a conflict of interest for the PM/RM: *projects versus people*.

Q_{1.25} Why did you say "in most cases"? When might it be okay to assign a person both roles?

A_{1.25} If an organization is in transition (growing or shrinking), it can be in the best interest of the business to temporarily (for weeks or a few months) assign some people to take on both roles until the organization begins to stabilize or is ready for the next change.

Also, it might be okay for one person to take on both roles if the department is relatively small but specialized, focused on serving a particular client or industry. If the small department has only a handful of employees, who also are the core project members on several small projects, then one person may be able to hold both positions because she may be able to easily handle both the PM and RM duties.

Q1.26 In my organization, we are required to perform the roles of both project manager and resource manager. I like your approach better, but in defense of our senior management team, it would be too costly to hire more project managers or resource managers so that those roles aren't shared. Do you agree?

A1.26 No, not in most cases. I submit that, in most cases, you can take those employees serving as PMs/RMs and assign some to be full-time PMs and the others to become full-time RMs. By allowing each to specialize in their chosen crafts, they will have far more passion for what they do and be able to take on more work. PMs can take on more projects and RMs more people. Here, everyone wins: Employees have someone who champions them (RMs), and the projects are given exclusive attention by PMs. Meanwhile, both PMs and RMs improve their skills.

If the senior managers believe that more people must be hired, then that is an admission that the current organizational approach, with the current staff numbers, is broken—that the job isn't getting done right with the PMs and RMs now on board. That means that commitments are being missed, quality is being sacrificed, budgets are being overrun, and morale is suffering. In this case, the senior managers will have to hire more folks—*because there never were enough folks to begin with!*

Missed commitment by RM **Q**1.27 What if a resource manager says that his employee (one of my project members) will be available next week to work on my project, yet each week the commitment is deferred another week?

A_{1.27} If the project is at risk because the project member's activities are in the critical path, escalate over the RM's head to resolve the conflict—informing the RM of the impending escalation before doing so. If the project member is not in the critical path, and you can give the RM and the project member leeway, then you may do so.

Q_{1.28} As a project manager, am I responsible for finding project members by reviewing resumes, for example? Should I be part of the interview process?

PM's role in interview process for new project members

A_{1.28} Organizations and companies approach this differently, but in my experience, the following approach works best. Resource managers have the primary duty to identify and interview potential candidates; that's one of the main reasons they are called resource managers. RMs are trained specifically to be experts in this area.

Having said that, it could be in the PM's best interest to be part of the selection and interview process to help ensure each candidate chosen has the knowledge, skills, experience, and cultural attitude that will best benefit the project. Of course, in a situation in which the PM has the time to get involved in the hiring process, and the RM can use the assistance, the PM can demonstrate professional maturity by helping the RM.

Q_{1.29} As a project manager, should I take my own minutes at meetings?

Taking minutes at meetings

A_{1.29} No, not in most cases. If the leader of a meeting also records the minutes, it can disrupt the meeting's progress. Taking your own notes wastes time and diverts your attention. But if the meeting is short or is focused on a single topic, it might be okay.

Q_{1.30} But if someone else takes the minutes, often the minutes are of lower quality than is acceptable to me. They may be incomplete, inaccurate, and difficult to interpret. What then?

A_{1.30} Ideally, PMs should have one or more project-management assistants—often called project analysts—to assist them with administrative activities. My usual preference is to have the project analyst (or other note taker) take the minutes and then polish and distribute them within one day of the meeting, or within two days if the meeting is a project tracking meeting. This means that the minutes will be sent out under the name of the minutes-taker, not the PM. But I recommend that the PM provide a template and examples to help set expectations for the minutes-taker and that the minutes first be approved by the PM. This process helps motivate the note taker to do a superb job because his name will appear as the author of the meeting minutes.

Q_{1.31} What can I do if my organization cannot or will not allow me to hire a project analyst?

A_{1.31} If you do the math, you will find that in most cases, it is cost-efficient and productive for an organization to hire one or more project analysts to support the PMs across an organization. This frees the PMs to be more effective and take on more projects. However, if your organization chooses not to do so for whatever reason, then look for an admin person or project member to assist. Many admin people would welcome the diversion from their regular duties. (See Chapter 5, "The Project Analyst," for more.)

PM's technical skills

Q_{1.32} How technical should a project manager be?

A_{1.32} A PM should be sufficiently technical to understand the terminology, technology, and processes relevant to successfully building a product, performing a service, or achieving a result. Having sufficient understanding of these areas can help the project manager earn the respect of his team and can significantly help with the planning, execution, and problem-management activities required on a project. Being sufficiently technical helps a project manager understand the project's dynamics and be better qualified and prepared to know when to ask questions, know what questions to ask, understand the responses, and know when to seek help. (See *Neal Whitten's No-Nonsense Advice for Successful Projects*, Chapter 17, "How Technical Must a Project Manager Be?" for more on this topic.)

Q_{1.33} **Is it preferred that the project manager have strong technical skills?**

A_{1.33} Not necessarily. My experience shows that being too technical can often be a handicap for PMs. There is the temptation to spend too much time and focus too much on the technical aspects of the project, sacrificing effective management across the entire project.

Q_{1.34} **Can the project manager be the least technical member of the project team and still be effective?**

A_{1.34} Yes, this is possible, as long as the PM is sufficiently technical to successfully lead the planning and execution of the project.

Q_{1.35} **I am a project manager responsible for five projects. I have just been assigned to own another three projects. I feel that I only have the capacity to satisfactorily lead five projects, not eight. Should I push back and risk looking bad?**

PM overloaded from leading multiple projects

A_{1.35} You are responsible for managing the commitments you make. If you believe that your workload is too heavy for you to successfully manage, it is your duty to speak up. It would be professionally immature and unethical to say nothing and then fail to meet your commitments.

**Creating a
matrix to
help show
workload**

Q1.36 It is not easy to articulate just how many projects I can handle at any point in time. Do you have any suggestions?

A1.36 Yes. Create a matrix. Along the horizontal axis, list your projects by name. Along the vertical axis, list the typical activities/tasks/items that you must conduct or handle on each project. Example items to list might be project tracking meetings, escalation meetings, work meetings, documents to review, action items to perform, meeting minutes to produce (or approve), e-mails to send/receive/process, coaching, reevaluating project plans, and participating in project reviews.

Now identify (in hours) how much time each week you expect to spend performing or managing each activity/task/item for each project. Add up all the time spent per project. Then add up all the time spent across all projects. Now you have a mostly quantitative measure of your workload to show your boss.

You can ask for help to be assigned to you, or you can ask to be relieved from some projects. Don't just dump the problem on your boss. Propose solutions, and volunteer to help implement the solutions. Be candid about your preferred solution, and explain why it is in the best interest of the business.

Q1.37 What if my boss says to do it all anyway?

A1.37 If this is a temporary situation, and you are able to, you should rise to the occasion and do what's required. However, make sure your boss understands that your being spread too thin will affect him, the projects, and you. If this is a long-term situation, creatively work to lighten your load over time.

In the worst-case scenario—one in which your situation shows no sign of improvement, even though you are creatively working to resolve it—then you might want to find another job. Jumping to another job within your company, or especially to another company, should only be considered as a last resort.

Q_{1.38} Why would my boss load me up with too much work?

A_{1.38} Many reasons may be at play: temporary business need; survival of the organization; the boss' failure to fully understand your limitations; or the boss' own overwork and stress, lack of leadership training, and weak job performance.

Q_{1.39} I have union (collective bargaining) people on my team. Should I be more sensitive in working with them than when working with any other group?

Working with a collective bargaining group

A_{1.39} Project members should be held accountable for their commitments, regardless of whether they are contractors, vendors, union members, part-time employees, or are assigned from the client organization. Consult your boss, project sponsor, legal staff, or other appropriate person to determine whether special rules or guidelines apply in your organization or company when working with members of a union.

Q_{1.40} Is a matrix organization environment good or bad for a project manager?

Matrix organization environment

A_{1.40} Let's first look at the definition of a matrix organization provided by *A Guide to the Project Management Body of Knowledge (PMBOK® Guide)*. A matrix organization is "any organizational structure in which the project manager shares responsibility with the functional managers [resource managers] for assigning priorities and for directing the work of persons assigned to the project."

This is a broad definition and gives great leeway to either the project manager or the resource manager in assigning and directing work. However, I believe the most effective implementation of the matrix organization typically includes the following parameters:

- The project manager is accountable for the success of the project; her primary focus is nurturing the project.
- Resource managers are accountable for the development of their employees, helping them reach their potential within the organization and company, as well as ensuring that they are meeting their commitments on assigned projects.
- Resource managers provide people with the required skills to projects and assign project-related jobs (e.g., designer, tester, trainer) to their employees.
- Project managers can assign project members activities/tasks/action items that are related to their job assignments.
- Resource managers typically work behind the scenes to ensure that their employees are doing quality project work in a timely manner—work that may be spread across many different projects.
- The project manager works directly with each project member on small teams or with each team leader on larger teams to ensure that quality work is being performed in a timely manner.

As you can see, there is an important symbiotic relationship between the project manager and the resource managers of the employees assigned to the project. A matrix organization can be a great structure for both the project manager and the resource managers. The key is for the PM and RM to understand and agree on the separation of powers and focuses.

RM jealous of PM's power $Q_{1.41}$ What if, in a matrix organization, a resource manager is jealous of the power and recognition that the project manager receives? What should the project manager do, and what should the resource manager do?

A 1.41 The PM should do nothing, as long as the RM is making sure that his employees assigned to the project are performing satisfactorily. The RM should fully support the PM with regard to employee issues and by fulfilling his own responsibilities. And I suggest the RM get over such pettiness, which is also a sign of professional immaturity.

Q 1.42 As a project manager, what's your advice if I am asked to take over a project that's in trouble?

Taking over a troubled project

A 1.42 Set conditions to cover yourself and to help you and your new team—including the senior stakeholders—be successful. For example, define a relatively short period of time during which you will reevaluate the project plan, get an understanding of the current problems, and determine how best to mitigate them. Let it be known that you intend to honor the current commitments, but you need to know the project parameters to figure out whether the expectations are realistic. Prepare senior stakeholders for a new plan with new commitments.

Q 1.43 What if the project sponsor says that I must inherit things as they are—including the commitments for scope, time, and budget?

A 1.43 Don't take that sucker punch. Although your project sponsor may mean well, this is bad leadership on his part. He should respect you for wanting to stop the hemorrhaging, repair the damage, and make an aggressive—but achievable—project plan.

Be constructive and open to ideas, but show that you have a backbone. If you cave on this, you are no better than the last project manager—actually worse. You should know better because you can see all the damage. And don't blame others: Nobody cares. You need to solve the problems and move forward. Keep in mind my definition of leadership: *Leadership is not about the ability of those around you to lead; it's about your ability to lead despite what is happening around you.*

I believe it is very likely that you will get your way as long as you do due diligence and maintain a great attitude. If you weaken, you aren't just selling out yourself, you are selling out your team, the project sponsor, the client, and anyone else who has a stake in the project's success. Oh, yeah—did I mention that you would be selling out yourself, and your career and potential . . . not to mention your personal time?

Budget accountability

Q 1.44 In A1.2, you list the primary duties of the project manager. I don't see mention of "budgets" anywhere in the list. Is that intentional?

A 1.44 As I stated in *Neal Whitten's No-Nonsense Advice for Successful Projects*, my view is that the PM should create, defend, and manage to a budget throughout the duration of the project. Some of the PM's duties I've listed imply this, including "leads the project planning activities," "leads the project tracking and problem-management activities," "promotes project management best practices," and "enforces effective change control." Many project managers manage to a budget weakly because their senior management does not require more detailed budget accountability.

CHAPTER 2

The Boss/Resource Manager

"*A primary duty of management is to help employees reach their potential in the organization and company, and to create a continuously improving, productive work environment that challenges employees to perform at their best.* **"**

Q_{2.1} Briefly, can you describe the job of a resource manager— my boss?

A_{2.1} The *resource manager* (RM) hires, fires, makes job assignments, coaches, counsels, evaluates, awards, promotes, and secures future work opportunities for direct reports, also called employees. The RM is a *nurturer* of people.

Q_{2.2} What are the primary duties of a resource manager?

A_{2.2} The RM:

- Hires and fires
- Performs resource planning and allocation; makes job assignments
- Defines roles and responsibilities
- Supports direct reports in meeting their commitments
- Teaches professional maturity
- Evaluates performance
- Compensates and awards
- Provides career counseling and development
- Promotes a productive work environment
- Serves as a channel for company communications
- Executes company policies and practices
- Secures future work opportunities for employees.

Primary duties of RM

This list was extracted from the book *Neal Whitten's No-Nonsense Advice for Successful Projects*, Chapter 15, "Duties of the Effective Resource Manager," where these items are described in more detail.

Focusing primarily on strengths, not weaknesses

Q2.3   As a resource manager, should I focus more on helping my employees improve their weak areas or develop their strengths?

A2.3   Far more time should be invested in developing the strengths of employees. An employee's contribution to the project and organization and company is far more influenced by her strengths than her weaknesses. Although employees must be made aware of their weaknesses, and constructive help should be offered, my experience is that most people will not work hard to overcome their "natural" weaknesses—even though they have the ability to do so. Instead, employees will build value and reputation based on their strengths, improving them all the time.

Q2.4   What do you mean by "natural" weaknesses?

A2.4   Every employee is naturally good at some things and less so at other things. Let's look at an example.

Matt is highly technical but has very weak interpersonal skills. His interpersonal skills can be considered a "natural" weakness. Of course, Matt must understand that if he doesn't work to overcome this handicap, it could be an obstacle if he wants to be promoted to a position that would require him to lead others. However, Matt's boss should champion and celebrate Matt's "natural" strength, his technical prowess. Matt's technical side will be his strong suit and the primary value he brings to his job and career.

Q_{2.5} As a resource manager, when I assign an employee to a project, should I mostly walk away and allow the project manager to manage my employee?

A_{2.5} Definitely not! Dropping your employee on the doorstep of the PM and disappearing is doing a disservice to your employee and to the PM.

Dumping employee on PM

Q_{2.6} Then how should my relationship with a project manager work?

A_{2.6} Although organizations' cultures can vary, my experience favors the following relationship: You nurture people, and the PM nurtures the project. This means that you help your employees reach their potential within the company and help them meet their commitments on the projects to which they have been assigned. Your focus is on people. The PM, on the other hand, focuses on the successful planning and execution of the project. Your role and the PM's role, which are very different, require you to work together throughout the project life cycle, sometimes one-on-one and many times independently from one another.

Q_{2.7} Can you give a specific example of how the resource manager-project manager relationship works?

A_{2.7} When a project begins, the PM must ask you for people to be assigned to the project. Your job is to find skilled project members in your domain of responsibility. This is called resource planning and allocation. You assign your employees to specific jobs within the project. Once your employees are assigned to the project, the PM assigns them activities/tasks/action items related to their jobs on the project.

Assigning job of employee

Q_{2.8} Can the project manager change the job that the resource manager has assigned to his employee?

A_{2.8} No. Let's say that Mary is a great tester. Every PM wants Mary to perform test work on his projects. But Mary wants to move toward becoming a designer. Her boss gives her a break and assigns her to be a designer on her next project. If the PM could have his way, he would assign Mary to perform test work. Why? Because Mary is a known expert in that area, and her testing would reduce the risk to the PM. Mary's skill as a designer is unknown, but she remains assigned as a designer because her boss is the only one who has the authority to assign her a job. Mary—as all employees do—needs someone to champion her and her career. This is what her boss is doing. The PM, however, is free to assign specific activities/tasks/action items related to her assigned job as a designer.

Q2.9   But what if the project manager can prove that Mary is not qualified to be a designer on his project? Has the project manager any recourse? After all, it's the project manager's project!

A2.9   Typically, a PM cannot *prove* that a project member cannot do the job assigned until that project member begins performing the job. However, to answer your question, the PM does have recourse. The PM should address the issue with Mary's boss, and if the RM doesn't want to help, then the PM can escalate over the RM's head until the issue is resolved.

However, it's more likely that the PM cannot prove that Mary is not qualified, but is concerned that she might not be. In this case, the PM should approach the RM, explain the concern, and recommend that the RM assign Mary a buddy or mentor to help ensure her success. Most RMs—and employees—would welcome that idea. The RM should work with Mary throughout the project to ensure that she is performing acceptably.

Assigning a weak-skilled employee to a project   **Q**2.10   If a project manager has a project member position to fill, and that project member is expected to come from my department, is it acceptable for me to assign someone who has weak skills? Please keep in mind that I am not a miracle worker. I have many employees, and it is very difficult to find the best job for each of them.

A2.10 Hang on for a moment while I grab my violin. Get real! Nobody ever said that you as an RM have an easy job; it's a constantly challenging job. However, when a PM requires a person with particular skills, it is your job to find that person; it is not the PM's job. The right person can be someone who already reports to you, someone down the hall who works for another RM, a new hire; or a contractor. Your job is to satisfy the skill needs. If you do not, then the PM must escalate over your head to resolve the issue.

Q2.11 What if I "win" and the project manager "loses"; that is, the project manager must work with the weak-skilled project member?

A2.11 Your job is not over. You must now do everything reasonable to help your employee be successful so that the project can be successful. If you do not, then the PM must escalate over your head to obtain an appropriate resolution. Another recourse the PM has is to delay the project to make up for the handicap of the weak-skilled project member. However, final approval to extend the project must come from the project sponsor.

One more thing: It's not about winning or losing, it's about doing the right thing—which is almost always what's best for the business. To take this to an extreme, project failure means company failure, which means there is no longer any need for resources—including *your derriere.*

Q2.12 As a resource manager, I often assign my employees to projects based on requests from project managers; however, many times my employees sit idle while the project manager and project team decide what to do with them. This is a big waste of my skilled employees' time; moreover, I do not have excess staff and can't afford this situation. What can I do?

Employees are idle on projects

A$_{2.12}$ Unfortunately, this situation can be common when a project starts up or if problems arise. Try doing the following:

- Make sure your employees have anticipated the type of project work they will be required to perform and that they have developed any supportive processes, procedures, or tools that can help them be more productive and do quality work when they are called upon to start the work.
- Do not release your employees to work on a project until their services are really required.
- Create a "skills pool" listing those employees who have time available to work on projects in need, and lend your employees out until they are needed on their originally planned projects.

When your employees are idle, it's not just the organization that suffers from their lack of contribution; the employees themselves suffer. Their skills are not being developed, they feel wasted and unappreciated, and morale can head south.

Q$_{2.13}$ **Are you saying that resource managers must work to avoid or address this situation?**

A$_{2.13}$ RMs are in a position to help repair this situation; however, PMs (and team leaders, if appropriate) must ensure that employees are effectively utilized for the amount of time that their services are required. Idleness is not easy to avoid, but RMs and PMs must work together to appropriately address it.

Accountability for commitments made by employees

Q$_{2.14}$ **As a resource manager, am I accountable for the commitments made by my employees?**

A$_{2.14}$ Yes. If they are inexperienced, you must work closely with them so that they learn how to make commitments and follow through on them. If they are seasoned and have shown their reliability, give them broad latitude to make commitments. However, never fully walk away from your employees. Like all of us, they are works in progress and need at least occasional coaching and counseling.

Q₂.₁₅ If I am accountable for the commitments made by my employees, should I make commitments for them?

Making commitments for employees

A₂.₁₅ No. You can participate in the decision-making process that precedes many commitments, but commitments must be personally made by your employees. However, if you believe a commitment is inappropriate or cannot be met, then do not allow it to be made.

Q₂.₁₆ As a resource manager, if I have an employee assigned to three projects, and I think one of those projects is more important than the other two, do I have the authority to direct my employee to break his commitments on two projects so that the "most important" project can be protected?

Managing priorities of commitments

A₂.₁₆ You have the right to manage your resources so that they satisfy your department's commitments. However, you and your employees remain accountable for managing all of your commitments, not just the ones that you feel are important this week.

Q₂.₁₇ Do the project managers of the two "less important" projects have any recourse?

A₂.₁₇ Yes. They must immediately work with you to ensure that the needs of their projects can still be met. If they believe you cannot or will not satisfy their needs, then they must escalate the issue over your head to obtain an acceptable resolution.

Q₂.₁₈ As a resource manager, should I strive to make my employees close personal friends of mine?

RM-employee relationship: how close?

A2.18 No. In my experience, attempting to develop a close relationship with all of your employees is nearly impossible if
you have many employees. Moreover, this will cause problems among your employees as they compete for your time
and attention. Your employees are not looking for a best
friend; they are looking for someone who will champion
them, someone who will help them reach their potential in
the company. Being too close to your employees can make
it much more difficult to be candid with them about their
strengths and weaknesses and to provide the necessary
nurturing.

**Poor-
performing
employee**

Q2.19 As a resource manager, what should I do if I have an
employee who is not performing satisfactorily?

A2.19 You are accountable to fix the problem. There can be many
possible solutions, such as ensuring that the employee is
receiving sufficient training, assigning a buddy or mentor to work closely with the employee, finding a job more
suitable to the employee's skills, or firing the employee.
Whatever you do, do it relatively quickly; do not allow poor
behavior to continue—and do not wind up spending more
time overall with poor performers than you do with good
performers.

Q2.20 I struggle when working with poor performers. I have
a tendency to avoid drama and suspect that I am not
as effective as I should be in this area. Any additional
advice?

A2.20 Change your behavior or change your job! As an RM and
leader, you do not have an option. You must address poor
performance head-on and with the appropriate sense of
importance and urgency. You own this duty in your organization. If you do not address poor performance, no
one will. Avoiding this duty sends a message to other
employees that mediocrity is acceptable. Your credibility
and leadership will be seen as weak, and the morale and

productivity of others will be negatively influenced. Seek guidance and support from your boss, your peers, your HR (human resources) department, or a trusted and respected friend.

You are not alone in feeling this way. Many years ago, when I first became a resource manager, I encountered an employee who was very difficult to work with and was a consistently poor performer. I diligently worked with this employee in an attempt to help him turn his performance around. Upon counsel from my boss, I finally went to the local HR folks and got their support. I then told the employee exactly what would happen if he did not improve his performance to the expected level. I said that he would have five minutes to clean his personal effects out of his desk while I watched. I would then escort him to HR where he would be processed to exit the company, and then he would be escorted off the property.

The employee was on a "measured mile" plan that required me to check in with him at least daily. One morning, when I checked on him, it was all too apparent that he had no interest in improving his performance. I told him that this was the last straw—the clock was ticking, and he had four minutes and 50 seconds to clean out his desk. After I walked him to HR, I called a department meeting to tell the rest of my staff that he was no longer an employee. I did not say much more, because the matter was personal and confidential.

This whole ordeal was really hard on me. That afternoon, many of the department members visited me individually. I thought I knew what they would say—that I was too hard on him and should have cut him more slack. *They said the opposite!* They said they wondered when I was finally going to do my job and fire him. They said that they had been doing his work for more than six months!

Step up to the plate and pull your weight. All eyes are on you, expecting you to do your job.

Q2.21 I am a super-busy resource manager. What if I simply transfer the problem employee to another resource manager?

A2.21 Where's your accountability? Step up to the problem and solve it. That's what leaders do, and that's what the business requires of you. In the rare case in which your job is critical to the business, and you openly, without hiding any issues related to the employee, transfer the employee to an RM who has better skills or more time to work the problem, then that might be okay. But these transfers should occur very infrequently.

Practicing altruism

Q2.22 As a resource manager, I have been told that my job includes helping employees advance over my head if they appear to have the potential. This approach seems destructive to my career. Why should I stick my neck out for others if no one does it for me or if it can harm my own career?

A2.22 Because it is your job! Your job includes nurturing your employees to help them reach their potential in your organization and company. It would not be unusual for an RM to encounter an employee who has more potential than the RM. An attribute of the best RMs is altruism—unselfish regard for the development and welfare of their employees. If you owned the company, you would want your RMs to behave in this professionally mature manner. By the way, this altruistic behavior also helps the organization and company survive—which keeps you employed.

Frequency of performance evaluations

Q2.23 How often should resource managers evaluate the performance of their employees?

A2.23 Most organizations typically strive for their resource managers to formally evaluate employee performance every six months or year, more commonly yearly. Of course, the frequency of performance evaluations can vary widely depending on many factors such as the industry, the company, the performance measurements, and the job level and skill of the employee, to name a few. I favor at least quarterly (four times per year) evaluations for most employees in most businesses. Quarterly assessments promote communication between RMs and their employees, and provide frequent opportunities for employees to increase their rate of growth and overall value to the organization.

Q2.24 Quarterly seems a difficult goal to achieve. Any advice if I plan to perform the evaluations less frequently?

A2.24 Without knowing your industry and circumstances, I cannot say that your approach is inappropriate—it may be fine. However, here is some advice that may buy you some "extra" time between formal evaluations:

- Never surprise an employee with a negative evaluation rating. Constructively coach that employee in the time leading up to the formal performance evaluation.
- Provide performance feedback whenever the opportunity arises—this may even be daily or weekly.
- Be honest with negative feedback, but be especially generous with positive feedback; strive to give far more positive feedback than negative. Providing frequent feedback sends the signal that you care.
- Offer your employees intermediate performance reviews with just a few days' notice.

Q2.25 As a resource manager, how do you recommend I stay involved in my employees' assignments? I do not want to meddle in the projects to which they have been assigned.

Coaching, counseling, and tracking employees

A2.25 When an employee is first assigned, work with him to ensure he has the proper skills and has done enough estimating and planning. Then work with the employee weekly to ensure that he is meeting his commitments and is performing satisfactorily. The weekly meeting could be as brief as 15 minutes or as long as an hour.

Q2.26 But wouldn't that mean that my employee is sitting through two tracking meetings: mine and the project manager's?

A2.26 Yes, but the meetings serve different purposes. The PM's meeting is all about the project. Your meeting is more about helping to develop the employee's professional work habits and helping to ensure that he is meeting his commitments across all the projects to which he has been assigned.

Q2.27 Whoa! I have 30 employees. I don't have that kind of time to spend with each employee.

A2.27 Then don't plan on being a highly effective RM and developing top employees. It may help to adjust the frequency and length of meetings, tailor your interaction based on the needs of the employee, or do it over lunch—but make sure you do it!

Number of employees per RM

Q2.28 It sounds like you are not a fan of resource pools, where many employees report to one resource manager. How many employees can a manager typically manage effectively?

A2.28 It varies depending on the specific situation and industry; of course, it also depends on what is meant by "manage." My model of the resource manager's duties requires that a manager have 10 to 15 employees—closer to 10 employees for new managers and up to 15 employees for seasoned managers. However, if an organization is growing or in transition, a manager can temporarily have smaller or larger numbers. When organizations resort to assigning 50—sometimes 200—employees per manager, there will be a long-term price to pay.

Q2.29 There is no way our company could possibly have such a low ratio of employees to resource managers. We would not remain competitive because our costs would be too high. Is lowering the ratio really worth it?

A₂.₂₉ Short-term, you might keep costs down by having fewer RMs, but long-term, you lose. Why? Because having consistently high ratios of employees to RMs means that employees won't get the nurturing they need in areas such as training and employee effectiveness. What might suffer? Employee productivity, reliability of commitments, quality of products and services, maintenance and support costs, continuous improvement of processes and methodologies, customer satisfaction, and employee development. Employees might feel less appreciated, and attrition could rise. After all, the number one reason employees leave a company is that they do not feel appreciated. High attrition is a serious problem for most companies: They lose many skilled people, and the cost to continuously hire and train replacements can be a great competitive handicap. You do the math.

Q₂.₃₀ Do you believe in the adage that employees don't quit companies, they quit bosses?

A₂.₃₀ Yes, for the most part. As people, we strive to put a human face on an otherwise faceless corporation or entity. For most employees, that face is their boss. If you and your boss have a great relationship, and you feel that your boss champions you, you likely have a similar feeling about your company. However, if you have a weak or poor relationship with your boss, it's likely that you have a similar feeling about your company, and you are far more motivated to look for greener pastures.

Employees don't quit companies; they quit bosses

Q₂.₃₁ I'm not comfortable with your view that companies are typically faceless corporations and entities—implying that they don't "care." Companies build products and produce services that benefit their clients—and often society—in many ways. Wouldn't you agree that these companies do care—that there *is* compassion, if not in the boardroom

Companies can't "care"; only people can care

then at least in the company employees who actually produce the products and services?

A_{2.31} Do companies care? No. Do the employees of these companies care? Maybe. Employees at the best companies feel a sense of pride, purpose, contribution, and appreciation of what they bring to the company—and they often do care. They see human faces—mostly their immediate bosses, but senior management as well—as their liaison to an otherwise faceless company.

Employees want to care and want to work for a company that cares, but don't assume that "caring" is a natural state for a company. Companies can't "care"; only people can care. Furthermore, don't get confused by the fact that people work for companies, and people can care, so therefore companies care. Companies have no heart. Only the people at companies have heart—if they choose to demonstrate that heart.

This question is a great example of why leadership is so important in attracting, developing, and retaining the best employees. As stated elsewhere in this book, the people who lead the company make all the difference. If you have the best leadership, you will have the best employees. If you have weak leadership, the best that employees give is often far from the best they are capable of offering. So I repeat: Companies as entities don't care, but people who work there can care. Employees cannot bond to a faceless corporate entity, but they can and do bond with their bosses, who are approachable faces.

Interviewing a new-hire candidate in a group setting

Q_{2.32} Is it more effective for the resource manager to interview new-hire candidates one-on-one or in a group setting?

A_{2.32} One or two one-on-one interviews are fine when probing the candidate's personal side. But my experience shows that most interviewing should be done in a group setting centered on the candidate. The group can be made up of management and non-management, and the topics discussed may be quite broad, covering anything from technical issues to team dynamics to attitudes. It is good to see the candidate surrounded by potential peers and observe the interactions. Of course, prior to the interview, the interviewers must have decided who has the lead role in the group interview and how the interview will be conducted.

Q₂.₃₃ But isn't the group setting too intimidating an environment? It seems to border on "cruel and unusual punishment."

A₂.₃₃ You want to know what to expect from the candidate. With several folks asking questions, there is little time for the candidate to choreograph the answers. This interview environment most resembles the real workplace, and you can learn a lot about the candidate and how well he or she will fit into the culture. True cruel and unusual punishment is hiring the wrong candidate and having to let him or her go months later. Everyone loses in this scenario. Group interviews help the candidate and your company find the right match-up.

Q₂.₃₄ For a resource manager looking to hire new employees, which is more important: attitude or skill?

Attitude versus skill

A₂.₃₄ Both are important, but let's put them in perspective. Say that I am looking to hire a person with exceptionally high skills in a certain field. I narrow the selection to two candidates. One candidate is clearly outstanding in the field, but has a poor attitude. The other candidate has an acceptable level of skill in the field, but has a great attitude. I would hire the candidate with the great attitude. Why? Because someone in a leadership position with a poor attitude can easily undermine a project or organization and reinforces the saying about a bad apple spoiling the entire barrel of apples. But if I have a project or organization made up of people with great attitudes, I can accomplish anything with that team.

Tooting your own horn

Q2.35 Should I tell my boss when I do something noteworthy?

A2.35 Yes. Your boss should care about your performance and overall personal development; however, do not run each time to notify your boss. Weekly or monthly status reports, as discussed in Q&A 21.32-21.35 (Chapter 21, "Personal Development, Job, and Career") may be fine. Truly noteworthy and unique events can be communicated right away. However, do not allow your "self-promotion" to upstage more important business events.

Seeking help from your boss

Q2.36 How should I tell my boss if I am in over my head?

A2.36 First of all, I commend you for recognizing your duty to be truthful about your situation. This is an act of professional maturity. But don't be overly hasty in bringing your boss into the mix, unless you think the situation is important and urgent. Perform due diligence and be as creative as you can in understanding the situation and the alternatives you can consider to resolve the problems. My experience is that most problems are not as bad as they seem at first.

If you believe it's time to tell the boss, I recommend the direct approach, in which you openly discuss with your boss the problem you are having. Propose your preferred solution and have another option or two in mind that you can pull out if necessary. Tell your boss exactly what help you are asking her to provide.

We all find ourselves in these situations at one time or another. If you owned the company, how would you want your employee to behave in your current situation? Bingo! Now you know how to act.

Q2.37 Should I tell my boss that I am interested in getting appropriate coaching so that I can earn a better performance evaluation, learn about promotional opportunities, get a salary increase, or find a mentor?

Disclosing your career interests

A2.37 Yes. Don't assume your boss understands your career interests. The saying about the "squeaky wheel" getting the oil is true. However, do not approach the subject with an attitude of "What can you (the boss) do for me?" Instead, think, "What can I do to advance the business and help you (the boss) look good in the process?" Remember why you are employed. It is not about you; it's about the business.

Q2.38 As a resource manager, should I have goals and objectives for my department?

Setting department goals and objectives

A2.38 Yes! Yes! Yes! I am often amazed at how few RMs have goals and objectives. If you worked for me, I would expect you to have: (1) a vision statement, (2) a mission statement, (3) goals, and (4) objectives that relate to your department or organization.

The vision statement is just one or two sentences that state what your department strives to become someday. You may never precisely attain the vision, but it keeps you focused and moving in the right direction. The mission statement, for most departments, can be a sentence or a paragraph long. It defines the work that your department does in support of achieving your vision. I would also expect you to have three to five goals that you want to achieve for this fiscal year. Then I'd expect you to state specific objectives (measurements) you have committed to to ensure that you achieve your goals.

Q2.39 Why are goals and objectives so important?

A_{2.39} I often ask people if their department, organization, or company is more effective today than it was one or three years ago. That is, are you more productive? Are your products of higher quality? Are you learning from your mistakes and not repeating the same ones? Are your commitments more reliable? Are your customers more satisfied? Is the morale higher?

Most people tell me that they are not sure, but they think things are better. I ask them if they *think* the situation is better because they are getting used to working in the environment, or is it *truly* better. To the people who say that things are better, I ask how much better? Most people cannot say. This is why you need specific goals and objectives. Without them, most organizations drift—they are not deliberate.

The world we work in is far more competitive each year—or should I say each day! Your organization must be more effective today than it was yesterday, and still more effective tomorrow than it is today. Goals and their corresponding measurements help you plan for and know that you are achieving improvement in areas important to your business.

Q_{2.40} Can you be more specific about what a goal could be?

A_{2.40} Here are some examples of goals: improve productivity by 25 percent; improve quality by 30 percent; reduce software code-fix turnaround time by 33 percent; increase throughput speed by 50 percent; reduce costs by 40 percent; decrease time-to-market by 20 percent; increase market share by 10 percent; improve return on investment (ROI) by 20 percent; improve customer satisfaction by 20 percent; and increase morale by 10 percent.

Q_{2.41} Can you also give an example of corresponding objectives for a goal?

A_{2.41} Let's look at the goal of "reduce code-fix turnaround time by 25 percent." Assume that this is a goal of a software maintenance or support department. Today it takes, on average, eight hours to identify a defect, produce a fix, and verify that the fix does indeed correct the problem. Objectives are typically formally measured every month or every quarter. In this case, monthly measurement would work fine.

A chart is produced that shows the average fix turnaround time at the start of the fiscal year to be eight hours. By the end of the fiscal year, it needs to be reduced to six hours—a 25 percent improvement. The target improvement expected each month would be shown on the chart for the 12 months. Each month, actual turnaround times would be charted, and the trend would show whether the department is on track or not.

Q_{2.42} **Would the objective of 25 percent improvement also require a list of planned actions?**

A_{2.42} Yes. Planned actions for this objective might include:

1. Improving the skills of those working on the objective through formal training classes

2. Incorporating productive debug aids/tools into the products being supported

3. Creating SWAT or tag teams to work together to accelerate fix turnaround time

4. Offering a bonus to the team at the end of the fiscal year if the goal of 25 percent improvement is reached.

Q_{2.43} As a resource manager, I am considerably technical. Is it a good idea, as a walk-around resource manager, to suggest enhancements, techniques, and solutions to my employees?

Drawing the line on directing employees

A2.43   Perhaps, but be careful here. If you are suggesting changes that affect project scope in any way, those changes should typically go through an established change control process. But if you are suggesting to an employee how to improve productivity and quality, that would likely be a good thing—and could be viewed as part of your coaching and counseling duties.

When an RM provides too much direction, it can become micromanaging—which is a big turnoff to employees. Moreover, understand that as an RM, you wield a lot of influence over your employees—more than you may realize. The suggestions you give your employees are likely to be adopted more because of your position of power than because of the ideas' merits; consequently, your well-intended ideas could have unintended consequences.

Serving your boss

Q2.44   Do you believe that you are employed to serve your manager or that your manager is employed to serve you?

A2.44   Both! Throughout this book are examples of the duties that each of us has to make our boss look good and help the organization or company thrive. However, there are also many examples of how your boss needs to help you reach your potential in the company and help create a productive work environment to encourage employee effectiveness and continuous improvement. It is a symbiotic relationship that must work in both directions to create an optimal enterprise.

Reducing or preventing downsizing of employees

Q2.45   As a resource manager, what role, if any, should I play in preventing downsizing?

A2.45   A big one! Your employees are giving their best to manage the day-to-day operations. I believe that it is management's duty to do their best to look out for their employees—as long as their employees are performing well. Unfortunately, most companies don't feel this way—or if they do, their practices do not reflect it.

Most companies are quick to solve many of their business problems by downsizing employees—employees who are otherwise strong performers. I think this behavior is seriously shortsighted. It doesn't require much thought, skill, or talent to reach for the "downsize" solution. *Not* resorting to downsizing requires true leadership. Creativity, innovation, and resourcefulness are needed to make a business more competitive, focus on giving customers more of what they need, search out new markets, and retrain and retool employees.

Q_{2.46} **But I am only one manager of many. What, realistically, can I do to make a difference?**

A_{2.46} Change in an organization or company doesn't just happen; it is made to happen. Seeds can be planted anywhere and at any level in an organization. I agree that downsizing can't be significantly reduced or eliminated by wishing it away, but where are the creative proposals to counter downsizing? Where are the incentives to bring out the best in employees? Where are the profit-sharing plans and the stock options? The best ideas are often in the bowels of a company, not in the boardroom.

Q_{2.47} **You clearly appear to be a fan of management sharing the fruits during good times, but what can be done during the bad times that companies must invariably face?**

A_{2.47} Just as some in management may not like my views on downsizing, some of the non-management troops may not like my views on sharing the pain. When an organization or company falls on hard times, I think employees should give something back. For example, some sacrifice may be required in terms of working overtime, giving up some conveniences, and deferring salary increases. Or if the company has an extended period in the red, then its employees—including management—may give up some pay.

If, after attempting all reasonable options, an organization still faces downsizing to protect its solvency, I prefer cutting salaries by 10 percent rather than downsizing the workforce by 10 percent. I believe in all members of a company—management and non-management alike—sharing the responsibility when an organization's or company's survival is at stake.

Q2.48 Do you believe that there are times when downsizing is justified and will be required, no matter how creative the attempts at prevention?

A2.48 Yes. But let's exercise this option infrequently. Today downsizing is part of many companies' standard operating procedures.

Q2.49 What do you say to those in management who assert that you just don't understand that staying afloat without downsizing is a lot tougher than you let on?

A2.49 I say show me what you have done to anticipate and resolve the problems. What have you considered or tried? Where are your own sacrifices? Did you look for better ideas outside your company?

I know it's not easy. It's never easy, but there are almost always other options. Someday I can see it becoming standard operating procedure for companies to have an elite staff of highly creative folks whose sole job is to keep revenue strong and to develop contingencies for likely problems. Being proactive will yield better results than will the typical "firefighting" that occurs after the damage has been done and significant casualties have been incurred.

CHAPTER 3

The Project Sponsor

66Never underestimate your power as a leader to influence the outcome of events both big and small.99

Q₃.₁ What is the project sponsor's job?

A₃.₁ The *project sponsor* champions the project from a business perspective and helps remove obstacles that might impede its overall success.

Q₃.₂ What are the primary duties of a project sponsor?

A₃.₂ The project sponsor:

- Ensures the strategic significance of the project
- Provides approval and funding for the project
- Solicits support from key stakeholders
- Supports broad authority for the project manager and team
- Resolves appropriate conflicts
- Is accessible and approachable
- Supports periodic project reviews
- Supports the post-project review
- Encourages recognition.

This list was extracted from the book *Neal Whitten's No-Nonsense Advice for Successful Projects*, Chapter 16, "Duties of the Effective Project Sponsor," where these duties are described in more detail.

Duties of the project sponsor

The need for a project sponsor

Q3.3 Should a project have a sponsor?

A3.3 Yes. A sponsor is typically someone in middle or senior management who champions the project. If a project has no sponsor, then it is subject to the whims of the political climate at the moment—which can put the PM and other project members in a bad position.

Finding a project sponsor

Q3.4 There is no sponsor for my project. As a project manager, how do I obtain a sponsor?

A3.4 Talk with your boss about the best course of action to pursue. It is possible that your boss can fulfill the role of project sponsor.

Weak relationship between PM and sponsor

Q3.5 As a project manager, what should I do if I have a weak sponsor or a weak relationship with my sponsor?

A3.5 A sponsor can greatly benefit a project and significantly increase its likelihood of success. You want to have a good working relationship with your sponsor. Arrange to meet with your sponsor, and bring along a short list of primary duties you believe he should perform—such as those listed in Q&A 3.2. Discuss and fine-tune each item on your list. When you leave the meeting, there should be a clear understanding of what each of you expects and needs from the other.

PM disagrees with sponsor decision

Q3.6 What if the project sponsor makes a decision that I, the project manager, think is not a good decision?

A3.6 You have the duty to talk with your sponsor and give him your opinion of the decision. It could be that the sponsor, having more information than you, has made the appropriate decision. Therefore, discussing the logic behind the decision may satisfy your concerns. If you still believe that the decision is poor, and you are unable to convince the sponsor to alter his decision, then your options are limited. Perform the very best you can under the circumstances.

In the unlikely case that your sponsor is directing you to do something illegal or unethical, immediately go over your sponsor's head. Typically, you should talk first to your immediate boss. If you are drawn into an illegal or unethical situation, you are certain to be implicated along with your sponsor, so *never* become a party to illegal or unethical behavior. (See Chapter 18, "Ethics and Integrity," for more on this subject.)

Q_{3.7} My project sponsor is high up in my management chain. Whenever the client executive has a concern about the project, she immediately does an "end run" around me, the project manager—and everyone between me and my sponsor—and goes directly to the sponsor. This undermines my credibility and makes it very hard to run the project in the most effective manner. What should I do?

Client/ sponsor relationship disruptive to PM

A_{3.7} First, you might want to consult your immediate resource manager for tips on how to deal with this problem. But ultimately, you (or some manager on your behalf) need to confront your sponsor (in a professional manner) about the situation. If your sponsor realizes how disturbing, disruptive, and unproductive the situation is, he may work with the client to define a more appropriate and effective communications path. Your sponsor could also bring you in on the discussions—demonstrating his confidence in you and supporting your inclusion in the communications path.

When you discuss this situation with the sponsor, it is important that you also bring a solution to the problem. However, depending on your effectiveness as a project manager and the relationship between your organization and the client, it is possible that the problem may continue.

Keeping sponsor informed of project problems

Q_{3.8} As the project manager, should I keep the project sponsor informed of all project problems?

A_{3.8} Definitely not. The project sponsor is very busy and cannot deal with every problem that arises. When most problems first surface, they appear more important than they turn out to be. Choose carefully the type of problems that the project sponsor needs to be made aware of quickly. Discuss with the sponsor the criteria to be used to determine if he needs to be notified immediately of a problem, as well as how that notification should occur. Perform due diligence by proposing both the criteria and communications path to make the decision-making process less burdensome to the sponsor.

Project status report as a means of communicating with the sponsor

Q_{3.9} If I, a project manager, send a weekly project status report out to the project sponsor and others, and it contains important information that the project sponsor needs to know about and perhaps act upon, is this sufficient communication with the project sponsor?

A_{3.9} Typically not, unless you and the sponsor have already agreed to this communications process. Otherwise, you must not assume the written reports will be read on a timely basis. Nor should you, in most cases, drop problems in the lap of your sponsor without being more formally involved in their solution. Moreover, you probably should not notify your sponsor of a problem at the same time everyone else is notified. Professional courtesy dictates that you not blindside the sponsor.

Q_{3.10} As the project sponsor, how involved should I be with the project?

A_{3.10} Your level of involvement depends on a number of factors, such as the importance of the project to the business, the complexity of the project, and the skills of the project manager. However, as the project's champion, you must always be accessible and approachable to the project manager and other key stakeholders, such as the client. Do not leave the relationship between you and the PM to chance. Ensure that the PM and you have a clear and open line of communication and that both of your expectations are clear.

Involvement of the sponsor with the project

Q_{3.11} As the sponsor, should I attend weekly project tracking meetings?

A_{3.11} In most cases, your attendance should not be required. However, your occasional presence for all or part of a meeting can benefit both you and the project members. You can see firsthand how things are progressing, and the team will see that you care about the project and the team's contributions.

Sponsor's attendance at project tracking meetings

Q_{3.12} If the project is having problems, who is most accountable: the project sponsor (me) or the project manager?

A_{3.12} That depends on the nature of the problems. If there are major problems with funding, or the relationship with an external client, or support from within the company (if the project's client is internal to the company), to name a few, then you might be most accountable. If the problems are related to the planning and execution of the project, then the PM might be most accountable. However, regardless of where most of the fault lies, you have an ongoing duty to understand the project's major problems and to en-

Most accountable for project problems: PM versus sponsor

sure that they are receiving the appropriate attention and resolution.

**PM's
relationship to
sponsor**

Q3.13 I am a project sponsor. Does the project manager work for me or for his resource manager?

A3.13 The PM is assigned to bring your project to a successful conclusion. For purposes of the project, the PM works directly for you. The two of you should strive to have a close, productive relationship. For personnel-related issues, such as career development, training, salary, and promotion issues, the PM works directly with his resource manager. The PM's performance evaluation is expected to be administered by the PM's resource manager, with input from you.

CHAPTER 4

The Business Analyst

❝What ties your customers to you is when they feel you want to help them get to where they want to be.❞

—Ron Karr, sales consultant and trainer

Q_{4.1} What are the duties of a business analyst?

A_{4.1} The *business analyst* (BA) champions the client. She is the client's advocate, and she:

- Defines and maintains focus on the client's requirements—the problems to be solved
- Owns the business-process direction designed into the product
- Manages client expectations
- Drives the production of work that meets minimum requirements
- Ensures the product, service, or result satisfies the client's business needs
- Is a catalyst for resolving business-related product problems and conflicts.

For more on the duties of the BA, see Neal Whitten's *The EnterPrize Organization: Organizing Software Projects for Accountability and Success*, Chapter 14, "The Business Architect." (The business architect and the business analyst are one and the same.)

Primary duties of the BA

Q_{4.2} The business analyst appears to be defined here as having a bigger role than BAs actually have in many organizations. Do you agree?

A4.2   Yes. However, I have seen many companies, including many of my clients, embrace a more serious and influential role for the BA.

Ensuring an effective requirements document

Q4.3   Are you saying that the business analyst writes the requirements document—the document that identifies the problems to be solved?

A4.3   Not necessarily. The BA is responsible for *ensuring* that the requirements document is written and approved. This means that the BA could write the requirements, write them jointly with the client, have the client write the document, or take some other approach.

Understanding the client's business-related processes

Q4.4   What do you mean when you say the business analyst "owns the business-process direction designed into the product"?

A4.4   The BA must understand the business of the client in terms of how the new product or enhancement will affect that business. The BA must ensure that the new product has been correctly designed and will be well-received by the client. For the most part, clients do not want to be forced to change their business processes to conform to new products; they expect those products to be designed to fit seamlessly, when possible, into existing business processes. It is arrogant for the producers of products to ignore or give little attention to the effect of their products on the client's day-to-day operations.

Providing work that *meets* *minimum* *requirements*

Q4.5   What do you mean by work that meets *minimum requirements*? It doesn't sound very exciting. It sounds like producing "C"- or "D"-grade work.

A_{4.5} On the contrary, meeting minimum requirements is producing A-level work. The BA, working with the client, ensures that minimum requirements are defined for product content so that the product satisfies the client's basic needs and does not contain unnecessary extras that do not meet its scope, schedule, cost, and quality requirements. Providing work that meets minimum requirements is producing what the client needs (not necessarily what the client originally wanted). It is satisfying the *mission critical* or *essential* requirements, and it supports the adage that it is better to under-promise and over-deliver than to over-promise and under-deliver.

Q_{4.6} **Can you give an example supporting the assertion that "meets min" is really a good thing?**

A_{4.6} Clients almost always prefer lower-risk projects, delivered reliably, than high-risk "kitchen sink" projects. The "meets min" concept supports this theme.

For example, consider a case in which a client requests 100 features in a new or enhanced product, when 60 specific features are truly the "meets minimum" requirements—the needs. The extra 40 features are nice to have, but not essential for a successful product. The product can be available in six months if it's produced with the 60 necessary features, but producing it with 100 features may stretch the delivery to 10 months. Typically, it is in the best business interest of the client to go into production in six months with a solid product that meets the essential needs—not to delay production at least another four months to offer a more feature-rich product. In this scenario, the "meets min" product is expected to capture market share and increase cash flow sooner.

As a general rule, the larger and longer the project, the greater the likelihood of increased risk and quality problems and the greater the temptation to continually rework the requirements. For more on "meets minimum requirements," see *Neal Whitten's No-Nonsense Advice for*

Successful Projects, Chapter 21, "Meet Minimum Requirements: Anything More Is Too Much."

**Producing
results that
conform to
requirements**

Q4.7   I am accustomed to the business analyst having to ensure
that the product produced conforms to the requirements.
Why didn't you mention this responsibility?

A4.7   This duty is implied in the listed bullet point "Ensures the
product, service, or result satisfies the client's business
needs."

Q4.8   In our organization, the business analyst helps define
and participates in product testing to ensure the product
conforms to the requirements. Do you think that the
business analyst should do this?

A4.8   Yes, but there is considerable leeway here. Ensuring that
the product conforms to the requirements does not necessarily require the business analyst to define the testing
or participate in that testing. The BA has approval rights
over the test plans and adherence to them, but the BA's
direct participation in testing activities is an organizational
decision.

**The power of
the BA**

Q4.9   If my job as a business analyst is to be the client's
advocate, what power do I have to assert my views on
behalf of the client?

A4.9   You have plenty of power! For starters, you direct the
development of the requirements and negotiate their approval. You have approval rights on many key areas of the
project, such as the project plan; processes and methodologies to be followed; the quality process to be followed;
and the test plans, to name a few. You are a core member
of the project and are expected to participate in routine
project tracking meetings. You serve as a check and bal-

ance over the project to ensure the client is being served properly.

Q4.10 Could the role you are defining for the business analyst lead to a contentious relationship with the project manager and other members of the project?

Promoting a healthy contentious relationship

A4.10 Yes, but I would describe the relationship a bit differently. The BA's job is to look out for the client. No one else working on the project has such a strong tie to the client. The project manager's relationship with the client is nearly as close as the BA's, but the PM's greatest loyalty is to the project sponsor. Obviously, everyone on a project team wants to satisfy the client and run a successful project. However, the team dynamics in achieving a successful project play out differently depending on your role on the team.

A healthy contentious relationship between project members is a good thing. It keeps everyone on their toes and encourages team members to do their best work. So do not assume a contentious relationship is bad. It's not, nor would we want to make it so. When a disagreement arises between two parties, it can be ironed out 95 percent of the time. If it cannot, escalations are initiated. Escalations are good business tools and should not be taken personally by either party to the disagreement. It's not personal; it's business.

Q4.11 As a business analyst, what if the project manager and I cannot agree on the resolution of an issue? What course of action should I take?

Disagreeing with the PM

A4.11 It depends on the issue. If the PM disagrees with your position on an issue that requires your approval in order to proceed, then the PM must escalate that issue over your head in order to resolve it. Generally speaking, if the PM takes a position you disagree with on an issue that is within his domain to decide, then you must escalate over the PM's head. You may have considerable clout and power on a project, but that does not mean you have absolute power. And while the PM has the most power on a project, even he does not have absolute power. These checks and balances on each of your powers are healthy and strengthen the outcome of a project.

Fostering a good relationship with PM

Q4.12 As a business analyst, it appears that I should strive to foster a good working relationship with the project manager. Do you agree?

A4.12 Absolutely yes! You both have positions of power on the project and need each other. I expect you both to work closely together and develop a great working relationship.

Being the client's advocate

Q4.13 As a business analyst, and the client's advocate, is it my job to always do what the client requests?

A4.13 Yes, provided that the request is legal and ethical—and in your company's best business interest. Moreover, you have the duty to ensure that both the client's requests and the execution of those requests are in the client's best interest. If you think otherwise, then work with the client to propose alternatives. Do not knowingly allow the client to make a decision that will be harmful.

Combining the roles of BA and PM

Q4.14 I am a project manager, and I am also the business analyst for that project. Is this wrong?

A4.14 Not necessarily. On smaller projects, it can be customary for one person to take on both positions. On larger projects, however, the PM does not have the time or resources to take on so much work and must primarily focus on the planning and execution of the entire project.

Q4.15 **On smaller projects, then, is it a handicap for one person to take on both the project manager and business analyst roles?**

A4.15 Maybe. The BA position requires specific skills, as well as the time to focus specifically on the client's needs. On small projects, it is more likely that the PM will be able to meet the demands of the BA position.

CHAPTER 5

The Project Analyst

❝A leader's accomplishments are directly related to the talents and dedication of those performing the work. ❞

Q_{5.1} What is the project analyst's job?

A_{5.1} The primary role of the *project analyst* (PA) is, simply stated, to help the project manager. By supporting the PM, the PA can significantly free up the project manager to become a more effective leader.

Primary duties of the PA

Q_{5.2} What are the primary duties of a project analyst?

A_{5.2} The PA:

- Provides the primary interface with project management tools
- Assists project members in the preparation of their plans
- Collects member plans to create the project plan
- Routinely analyzes the progress of plans
- Plays a supporting role during project tracking meetings
- Produces project-tracking-meeting minutes
- Provides a set of "constructive eyes" for the project manager
- Backs up the project manager
- Makes the project manager look good.

Q_{5.3} This book addresses some mighty powerful players on the project scene: the project manager, resource managers, project sponsor, client, business analyst, contractors, vendors, and of course, the all-important project member. Why did you add the project analyst to the group?

PA frees PM to be more effective

A_{5.3} This book is about professional behaviors for project stakeholders. The project analyst can play a significant role in helping the project manager—and, therefore, projects—be more successful. Although some organizations have embraced the PA concept (or an equivalent position), many have not. The PA role is a powerful one that is often overlooked or underutilized. Project managers are typically high-wage earners who perform many basic tasks that could be performed by a project analyst—and might, in some cases, be performed *better* because of the specialized skills that the project analyst brings to the team.

Many project managers are stretched to their limits but continue to perform the type of activities better performed by a PA. The PM must focus primarily on leading the project to a successful conclusion and less on support activities that consume far too much of his time and energy. Enter the project analyst!

Q_{5.4} Can the project analyst also be known by other titles?

Names for the PA role

A_{5.4} Some typical project analyst duties might be performed by project members in positions titled project administrator, project scheduler, project coordinator, and project associate, just to name a few. Of course, the position title is not what's important, but the duties performed by the project member in this position.

Q_{5.5} Can you explain the project analyst's duty to provide the primary interface with project management tools?

Primary interface to project management tools

A_{5.5} It is often highly unproductive for PMs to spend time entering and modifying data in project management tools. A project analyst could likely work with these tools more skillfully, efficiently, and for less cost, which frees the PM to lead the project and perform the duties listed in Chapter 1, "The Project Manager."

It is important to note that nothing in the project plan should be added, deleted, or modified without the PM's authorization. The PM should always be fully aware of and approve all information that populates the plan and other project tools. The PM can request that the PA generate specific reports from project management tools that can help track and manage the project plan's progress.

Assists in preparation of plans

Q_{5.6} What about the project analyst's role in assisting project members in the preparation of their plans?

A_{5.6} The project analyst can help the project manager ensure that project members—including team leaders—receive proper training in how to develop effective plans for their portions of the project. The project analyst can hold formal training classes for project members, or she can work one-on-one with project members to help teach them the planning skills they need. Of course, any instruction of project members must be supported and approved by the project manager. This training can also include teaching project members how to use the chosen project management tools.

Q_{5.7} Does the project analyst also help the PM review the project members' plans?

A_{5.7} Yes. After a project member has created a plan or a team leader has created a plan with her team, the plan typically should be reviewed and approved by the appropriate resource managers. Afterwards, the project manager must review the plan and be sure it is complete, accurate, sufficiently detailed, reasonable, and likely to be achieved.

The project analyst may assist the project manager in "scrubbing" these plans and ensuring that any problems found are logged, assigned to the proper project members, and tracked to closure. Depending on the project analyst's prior experience, he may scrub the plans by himself, which frees the project manager to scrub other plans or perform other duties.

Q5.8　Can you tell me more about the project analyst's duty to collect member plans to create the project plan?

Constructs overall project plan

A5.8　At the direction of the project manager, the project analyst collects all plans from the project members or team leaders and loads them into the chosen project management tool(s). In some cases, each plan might already have been developed using the chosen project management tool, so it may be relatively simple to combine the plans. In other cases, the individual plans may have to be entered from scratch. The project manager, with assistance from the project analyst, determines which activities from each plan need to be added to the overall project plan.

Q5.9　Aren't all activities from the individual plans added to the project plan?

A5.9　My experience has shown that it is not effective to load all the activities from each plan into the project plan unless it is a small project. On a larger project, the PM will have too many details to track if every activity is added to the overall plan. Project members or team leaders need these details documented to successfully manage their domains, but the project manager may only need to track key activities and any dependencies that one individual plan has on another plan. For larger projects, it may be best to uplift as little as 20 percent of an individual plan's activities to the overall plan.

Routinely analyzes progress of plans

Q_{5.10} What can you tell me about the project analyst's duty to routinely analyze the progress of plans?

A_{5.10} Under the direction of the PM, and working closely with project members and team leaders, the project analyst may regularly review the progress being made on some or all of the individual plans. The project analyst acts as a check and balance to help ensure that approved plans are being implemented as planned and that any problems are identified and are receiving the necessary attention.

For example, the project analyst assesses the effect of schedule slippages on the overall project plan and helps the designated project member or team leader mitigate his problems. The project analyst's focus is on helping the project member or team leader be successful. It is important that the project analyst's energy is focused on resolving problems and learning from mistakes, not in finding fault or attacking people.

Project tracking meetings

Q_{5.11} What role does the project analyst play during project tracking meetings?

A_{5.11} The project analyst supports the project manager during project tracking meetings. For example, the project analyst records the meeting minutes while the project manager directs the tracking meeting. (The person running the meeting should not take a lot of notes. Why? Because, as mentioned in Q&A 1.29 of Chapter 1, "The Project Manager," the meeting's leader pausing to write slows down the pace of the meeting. Note taking also diverts the leader's attention and hinders her ability to ask questions and interface with the meeting participants.)

The project analyst can also help by recording "action items" as they are mentioned during the meeting. The list of action items should be visible to everyone at the meeting. It can be made, for example, on a flip chart, white board, or large-screen computer monitor.

The project analyst may actively participate in discussion during the tracking meeting. Anything that the project analyst can do to help the project manager have a more productive meeting is encouraged.

A project analyst might also make sure that a suitable meeting place is available for each project tracking meeting and that the proper seating and materials are available.

Q₅.₁₂ **Isn't it the job of the project manager, rather than the project analyst, to produce the minutes of the project tracking meeting?**

Minutes of project tracking meeting

A₅.₁₂ The project analyst typically drafts the meeting minutes and presents them to the project manager for approval. The project manager may choose to modify the information appearing in the minutes or their style or tone. Once approved, the project analyst distributes the minutes to the appropriate audience.

Along with the meeting minutes, the PA may prepare exhibits that the project members will use at the next project tracking meeting. These exhibits could include action items updated with the most recent status, customized project checklists that each project member or team leader will update and present at the next meeting, and other exhibits as needed.

The project analyst may also help prepare periodic (monthly, weekly, or as often as needed) reports to senior management and the clients. These reports are important communication tools and must include metrics that show the plan and the progress being made toward the plan.

**Expands PM's
reach**

Q_{5.13} How does the project analyst provide "constructive eyes" for the project manager?

A_{5.13} The project manager relies on all project members to communicate accurately, honestly, and in a timely manner. This includes asking for help when it is needed, especially if problems are not being resolved with the sense of urgency and importance they require. The project analyst is always alert to areas within the project that require the project manager's attention and appropriately informs the project manager.

Backs up PM

Q_{5.14} How does the project analyst back up the project manager?

A_{5.14} If the project analyst has achieved a certain level of skill and experience in assisting project managers, then he might act as the project manager's backup when the PM is not available. For example, if the project manager is out of the office or attending to duties, then the project analyst might substitute for or represent the project manager—if not in a decision-making capacity, then at least in a data-gathering capacity.

**Focuses on
making the
PM successful**

Q_{5.15} What does the project analyst do to make the project manager look good?

A_{5.15} The primary duty of the project analyst, as described in just a few words, is to make the PM look good. The PA's function is to help the PM be successful so that the project will be successful. The PA is the tireless and loyal supporter of the PM.

Q_{5.16} What do you think is the proper ratio of project analysts to projects or to project managers?

A_{5.16} The correct ratio varies depending on the complexity and sizes of the projects and the skill of the PMs. Depending on the number of team members on a project, there may be no, one, or multiple PAs assigned to work on the project.

For example, one PA may be able to support a handful of small projects that have five to 15 core members each, or support one high-maintenance mid-size project with 50 to 75 core members. Large projects may benefit from multiple PAs. Designating PAs can free up PMs to take on more projects and to perform more effectively on their current projects.

Q_{5.17} I can certainly see the benefit of a project manager having the services of a project analyst, but don't you believe that most organizations cannot or will not incur the extra expense of hiring project analysts to support their project managers?

A_{5.17} If PMs are to be consistently successful leaders, they must always be searching for methods that can optimize their effectiveness. In my experience, it is more cost-effective for most organizations to hire PAs or train interested employees to become PAs than to leave PMs to perform many tasks typically done by PAs.

Q_{5.18} Should a project analyst report directly to a project manager, thus making the project manager also his resource manager?

A_{5.18} No. As I have discussed elsewhere in this book (Q&A 1.24, Chapter 1, "The Project Manager"), it is best for a person to not take on the positions of both PM and RM. PAs report to resource managers and are assigned to PMs. Preferably, all PAs should report to the same resource manager so that their specialty skills are uniformly developed and their careers are nurtured. Project analysts are likely to come from project management organizations (PMOs) or similar groups.

CHAPTER 6

The Client

We tend to forget who pays our salaries. It is the customer .... The minute we forget that, the reason for our being here is gone.

—Lars Nyberg, manufacturing company executive

Q6.1 As a project manager, what can I do if a client internal to the organization or company is not willing to dedicate enough people to work with me and other members of my project team?

Insufficient dedicated resources from client

A6.1 Make sure the client fully understands its roles and responsibilities throughout the life cycle of your project. The client shares the responsibility for the success of the project. Explain that by performing its duties, the client helps ensure that the right product, service, or result is delivered. And if necessary, explore alternative solutions such as hiring a vendor or contractor to work on behalf of the client.

If the client continues to give the project insufficient support, then discuss the issue with the project sponsor (if different from the client) and get the sponsor's support to help work this issue to closure. You must make it clear to both the client and the project sponsor how the final delivery will be affected if the client's participation is not adequate.

Q6.2 What if the client is external to the organization or company?

A6.2 The same answer given in A6.1 still applies. However, it is more likely that external clients will cooperate because "real" (external-to-the-company) money is at stake, and there usually are bigger consequences if they do not.

In the worst-case scenario, an external client might demand that you perform your best anyway, even though the client is not a sufficiently active project participant. As long as the client is aware of the risks, and you believe that the work can proceed in a satisfactory manner, then continue on with the project. However, if you believe the risks are too high and the client's investment may be in jeopardy, then talk with the project sponsor before you proceed further. The project sponsor should consult with his legal counsel, if appropriate. If the project sponsor is not sure whether to seek legal advice, then that means he *should.* Always err on the side of caution.

Confiding in client about company-sensitive information

Q6.3 We all know how important the client is. As the project manager, is it appropriate for me to tell the client that a critical employee from my company should be requested by name, full-time, in the contract? If not, the employee might only be available part-time or not at all, and that could harm the project.

A6.3 No. This behavior undermines your company. However, if you believe that the project will be harmed if the individual is not committed full-time to the project, then work through the appropriate channels within your company to ensure that person's availability or the availability of an equally skilled resource. After the commitment has been arranged internally, it is appropriate to add the employee's name to the contract.

Saying "no" to a client

Q6.4 From a requirements point of view, should the client always get what it wants?

A6.4 Not necessarily. Clients should get what they *need.* Most clients don't know the difference between what they need and what they want. Consequently, they want it all. The business analyst's job is to protect the client's interests. This includes making sure the client understands the difference between needs and wants and is given what is in its best business interest. More on clients' needs versus wants is discussed in Q&A 4.5 and 4.6 (Chapter 4, "The Business Analyst").

Q_{6.5} **As a project manager, I am never comfortable saying "no" to a client. After all, the client is paying the bill.**

A_{6.5} You aren't simply saying "no." You have the duty to tell the client what you think is in its best business interest. If, after hearing your opinion, the client still insists that it wants more of the requirements satisfied than you think would be in its best interest, then you must honor the client's request. But work closely with the project sponsor to ensure that you have done the best you could for the client and have sufficiently documented your position if related issues arise later.

Q_{6.6} **The last example seemed to relate to an external client. Is it ever okay to say "no" to an internal client?**

A_{6.6} Yes, but not without great thought and consideration. For example, say an information technology (IT) shop has 100 projects waiting to be implemented, but only has the capacity to work on 30 projects at any given time. If an internal client owns one of the 30 projects now underway and asks that substantial new functionality be added and offers to pay any extra costs and allow more time for delivery, what do you do? The answer will vary on a project-by-project basis and is typically determined based on the best business decision. But often the right answer is *not* to perform a substantial amount of new work for this delivery. Why? Because doing so can jeopardize the availability of project members who have already committed to work on other projects.

An IT shop must consider the bigger picture: The goal is to appropriately service all clients, and breaking commitments to other projects in order to continue to service an active project can create great hardship throughout a company. The added work can be scheduled as a new project.

Many IT shops are not well-respected across their company because they manage their commitments poorly and so are frequently late in meeting those commitments. Internal clients would rather hear "no" from time to time, as long as you meet your commitments reliably when you do say "yes."

Honoring a client's request that undermines the project outcome

Q6.7 As a project manager, if I have a client who specifically requests that my team conduct the project in a manner that I believe could harm the integrity of the delivery, should I honor that request anyway?

A6.7 Almost never! Your client doesn't always know what he needs or what is best for him. Your job includes looking out for the client's best interests, even though the client might not fully understand what's at stake. Don't intentionally allow the client to make bad decisions.

Q6.8 I understand what you're saying, but I still have a hard time refusing a client's request. Can you give an example of how to do so?

A6.8 Say you are leading a software development project, and the formal testing is typically made up of three tests run serially: a development test, an independent test, and a user acceptance test. Each test lasts six weeks. This means that formal testing is scheduled to last 18 weeks. However, the client wants to reduce the time required to deliver the final product into production. All obvious options have been exhausted. But the client, believing that anything is possible, instructs the PM to conduct both the independent testing and the user acceptance testing in parallel, thus saving up to six weeks of testing. Usually, this would be a bad thing to do, because each formal test must be completed and any major problems corrected before moving on to the next phase of testing.

Because this book is not about software testing, I will not list the many reasons why these two tests should not be conducted in parallel. In short, doing so can cause serious problems that would likely lead to an additional six weeks—or more—of testing. You should understand the risks of running both tests at once, and you must explain these risks to the client.

Q$_{6.9}$ But what if the client is adamant about doing it anyway, and is willing to assume all risk and accountability for the mess that could result?

A$_{6.9}$ Most clients would not intentionally do something so reckless. However, in this extreme example, with the approval of the project sponsor and with appropriate documentation of the risk, the PM would oblige the client.

Understand that in the long run, almost all clients appreciate and respect the integrity of the project manager (and business analyst) to do the "right thing," even though the right thing is not always what the client wants to hear. Don't idly volunteer to do stupid things. Remember that the client is the reason you have a job.

By the way, the project sponsor should consult with his legal counsel before making the final decision on whether to honor the client's request.

Q$_{6.10}$ Are you saying that, as a project manager, I *should* abide by the client's wishes even if I think doing so is not in the client's best interest?

A$_{6.10}$ In general, do not perform an action that you believe is not in the client's best interest and could harm the client without first working with the client and informing him of the risks. If the client chooses to take the risk and pay the associated costs, then defer the decision to the project sponsor. It is important that the project sponsor is aware of the legal implications, if any, in performing the client-requested actions. In the unlikely case that the client is asking you to do something illegal or unethical, do *not* agree to do so, and immediately inform your project sponsor and your boss (if he is not the project sponsor).

Client not satisfied with execution of project

Q6.11 As the client, what if I am not satisfied with how the project is being conducted?

A6.11 Work with the PM to resolve your concerns. If that doesn't help, then escalate your concerns to the project sponsor. In the unlikely event that you are unable to satisfactorily resolve the issue with the sponsor, take your concerns to the sponsor's boss. The path of escalation, whether initiated by the client or the sponsor, should be documented in the project contract, or in the "document of understanding" if the client is internal.

Client hiring PM consultant as a check-and-balance

Q6.12 As the client, I have a lot riding on the successful planning and execution of the project. Is it appropriate for me to hire a project-manager-like consultant to monitor the project's progress as a check-and-balance mechanism to protect my business interests?

A6.12 It's your call. As a PM consultant, I have had several clients who wished they had done just that. If they had had an extra set of experienced eyes, they could have saved a lot of time and money. Problems would have been revealed much earlier, when it would have been less expensive and time-consuming to mitigate them. Not all projects are run so sloppily that you need to hire a consultant, but if you have a substantial business investment at stake, the extra cost of the PM-type consultant can yield a tremendous return on investment.

Do not overlook alternatives such as insisting on in-depth project reviews, audits by other PMs internal to your company, and the establishment of an oversight committee, just to name a few.

Q_{6.13} **Should the client always come first?**

A_{6.13} Not always, but almost always. Typically, the client's wishes should come first. However, it is possible that the client's demands are contrary to your company's best interests. In these cases, the client does not come first. The survival of your organization and company does. If your company goes out of business because you chose to satisfy certain client demands, you have created a bigger problem—for both your company and your client's company—than you would have if you had put your own interests first.

Client always coming first

CHAPTER 7

Contractors

❝Treating contractors like second-class project members will surely yield second-class results.❞

Q₇.₁   What is your definition of a contractor?

A₇.₁   A *contractor* is a person who has been hired to perform one or more activities. This person typically resides at the purchasing company's location and works alongside other contractors and company employees. A contractor can work under the direction of a representative of the contractor's company or under the direction of the purchasing company. Contractors typically work on an hourly basis and are not paid directly by the purchasing company; the purchasing company usually pays the contractor's company for the work performed. The contractor then receives a portion of that payment from the company.

Hiring contractors into lead positions

Q₇.₂   My organization often hires contractors into lead positions. Doing so robs the regular employees of some of the best opportunities. How do you feel about this practice?

A₇.₂   If an organization has a lead position open, and there is a qualified employee available, it should offer the position to that employee first. "Family" should come first. However, my experience is that it is common for an organization to lack qualified employees who are available for a given project—they are committed elsewhere. In this case, the business needs must be fulfilled, even if that means going outside the company to find contractors. However, when-

ever appropriate, I would want to train company employees to eventually take over the best jobs being held by
contractors.

Q_{7.3} **Would you hire a contractor to take the lead project manager position on a project, knowing that the contractor will be leading mostly company employees?**

Contractor as PM

A_{7.3} Yes, if there was no qualified employee available to take the PM position. Company management has a duty to promote business success so that opportunities and jobs are not lost. Projects need qualified project managers to lead them. Again, I would have no hesitation going out-side the company for help if I could not find the necessary skills inside the company.

Q_{7.4} **What about hiring a contractor to be a resource manager over company employees?**

Contractor as RM

A_{7.4} This one gets sticky. Only under very unusual conditions would I place a contractor in an RM position. Why? The contractor would be handicapped in working with many of the other RMs because he would most likely be viewed as an outsider. His "outsider" status could be a problem when he tries to get salary increases, promotions, awards, or the best jobs for the employees working under him.

Q_{7.5} **Can you give me an example of an "unusual condition" under which you would hire a contractor as a resource manager?**

A_{7.5} If the contractor was a well-respected former company em-ployee with an understanding of the company's manage-ment, I would feel more comfortable hiring him as an RM. I would also consider hiring the contractor if he is uniquely qualified to manage a specific skilled group of employees. And I might hire a contractor as an RM if the company is temporarily increasing its staff size, and I do not want to hire RMs only to have to let them go sometime later. But in most cases, I would expect to hire full-time, experienced RMs, or grow them from within the employee base.

Treatment of contractors

Q_{7.6} Should contractors be treated differently from other project members?

A_{7.6} No. Contractors should be held just as accountable as any other project members, information they need to do their jobs should be readily available, they should participate in meetings that are relevant to their domains of responsibility, and so forth.

As a consultant, I was mentoring a PM, and one day we were walking to a meeting. The PM told me that there would be contractors attending. Just before we entered the room, she lowered her voice and said that she would point out the contractors when we got inside the meeting room. I then stopped, pulled her aside outside the room, and asked if the contractors were part of the project plan. She said that they were. I asked if the contractors were needed to make the project successful. She again said "yes." I then said, "Don't point the contractors out to me. It doesn't matter, because I will treat everyone on the project the same. We are all in this together."

People perform at their best when they are treated the same as everyone else.

Treating contractors the same as project members

Q_{7.7} Are you saying that you treat contractors *almost* the same as project members who are full-time employees?

A_{7.7} No. I *always* treat them the same as other project members. For example, if it is customary for the project team to go out to lunch together each Friday, then a contractor just hired on the project is invited along as well. If the project team reaches a major milestone, and the team celebrates with snacks or small gifts, the contractor also is included.

Q_{7.8} I was taught that it is important that contractors *not* be treated exactly the same as employees because there are government rules about such things. What do you say to that?

A_{7.8} Do not treat contractors the same as *employees*. If the organization or company has a special event or gives out a trinket to each employee, the contractor does not participate (unless legal counsel has first been consulted). However, when it comes to the *project*, contractors should be treated the same as any other *project member*.

Not treating contractors the same as company employees

Q_{7.9} Do you believe contractors are often treated as second-class project members?

A_{7.9} This is a common practice in many organizations—fortunately, not in all. Some full-time employees resent contractors for a number of reasons. They believe that contractors:

- Get the best jobs
- Are paid too much
- Are paid for overtime, but employees are not
- Do not have to put up with the political drama
- Are not as motivated to perform well or produce high-quality work.

Resentful employees should keep in mind that without contractors, their businesses would suffer. Contractors are needed to fill skill voids. Employees who believe that contractors are getting a great deal can quit the company and become contractors! Guess what? You won't see a mad dash to exit. Most contractors would love to be full-time employees. When business slows down, the contractors are the first to be let go—as they should be. Again, "family" comes first.

Do not begrudge contractors. Understand the value they bring to the business and accept them as fully functioning members of the project team.

Don't begrudge contractors

<table>
<tr>
<td>

Uncooperative contractor

</td>
<td>

Q 7.10   As a project manager, what should I do if a contractor will not cooperate or "play well with others"?

A 7.10   Contractors should be held to the same high standards and expectations as other project members. If a contractor is harming the project, work with him to resolve the issue. If that does not work, escalate to the contractor's resource manager. This person might be an RM in the contractor's company or an RM within your company. If you are unable to obtain a satisfactory resolution, continue to escalate the issue until it is resolved. Include the project sponsor if necessary.

Q 7.11   What if I am not a project manager, but as a project member, I am having problems with a contractor?

A 7.11   Again, thoughtfully work with the contractor in an attempt to resolve the issue. If you are unsuccessful, then go to the PM for help. The PM will work with you in helping to resolve the issue.

</td>
</tr>
<tr>
<td>

Cost-effectiveness of contractors

</td>
<td>

Q 7.12   Are contractors really more cost-effective than full-time employees?

A 7.12   Sometimes they can be, but whether they are depends on so many factors that are outside the scope of this book. Focus on the following: Contractors are usually hired because the company doesn't have employees with the required skills available to perform the work. They are hired so that an organization or company can meet its business objectives. Most people reading this book should not second-guess the hiring of contractors; instead, you should focus on performing satisfactorily within your domain of responsibility, and leave it to senior management to make appropriate business decisions about the use of contractors.

</td>
</tr>
</table>

Q_{7.13} Are you saying that the project manager should not care whether contractors are used?

A_{7.13} In most cases, this decision is made by management and the sponsor—perhaps with input from the PM. Someday, I would like to see the PM take a more entrepreneurial role in an organization or company and be the primary decision-maker on whether to hire contractors. Today, however, very few companies are mature enough to give PMs this level of business accountability.

CHAPTER 8

Vendors

❝When formulating a contract with a vendor, you get what you negotiate—nothing more, but often less.❞

Q8.1 What is your definition of a vendor?

A8.1 A *vendor* is a company that is hired to perform some type of work typically defined in a document called a *statement of work*. The vendor usually manages its own activities and resides at a location apart from the company that has purchased its services.

PM's accountability over vendor

Q8.2 As a project manager, am I also accountable for work performed by a vendor?

A8.2 Absolutely yes! You are fully accountable for the project and, therefore, all of the pieces that make up the project.

Q8.3 That doesn't seem fair! The vendor committed to produce deliverables of specific scope, on specific dates, and with a specific level of quality. The vendor is hundreds of miles away and is an independent company. What can I do, realistically, about the vendor's performance?

A8.3 With that whiny, spineless attitude, not much! Here's how the vendor's performance should have been monitored: First, set the expectations for the vendor. These expectations are recorded in the contract. Then you track the vendor's progress against those commitments. The vendor should be tracked in the same way as all other members of the project. At least weekly, the vendor should give you a status report. If the vendor seems to be headed for a missed commitment, you must insist on a recovery plan that can be measured and tracked.

Q8.4 What if the vendor consistently delivers on time, but the work is lower quality than required? As a project manager, what could I have done to prevent this?

Low vendor quality

A8.4 Before the vendor is officially accepted as a member of the project, assess its capability to perform by *qualifying* it. Evaluate the vendor's ability to remain solvent and to successfully meet its commitments to your project, look at its performance record with past projects and clients, ensure that it has quality processes that can yield deliverables of acceptable quality, and interview current and past clients of the vendor.

Once you have determined that the company is qualified to be your vendor, make sure that it satisfactorily follows its approved quality processes. The vendor should provide periodic exhibits to prove that it is on track and is working within the expected quality parameters. These exhibits could include documents, prototypes, reviews, inspections, and product-specific deliverables. If you track the vendor's progress, you are much more likely to detect any quality problems before they can really hurt the project.

Q8.5 As a project manager, what recourse do I have if the vendor and I disagree on an issue?

Resolving disagreements with vendor

A8.5 First, do your best to resolve the issue by working directly with a representative from the vendor. If the problem remains, then, working with your project sponsor, escalate the issue up the vendor's management chain. The contract should define the escalation path up the vendor's chain of management, as well as how the vendor is expected to escalate up your management chain, if needed. If the escalation process and paths are not already documented, then you should do so as soon as possible.

PM behavior when working with vendors

Q8.6   I think you're expecting too much from the project manager when it comes to working with and managing vendors. How *should* a project manager behave when working with a vendor?

A8.6   Here is an example of what a PM should *not* do. Let's say that he just completed a project that was delivered late, over budget, and with lower than expected quality. He tells his boss that these problems were not his fault and that there was nothing he could have done to prevent them. The PM says that the vendor, located halfway around the world, was at fault. He explains that the vendor repeatedly insisted that it was on schedule and was following good quality processes—yet every delivery was late and of low quality. The boss says to the PM, "I don't recall you ever walking into my office and requesting funding to fly to the vendor's location for a day, a week, or a month—whatever it takes—to personally participate in resolving the problem."

Don't leave things to chance. Assert yourself and lead the project to a successful outcome in which everyone wins. Verify that things actually are as the vendor is telling you they are. Practice the mantra: *If it is to be, it is up to me!*

Q8.7   But what if the vendor doesn't want the project manager to interfere?

A8.7   As the PM, you shouldn't care what the vendor wants. When a vendor is failing to do what it is contractually obligated to do, your job is to ensure that the vendor recovers and that the project will be successful. Make it so.

Q_{8.8} As a project manager, what can I do if the vendor removes a critical project member from its portion of the project?

A_{8.8} Immediately discuss the issue with the designated vendor representative. If you are unable to resolve the issue, escalate up the vendor chain of management, with support from the project sponsor, to resolve the issue.

Q_{8.9} You leave me with the impression that, as the project manager, I can always get the vendor to do what I want. Do you really believe I can always get the vendor to fulfill its commitments?

A_{8.9} Yes, most of the time—but only if you get off your duff and lead the project like you mean it. You must act as if your job and the jobs of all the project members depend on your ability to lead the project to a successful outcome. Will you prevail 100 percent of the time when dealing with a problem vendor? Not likely. But when you do not prevail, you should escalate any problems to the project sponsor and vendor senior management. That is your role.

Q_{8.10} As the project manager, should I have a project member who constantly oversees the vendor's performance to ensure that it meets its commitments?

A_{8.10} Yes, in most cases. On small projects, that project member can be you. On larger projects, the project member designated as the liaison to the vendor can monitor its progress.

Q_{8.11} What is a case in which it might be okay for no one to oversee the performance of the vendor?

A_{8.11} There may be limited oversight of the vendor's performance if the vendor's contribution to the project is relatively minor or of low risk, or if the vendor has a proven record of high reliability.

PART TWO

The People Side

Part Two, consisting of 15 chapters, deals with more personal topics, providing advice for individual project members and employees. You will likely find many topics and issues that hit close to home; here's a sampling of what you can expect to find in each chapter.

CHAPTER 9: ACCOUNTABILITY, DEPENDENCIES, AND COMMITMENTS

Tracking dependencies; informing the receiver of the status of a dependency; learning information late; the uncooperative stakeholder; a project member's domain of responsibility; being unable to meet a committed date; discovering overcommitment; being invited late to a project; reviewers versus approvers; new urgent work versus existing commitments; obtaining commitments from others; project members undermining project manager and team decisions.

CHAPTER 10: LEADERSHIP STYLES, ATTRIBUTES, AND BEHAVIORS

Your company's most important asset; consensus management; micromanaging; benevolent dictatorship; the making of a leader; saying "I don't know"; listening to another point of view; holding back knowledge for power; ego; the "handicap" of being a woman or being young; motivating project members; criticizing the work or behavior of others; procrastination; determining your top three priorities; thinking for yourself; courage; delivering bad news; learning to say "no"; managing expectations; being a role model.

CHAPTER 11: SHARING POWER

Going against human nature; the downside of sharing power; having two or more project managers on a project; committees lacking a person with final authority.

CHAPTER 12: INTERPERSONAL COMMUNICATIONS

Is it okay to complain?; professional immaturity; asking for help; helping others when there is no direct benefit to you; attitude; speaking ill of others; random acts of kindness; saying "please" and "thank you";

admitting to mistakes; losing your temper; undermining a person's reputation; not liking a coworker; a coworker not liking you; making and taking things personally.

CHAPTER 13: RESOLVING CONFLICT THROUGH ESCALATIONS

Determining the party that initiates the escalation; knowing when to stop escalating; your boss' role in escalations; concern about harming relationships; escalating over your boss' head; escalation doesn't mean either party is wrong; the project manager's role in escalations; escalating to the CEO.

CHAPTER 14: MEETINGS

What to do if there are too many meetings; the best times of day to schedule meetings; attendees arriving late or leaving early; attendees who won't "play fair"; recording minutes; tips on conducting local meetings; tips on conducting remote meetings; what to do when a boss takes meetings on a tangent.

CHAPTER 15: CELEBRATIONS

The need for celebrations; celebrating late achievements; initiating celebrations; types of celebrations; disinterested project members.

CHAPTER 16: OVERTIME WORK

The business of working overtime; how much overtime is required; how much overtime is too much; avoiding burnout; overtime's effect on productivity and quality; the link between overtime and career success; planned overtime.

CHAPTER 17: MENTORING

Value of a mentor; finding a mentor; your boss as your mentor; rejection from a potential mentor; good chemistry between mentor and mentee; accessibility of a mentor; the boss' access to mentor's information; upsides and downsides of being a mentor.

CHAPTER 18: ETHICS AND INTEGRITY

Encountering illegal or unethical behavior; becoming a whistle-blower; conferring with a trusted third party; what to do if your boss asks you to engage in bad behavior; what a project manager or project member asked to perform questionable work should do; lying and distorting information; company's interests versus personal interests; announcing that you are leaving the company.

CHAPTER 19: TELECOMMUTING/WORKING FROM HOME

The choice to work from home; factors that affect working from home; obtaining your boss' permission; business decisions that drive the telecommuting decision; working "extra" hours from home.

CHAPTER 20: AWARDS AND RECOGNITION

Identifying award candidates; seeking an award; methods of recognizing award recipients; insufficient awards; are awards worth it?; envy of other's recognition; not feeling appreciated; offering bonus and penalty incentives.

CHAPTER 21: PERSONAL DEVELOPMENT, JOB, AND CAREER

Your boss and your career; unsure of your career interests; seeking a new assignment or job; unsure of your job duties; what's more important: career or project?; disliking a project to which you are assigned; disliking your job; trolling your resume outside of the company; paying for professional memberships or certifications; the amount of training to expect from your organization; creating a nonexistent job; discovering your talents; age and one's ability to achieve; balancing personal and professional lives; continuous personal improvement.

CHAPTER 22: PROMOTING CHANGE IN YOUR ORGANIZATION

Bringing ideas back to your team and organization; initiating change at the top of the organization; management's role in promoting change; obtaining stubborn management's buy-in; sharing best practices with other companies; lack of respect for the project management craft.

CHAPTER 23: MERGERS AND ACQUISITIONS

Anxiety impeding a project's progress; what to do when process-improvement initiatives are halted.

CHAPTER 9

Accountability, Dependencies, and Commitments

❝ *You manage your commitments; nobody manages them for you.* ❞

Q₉.₁ How do I determine my domain of responsibility?

A₉.₁ Simply stated, your *domain of responsibility* includes all responsibilities and commitments that fall within the scope of your assignment. It includes any activities and actions necessary to support your meeting your commitments.

A person's domain of responsibility typically is far broader than first assumed. There is a simple but powerful saying that is made up of ten 2-letter words: *"If it is to be, it is up to me."* This saying can help you define the boundaries of your domain as you work toward the successful achievement of your commitments.

Q₉.₂ If routine (typically weekly) project tracking meetings are held on a project, are they the mechanism for a project member to track the status of a dependency on another project member?

A₉.₂ The project tracking meeting is certainly an important and useful mechanism to help project members stay abreast of the progress of dependencies. However, do not use this meeting as the only method of tracking dependencies. A project member with a dependency on another project member should be in regular communication with that project member—especially as the dependency's due date nears. Moreover, the project manager is expected to stay on top of the progress of activities/dependencies that are approaching completion.

Q9.3 If a project member (receiver) has a dependency on a deliverable from another project member (deliverer), what duty does the deliverer have to keep the receiver informed of the progress being made in preparing the deliverable?

A9.3 The deliverer (the person responsible for creating the deliverable) has the duty to inform the receiver (the person dependent on receiving the deliverable) if there is any likelihood that the deliverable will be late or incomplete. The deliverer should inform the receiver as soon as the deliverer sees a potential problem. Why? The sooner the receiver is aware of a potential problem, the sooner plans can be discussed to help ensure the complete deliverable is available on time or an alternative plan is set in motion.

Q9.4 Should the deliverer also inform the project manager of a possible problem, or is informing the receiver enough?

A9.4 The deliverer should definitely inform the PM. The PM must be aware of all problems and potential problems that could harm the project. His help may be needed to negotiate and resolve the problem. Moreover, the PM sees the bigger project picture and must also focus on downstream effects on other project members and on the overall project schedule plan.

Q9.5 Say that a project member (deliverer) repeatedly says that he is on schedule to deliver a critical-path item to another project member (receiver) who has a dependency on that item—but the item is delivered three days late. Is the project member receiving the late delivery responsible for maintaining the critical-path schedule, even though it wasn't his fault that the dependency was delivered late?

A9.5 Yes, the receiving project member is responsible for doing what is reasonable to maintain the critical-path schedule. Meanwhile, the project manager should be aware of the situation and, if necessary, should help ensure that the integrity of the project schedule plan is preserved.

Q9.6 But this isn't fair to the receiving project member. It wasn't his fault that the delivery was late. Why should he be held accountable for maintaining the overall schedule integrity?

A9.6 The first priority here is not placing blame. It is resolving the problem so that the overall project does not suffer. To that end, the PM should typically be informed of the situation and may be instrumental in working with all affected parties to repair the situation. Don't forget to inform and include downstream project members who also may be affected. The project member who originally caused the delivery to be late can also be included in the resolution.

Q9.7 What if a stakeholder does not give me information in a timely manner that I need to perform my job?

Learning information late

A9.7 As soon as you realize that there is a problem, the first thing to do is recover as best you can. Then discuss with the stakeholder the hardship you face because the information came to you late. Ask the stakeholder to keep you informed in a timely fashion next time. Make sure that you and the stakeholder understand the new process or mechanism to be followed. Also, make sure that your agreement is documented and the appropriate parties are informed of the agreement.

Q9.8 What if the stakeholder refuses to change or create a process to appropriately address my needs?

Uncooperative stakeholder

A9.8   First work to resolve the problem with the stakeholder. Give her ample opportunity to help you. If it is clear that you are being ignored, and you cannot accept things the way they are, escalate the issue to the appropriate person. Do not overlook your own role in resolving the conflict—you personally might need to create or alter an existing process and champion that process to get the support you need.

Sharing information that is outside my domain of responsibility

Q9.9   I am not the project manager. What if I know that a project member will likely be late on a deliverable to another project member, but the receiving project member is not aware of the situation? The late deliverable will not affect me directly. Should I tell anyone?

A9.9   Usually, you are not technically responsible for informing affected parties. Why? Because doing so is outside your domain of responsibility. However, because there is a clear benefit to the overall project, you can see the upside in getting involved and contacting the appropriate stake-holders.

Q9.10   Who are the stakeholders that should be contacted?

A9.10   In most cases, you should first encourage the deliverer to inform the PM and other parties who would be affected by a late deliverable. If this doesn't work, then notify the PM. It will then be her duty to work with all affected parties to ensure the issue is appropriately handled.

Domain of responsibility defined by RM

Q9.11   Can you give an example of a case in which an unaffected project member clearly has the duty to inform other project members of potential problems?

A9.11   If the project member has been told by his boss that he is expected to go beyond his specific activities and tasks and to look out for the overall well-being of the project, then he has an expanded domain of responsibility. That project member now has the duty to inform appropriate parties when he discovers a problem or potential problem outside his own core activities and tasks.

Q9.12 What if the project member has been told not by his boss, but by the project manager, to look out for the well-being of the project? Should the project member comply with the project manager's request?

Domain of responsibility defined by PM

A9.12 Yes. The PM is accountable for the overall project, which includes defining and enforcing the project culture and the behaviors expected from its members. The PM should also tell the project member's resource manager that she has placed this expectation on the project member so that the RM can work with his employee to support the PM.

Q9.13 Do you believe a project member's domain of responsibility should include looking out for the health of the overall project, not just his assigned activities and tasks?

Project member's domain of responsibility

A9.13 Yes, but this only works optimally if *all* project members are aware that they are expected to take on this expanded role. However, project members need to understand that they must not take their eyes off their primary focus: their own assigned activities and tasks.

Q9.14 What is the best way to ensure that all project members understand that they are responsible for looking out for the health of the overall project?

A9.14 Their bosses should let them know that their overall performance evaluations will be based in part on their concern and subsequent actions related to the overall health of the project. Also, a culture-training class (see Chapter 27, "Project Culture") given at the beginning of a project should reinforce this duty. Every project team member should understand that the project manager is the only one who is fully accountable for the successful outcome of the project, but each member must also understand his role in successfully executing and completing the project.

Holding part-time stakeholders who have outside project conflicts accountable

Q9.15 I am a project manager. I have a project member who is assigned 50 percent of the time to my project and 50 percent to supporting applications that are active in production systems. Should I back off if this project member is going to deliver a critical-path item on my project late because he is being called upon to resolve a support problem requiring far more than 50 percent of his time?

A9.15 No. You should work to solve the problem. First talk with the part-time project member. If an acceptable solution cannot be reached, then the boss of the part-time project member must be included in the discussion. If the boss is not helpful, then the issue should be escalated until it is resolved.

The worst-case scenario for you? You are told to "live with it," which means that your project may suffer. In this case, you must work as diligently as possible to mitigate any damage to the project—all the while keeping senior stakeholders informed of any possible harm to your project and asking for their help, if needed.

Missing commitments

Q9.16 Is it okay to miss a commitment?

A9.16 No, not in most cases. Commitments should be viewed as sacred. If project members do not respect commitments, their projects are at great risk of failure.

Q9.17 When is it okay to miss a commitment?

A9.17 Two situations in which missing a commitment is the right thing to do are (1) when someone with authority over your work duties resets your priorities, or (2) when business needs dictate (the latter may or may not be related to the former).

Q_{9.18} As a project member, am I responsible for ensuring that all of my dependencies are sufficiently addressed in the project plan?

A_{9.18} Yes.

Responsibility for defining dependencies in project plan

Q_{9.19} But isn't that the job of the project manager?

A_{9.19} Not entirely. No one should be expected to understand your dependencies better than you. First and foremost, you must ensure that all of your dependencies are identified and satisfied in the project plan. The PM does have the duty to ask the right questions and help ensure that dependencies are properly planned, but you are accountable for communicating with others and insisting that your dependencies are appropriately addressed.

Q_{9.20} As a project member, what should I do if I believe that I cannot meet a committed date?

A_{9.20} Notify the project manager and those project members that may be affected. Work constructively with the PM and possibly your boss to obtain the help you need, and work with the PM and potentially affected project members to limit or repair any collateral damage.

Unable to meet a committed date

Q_{9.21} Won't it make me look bad to ask for help?

A_{9.21} Every project member has the duty to make sure their activities and tasks are being performed and completed as expected and needed. Asking for help is a sign of professional maturity, not weakness. Not asking for help—and putting the project at risk—will really make you look "bad."

Role of RMs in commitment of employees

Q9.22   What role do resource managers play with regard to the commitments their employees make?

A9.22   An important one. Resource managers should ensure that their employees are making reasonable, realistic commitments. It is common for employees to work on more than one project at a time, so it is even more essential for resource managers to make sure their employees are not spreading themselves too thin, causing projects to suffer.

Q9.23   Is it okay for employees to make significant commitments to projects without first informing their resource managers?

A9.23   Use caution here! The answer is entirely up to the resource manager. For example, employees assigned for the first time to a new job area, or weak or inconsistent performers, should consult their resource managers before making commitments. However, seasoned employees who reliably fulfill their commitments might be given wider latitude by their resource managers. If you are not sure what your boss would expect of you, then ask.

Specifying time of day of commitments

Q9.24   If I expect a delivery on a certain day or someone expects one of me, should I specify the time of day?

A9.24   Yes, if it matters—and it almost always does. When someone says she needs something from you next Tuesday, what does that mean to you? To some folks, it means that you can make the delivery by the end of the day on Tuesday. However, others think the end of the day on Tuesday is really 8:00 a.m. on Wednesday; that is, before the regular business day begins on Wednesday. But it is very possible that the requester meant that the deliverable was expected first thing Tuesday morning at 8:00 a.m. If specific delivery time is important, make sure both the deliverer and requester know what time delivery is expected.

Q9.25 What should I do if I am assigned to a project before I fully understand the magnitude of the commitment, and other duties prohibit me from fulfilling the expected commitment?

Discovering overcommitment

A9.25 Be truthful. Work with the PM in an attempt to negotiate an acceptable solution. If you are unable to resolve the issue, then include your resource manager in the discussion. Your boss likely has a far broader set of options that he might be able to suggest. Never stick you head in the sand and imply a commitment that you know you cannot fulfill.

Q9.26 I am often included late in projects and consequently get boxed into overly ambitious dates. What can I do?

Invited late to the project

A9.26 Plenty! The first order of business is to be as creative as you can be to comply with the challenging due dates. Work with the PM, your boss, and any others that can help you resolve this problem.

On the off chance that there are no workable solutions, then you must not commit to unachievable dates. Go back to the PM and your boss and negotiate for a more reasonable set of dates. As stated earlier, never say "yes" to a request that you know you cannot fulfill; if you do, you become the problem.

But there is another important task to perform. You must change the process that excluded you from early participation in the project. Ensure that your department or group is on the proper lists for inclusion at key decision points for future projects.

Q9.27 When it comes to commitments and accountability, should anyone on a project—for example, the vendor,

Treating all project stakeholders the same

contractor, client, part-time employee, college intern, senior manager, or full-time company employee—be treated differently from anyone else on a project?

A9.27 No. All are needed to ensure the project is completed successfully. If any of these stakeholders are having difficulty meeting their commitments, you must work with them to ensure the issue is satisfactorily resolved.

List of reviewers and approvers

Q9.28 If I own a document or deliverable, am I responsible for compiling a complete list of reviewers and approvers?

A9.28 Yes, you should initiate the creation of a complete list, but the PM has the duty to ensure that no one has been overlooked. Better to err on the side of having too many people on the list than to overlook a key player.

Approver will not approve

Q9.29 What should I do if an approver of my deliverable will not approve it?

A9.29 Do your best to work with the approver to address his concerns. If that does not work, escalate the issue to the PM or the approver's boss—whichever is the preferred approach in your organization. Approvers are in a power position because you need their approval before you can move on. If you cannot obtain their approval, then you have the duty to initiate an escalation.

Reviewer will not approve

Q9.30 What if a reviewer of my deliverable does not approve it?

A9.30 Work with the reviewer to resolve his concerns. If that does not work, then you do nothing. Reviewers are *not* in a power position because you do *not* need their approval before you can move on. If the reviewer cannot live with the outcome of your discussion, then it is up to the reviewer to initiate an escalation of the issue to the PM or your boss—again, whichever is the preferred approach in your organization.

Q9.31 What should I do if someone requests work from me that seems urgent, but doing the work will cause me to miss existing commitments?

New urgent work versus existing commitments

A9.31 If the requester has more authority than you do, you must comply with the request—but you have to inform the requester of any existing commitments that will suffer. You also must inform the PM and your boss (if different from the requester) that the focus of your work has been directed elsewhere. The PM or RM may escalate the situation so that you can refocus your attention on your original commitments. You also have the duty to inform project members who have a dependency on commitments you will miss.

Q9.32 As a project manager, how do I obtain commitments from project members?

Obtaining commitments from project members

A9.32 Commitments can be viewed as big or small. Big commitments include project members agreeing to perform major activities on your project. You direct project members to define their portions of the project plan in terms of the activities and tasks to be performed. After the activities and tasks are defined and you approve them, they are considered commitments to be fulfilled by the project members.

Small commitments are day-to-day tasks that project members commit to perform and that may or may not appear in a project plan or require documentation (such as an e-mail or meeting minutes), depending on how important they are and on the reliability of the performer. These commitments are made on the spot; those involved are well aware of their promise to perform. You are responsible for deciding if a small commitment should be documented.

Project members undermining PM and team decisions

Q_{9.33} As a project manager, I conduct many meetings over the course of a project. Unfortunately, it is common for attendees to barely participate in discussing and resolving problems. Afterwards, I hear that some of the attendees are undermining decisions from the meeting—decisions that they were not willing to comment on during the meeting. What can I do?

A_{9.33} This situation highlights a gross example of those project members' professional immaturity. This dishonest and unaccountable behavior should not be tolerated. It doesn't just undermine your meeting and your good leadership intentions; it undermines the project's and team's business objectives.

I suggest you confront these project members individually, in a professional manner, and ask for their personal help in future meetings. Let them know that their behavior undermines the project and that you need their contributions to make the project as successful as possible. Tell them that you know they can bring value to these meetings. When conducting future meetings, praise them for their participation and the ideas they contribute. If they remain passive and will not participate, ask them directly for their advice and counsel on the topics being discussed.

If a project member continues this highly unprofessional behavior, include his boss in addressing the situation. Repeated offenses could be grounds for dismissal.

When new projects are started, discuss this issue in culture-training classes so that everyone knows what behaviors are expected of them. (See Chapter 27, "Project Culture.") Remember that your handling of these situations will be watched closely by all members of your project team.

CHAPTER 10

Leadership Styles, Attributes, and Behaviors

❝Leadership is not about the ability of the leaders around you to lead; it's about your ability to lead despite what is happening around you.❞

Q₁₀.₁ I have heard that a company's most important asset is its people. Is this true?

A₁₀.₁ It's not true, although many companies promote this myth.

A company's most important asset

Q₁₀.₂ If a company's most important asset is not its people, then it could be one of many things. Is it the company's products and services, brand, shareholders, profit, intellectual property, innovativeness, quality, clients, or marketing?

A₁₀.₂ No. It's *leadership*. Everything you mentioned is clearly important. But nothing is as important as leadership. For example, if you have a company made up of mediocre leaders, but it has the best employees, it will still be a mediocre force in its industry. However, if your company is led by the best leaders, but it has mediocre employees, it will be a formidable force in its industry. And those mediocre employees? They will become the best because they will rise to the expectations of their leadership. Again, it's all about leadership. If you are reading this, then you are likely in a position of leadership. You have a great duty to lead well.

Leadership!

Focusing on your leadership

Q 10.3   As a leader, if I don't have strong leadership around and above me, then my job is far more difficult. Do you agree?

A 10.3   I agree that your job may be more difficult, but it is not impossible. Remember my definition of leadership: *Leadership is not about the ability of those around you to lead; it's about your ability to lead despite what is happening around you.* Effective leaders rise to the occasion.

Q 10.4   When you talk about leaders, are you referring to people who have others reporting to them?

A 10.4   Not necessarily. Of course, a person (such as a resource manager) who has others reporting to him on a "solid line," or a project manager or team leader, to whom others report on a "dotted line," are clearly in leadership positions. However, you can be a leader without anyone reporting to you if your job requires decision-making, negotiating, influencing others, being creative, and making things happen—to name a few.

Consensus management

Q 10.5   Is consensus a good thing?

A 10.5   Typically, no. When a team reaches consensus in solving a problem, a lot of "bad" things can happen. For example:

- The solution can be derived too quickly, without sufficient thought and concentration from the team.
- The team does not work hard to find the best solution— it settles for a compromise ("I can live with that").
- The team comes up with a solution that helps everyone get along and be happy, but can hurt the business.
- No one feels personally accountable for the outcome.

Q 10.6   Then why is consensus management so popular with organizations?

A10.6   Because we tolerate mediocre leaders. Many leaders are quick to promote consensus management because it removes the burden of decision-making from them and spreads it across a team. This approach does not tend to yield the most optimal result, even if the result is supported by the group. Consensus is a leadership style that focuses more on seeking everyone's approval than continuously seeking the best business solution.

Q10.7   If you are not a fan of consensus, are you then a fan of democratic rule?

Democratic rule

A10.7   Democratic rule may work well for many governments, but it is bad for running a project or business. The problem is that everyone votes from the perspective of his own domain of responsibility—which he should. But what is in a project member's best interest often is not in the project's best interest. We need solutions that favor what is best for the project—and ultimately the business.

Q10.8   How about micromanaging? If the leader has a good head for business, then wouldn't micromanaging be a good leadership style?

Micromanaging

A10.8   Micromanaging is a terrible leadership style. A micromanager manages or controls to a lower level and detail, which is viewed to be excessive and often meddlesome. No one wants to be micromanaged or work around a micromanager. People who are micromanaged lose their passion and their drive to do their very best. They do not feel committed; they allow the micromanager to be committed *for* them. Micromanaging is a great way to undermine the morale in an organization—fast!

Q10.9   Then what leadership style do you advocate?

Benevolent dictatorship

A10.9   Benevolent dictatorship. A *benevolent dictator* is a leader who actively solicits information and opinions from project members and others; listens to them; and demonstrates the leadership, courage, and boldness to personally make the right decision—then stands accountable for that decision.

Q 10.10 Are you saying that when the final vote is taken to determine a course of action, there's only one vote that counts: the benevolent dictator's?

A 10.10 Bingo! But understand that the benevolent dictator (BD) listens carefully to others and the ensuing discussion before making a decision. The BD then pursues the best business decision.

The perception of reaching a consensus

Q 10.11 If I adopted the benevolent dictator approach, I would miss the consensus approach because my team members feel good about their ideas being included in solutions. Do you agree?

A 10.11 No. In the final analysis, we need the best business solution, not a team that "feels good." However, I expect the BD, once he feels he knows the right solution, to work with the team in "seeding" ideas that others can grow and for which they can get credit. In the end, I want the BD to do his best to leave the team with the *perception* that it reached a consensus. I would like the team to "feel good," but not at the expense of reaching the best business solution. Remember that sometimes, some team members might not like the final decision made by the BD. That's business!

Having said all this, my experience is that the team's position and the BD's position will be one and the same at least 90 percent of the time. The team will still feel the camaraderie of supporting the best business solution almost all of the time.

The making of a leader

Q 10.12 Are leaders born or made?

A 10.12 This is often debated by the "experts." There are those among us who appear to have been born with attributes that help them become effective leaders. These qualities include high self-esteem, a knack for communication, and an outgoing, approachable personality—to name a few. However, my experience is that most people—including those born with a disposition toward these special attributes—must work at developing and fine-tuning the traits and skills that help make an effective leader. I believe that anyone can learn to become an effective leader. While some people may achieve more significant leadership roles than others, everyone can learn this essential craft.

Q 10.13 As a person who strives to be a consistently effective leader, I want to believe you when you say that anyone can learn to be a good leader. However, I don't know many leaders whom I truly admire for their abilities. Why aren't there more effective leaders around us?

A 10.13 Good leadership is a matter of choice and beliefs. If you believe that you cannot be among the best leaders, then you will limit your growth. It's a self-fulfilling prophecy. We are not victims unless we choose to be. We do not achieve goals, especially lofty ones, unless we demonstrate the passion, boldness, and courage to make these things happen. We all have the ability to define who we choose to be. Yes, genetics play a role. Yes, your environment growing up plays a role. But the biggest factor, by far, now that you are an adult, is your willingness and effort to develop yourself into a consistently effective leader.

Q 10.14 Should anything be mandated about projects?

A 10.14 Yes. At least these three actions should be mandated:

Three actions to mandate on projects

1. ***Hold post-project reviews.*** These should be conducted at the end of projects.

2. ***Apply lessons learned.*** At the start of new projects, the PM should review the most recent post-project reviews for lessons learned. The PM should then go be-

fore a review board of his peers and assure them that
the most notable problems on past projects will either
not happen on his watch or, if they do, they will be less
significant.

3. **Conduct culture-training class.** At the start of projects, the project membership must be trained formally
in key hard skills, soft skills, and processes that are essential to help ensure a successful project.

Q 10.15 It seems like overkill to mandate these three items for all
projects. Arguably, a project could simply be one person
doing one day's work. Do you agree?

A 10.15 I agree on both counts. My experience is that there is very
limited value in requiring that such small projects follow
the listed mandates. Instead, you and your organization
can decide the parameters that determine whether a project must abide by these mandates. For example, you could
decide that the mandates must apply to projects:

- That have at least two or three members and last at least
two to three months;
- That will cost at least $100,000; or
- That are considered to be one of the top 10 projects for
this fiscal year.

Q 10.16 Why do you believe so strongly in mandating these
actions? I believe that mandating tasks treats people like
children rather than adults.

A 10.16 Leaders must make decisions and insist on certain behaviors that they believe are in the best business interest of the
organization and company—regardless of how unpopular
the decisions are. Too many heads of organizations have
weak backbones and therefore do not provide the leadership required. If you leave these three mandated actions
up to chance, most people and organizations will not perform them.

There is no better way to learn from the past than to perform post-project reviews. You don't need a high-priced consultant to come into your organization to tell you what your problems are. You are already aware of them. The next step is to apply lessons learned—to do something about the good and bad experiences from past projects. Moreover, you need a forum to teach the culture that you want to instill across projects. A culture-training class provides all project members with a common understanding of how the project will be run and the role that each team member is expected to play.

Q 10.17 Is it okay to say "I don't know"?

Admitting "I don't know"

A 10.17 Absolutely yes! Who among us always has the right answer? Admitting that you do not know the answer, but taking the initiative to find the answer, is a sign of professional maturity.

Q 10.18 If I know I am right, should I bother to listen to another person's viewpoint?

Listening to another point of view

A 10.18 Probably yes. Although you might be right this time, you can't be certain until you hear from the other party. In most cases, we learn something from listening—even if it only serves to reinforce our position. Moreover, you want those around you to openly express their views and freely participate in contributing to a project's success. We like working on a project where others are willing—even wanting—to listen to our ideas. Besides, there may be more than one right answer.

On the flip side, there are (infrequent) times when we have talked enough and it is time for action. In these situations, you might not listen to additional viewpoints unless someone has a startling new discovery to share.

**Having
your ideas
challenged**

Q10.19 Should I welcome project members to challenge my ideas?

A10.19 Not only should you welcome project members to challenge your ideas, you should encourage them to do so. Typically, the folks around us are far more knowledgeable about many things than we are. You want to tap into that intellectual capital and use it for the good of the project.

**Soliciting
the views
of the least
participative
members**

Q10.20 As project manager, should I solicit the views of those who tend not to readily participate?

A10.20 Yes. Everyone has something of value to bring to the table. Intentionally draw the most reserved project members into discussions in a friendly and supportive manner. Let them know that you care about their views and value their contributions.

**Holding back
knowledge for
power**

Q10.21 Do you believe in the adage that you should never tell anyone all that you know about something—that knowledge is power? Should I hold back knowledge for power?

A10.21 No. This is a sign of professional immaturity. As a member of a team or organization, you should care about the value that you bring to your job. Helping others is a powerful way to increase your value—and to garner recognition and get more opportunities. As a mentor and consultant, I freely—and gladly—disclose all that I know to help those who seek my knowledge and experience.

Ego

Q10.22 As a leader, is an ego a help or a hindrance?

A10.22 Mostly a hindrance. When you go to work each day, leave your ego outside. It's not about you. It's about the success of your project, organization, and company. It's about good business. An overactive ego can get in the way of making sound judgments, establishing and maintaining good working relationships, and learning and growing from our mistakes.

> 66 *An unbridled ego can be a haunting liability.*
> *The less approval you demand from others,*
> *the more you are likely to receive.* 99

Q10.23 As a woman who must compete in many male-dominated environments, I am not seen as assertive, but as a "b***h." But my male counterparts are thought of as assertive when they behave the same way. What can I do to turn this thinking around?

The "handicap" of being a woman

A10.23 Unfortunately, there are people, in male-dominated environments or not, who have a hard time competing with or taking direction from a female—and there is little that you can do to immediately change this professionally immature bias. Instead, channel your energies and passion into performing your best and treating others with respect and dignity. In the long run, you will win over some converts.

Adopting this mindset includes listening to what others say about your behavior and actions, then looking inward and asking yourself if you can use their feedback to become a more effective leader and coworker. If you can, adjust your behavior accordingly. If not, move on.

Also consider discussing your concerns with a trusted confidant—perhaps a woman who has faced similar challenges and has emerged as a respected, successful performer. Of course, I would hope that your boss would be helpful and supportive as well.

Yet another option to consider is maturely confronting the offender in an attempt for both of you to learn and grow from the situation. But be careful. Although this action may bear fruit sometimes, other times it may fuel the other person's immature behavior.

Whatever you do, expect that there may always be someone—male or female—who will resent you and work to undermine your behavior and your success. You must believe in yourself and persevere in becoming and remaining an effective leader.

The "handicap" of being young

Q10.24 As a young person, I am not seen as a leader to be treated with respect, even though my teams and projects have received high marks for success. How can I deal with this "handicap"?

A10.24 Savor your youth. Do not wish it away; it will evaporate sooner than you would like. All of us were young employees once. You must channel your energies and passion into performing your best.

But a word of caution: Show respect for the knowledge and wisdom of those older than you. Be open to their ideas, and do not come across like a know-it-all. As much as you think you know now, you will know far, far more in five, ten, or twenty years. For now, you may have to work harder than others, but you will win over some converts.

Tracking others versus micromanaging

Q10.25 Is tracking others and following up on their commitments micromanaging?

A10.25 No, not if the tracking is performed appropriately. You must stay on top of your domain of responsibility. If you are dependent on another project member for a deliverable, you must get him to commit to delivering it. Periodically following up on that commitment is a sign of professional maturity. Not following up—and getting hurt because the delivery was late or incomplete—is a sign of professional immaturity.

Q10.26 Can I be an effective project manager and not be the smartest person on the team?

Being an effective PM versus being the "least smart" project member

A10.26 Yes. I'm proof that this is possible. There are probably always members smarter than me on a project—and I am thankful for that. I can even be the "least smart" and still be highly effective. It is not about how smart you are, but what you do with what you have. As a PM, I must make sure that my team follows good processes and learns from any mistakes made. I must not hesitate to tap into my team's intellectual capital to ensure that problems are resolved appropriately. I must say "I don't know" when appropriate—and then go seek the answer. I must ensure that the team works well together, and I must smooth out any obstacles. You don't have to be the smartest, but you'd better know how to lead your team.

Q10.27 What do you believe is the key difference between an experienced, seasoned project manager and a relatively new project manager?

Key difference between experienced and less-experienced leader

A10.27 An experienced PM will adhere to much of the guidance provided in this book; a less experienced PM is still figuring out for herself what works and what doesn't. But you asked for the key difference . . .

Let's say that I am an experienced PM. An inexperienced PM and I will have similar problems to deal with: availability of staffing, acquiring people with the right skills, technology issues, sufficient funding, poor estimates, project-scope creep, working with difficult clients or management, conflicting priorities, uncooperative project members, and so on. My experience does not mean that I am immune to these common problems.

The key difference between our behaviors is that I will likely confront problems more quickly, with the sense of urgency and importance that they deserve, while the less-experienced PM may tend to avoid conflict, causing many of these problems to drift. I will go after problems before they have a chance to solidify into more serious issues. I will *never* avoid necessary confrontation and will practice the philosophy that problems do not go away unless I take appropriate action to mitigate them.

Less-experienced PMs tend to be too soft and less sure of themselves and the appropriate action to take. The avoidance of necessary conflict is a hallmark of the less experienced.

Being a walk-around PM

Q 10.28 Should I be a walk-around project manager?

A 10.28 Yes. Too many PMs spend too much time dithering with PM tools instead of helping to clear obstacles on the critical path or prevent them from entering the critical path in the first place. By walking around, you learn a lot and can expedite the resolution of many problems. However, make sure that you do not resort to micromanaging. Inquiring, listening, and questioning are what leaders do.

PM's feedback to project members

Q 10.29 As a project manager, should I provide feedback to project members, even if I don't have to?

A 10.29 Yes, in most cases. Leaders are teachers, and your job includes teaching members within your domain of responsibility to learn from their behaviors and actions. Over time, you will see the benefits of your coaching: It will result in a more effective team. But take care not to be overly critical or concerned with small problems. As the saying goes, *don't sweat the small stuff*. At the same time, don't avoid talking with your team members about really important issues.

Q10.30 As a project manager, what role do I play in motivating project members to do their best work?

A10.30 I believe each person has the responsibility to be account-able for his own motivation. However, I do believe that leaders should create a productive and effective work en-vironment for members under their leadership. If a proj-ect member works hard to excel, the environment ought to support such behavior. The work environment should be one in which people look forward to coming to work and want to contribute to helping the team or project be successful.

This book encourages many actions that help to create an effective work environment, such as conducting post-project reviews and culture-training classes; and promot-ing awards, recognition, ethics, and integrity.

Q10.31 How can I critique the work or behavior of others without coming across as too negative or destructive?

A10.31 Here are some ideas:

- Begin with the Golden Rule: Treat others with the same respect and dignity that you would expect from them.
- Do not make the critique personal. It's not; it's business. Don't raise your voice or use words that would suggest the critique is a personal attack. Depending on the situation, you may want to begin the discussion by assuring the individual that your comments are not personal.
- Identify some positive elements of the person's work or behavior so that she sees that you are looking at the broader picture. For example, at the end of the discussion, if appropriate, say something like, "Barbara, you have come a long way and continue to improve. I really admire your great attitude and desire to learn and grow. I sure am glad that we are on the same team."

A note of caution: Never avoid confronting another person about a behavior or a problem with his work that he must correct for you to protect your domain of responsibility.

Dealing with a poor performer

Q 10.32   As a project manager, what do I do if a poor performer has been assigned to my project?

A 10.32   If the project member is already known to be a poor performer, begin your relationship on a positive note by making sure the project member understands the expectations you have of him and he has of you. He must understand his roles and responsibilities, his accountabilities, and his level of authority. You want to constructively work with the person and set him up for success, not failure. If the person does not perform satisfactorily or you feel that you have sufficient reason to believe that the person can not or will not perform satisfactorily, then you must have a discussion with the project member's boss—preferably with the project member present.

In a professional manner, ask the RM to help ensure that the project member does not fail. For example, the project member may need specific training, a buddy or mentor, or, in an extreme case, to be reassigned elsewhere so that an appropriate replacement member can be assigned to your project.

Q 10.33   What if the resource manager is unwilling or unable to resolve the performance issue?

A 10.33   Then you must escalate the issue higher until it is appropriately addressed.

Q 10.34   What can I do if I do escalate higher, but I am told that I must continue to work with the poor performer?

A 10.34   Enlisting help from your project team, look for ways to offload or swap some of the work assigned to the poor-performing member. In an extreme case, one in which you believe that you cannot stop the poor performer from doing irreparable harm to the project, you must talk to others up the management chain or to the project sponsor. These power players must know that the team member is likely to hurt the project *before* any harm occurs, while there is still time to take action to mitigate any problems.

Q10.35 **What if all this escalating still doesn't help, and the project sponsor says to do my best?**

A10.35 Then do your best. Just make certain that *you* are not the problem and that you have informed the power players of the problem *and* have offered solutions. Remember: *Leadership is not about the ability of those around you to lead; it's about your ability to lead despite what is happening around you.*

Q10.36 **What if a person's performance weakens *after* he is assigned to my project?**

A10.36 As you see a problem unfold, work constructively with the person. Perhaps a bit of coaching or mentoring by you or someone else can turn the situation around. However, if the problem persists, and you believe that the project will be harmed, then take the issue to the person's boss.

My style is to let the poor performer know that I am going to bring his boss into the equation so that the problem can be addressed appropriately. The goal is to have a three-way discussion so that all the relevant information is on the table. In the extreme case where the boss does little to help, then the PM must escalate the issue higher. As a PM, you remain accountable for the outcome of your project.

Q10.37 **Do you believe that procrastination is a bad thing?**   **Procrastination**

A10.37 In most cases, procrastination is a good thing. I am amused when a new year begins and various media are full of articles and snippets about how to avoid procrastination.

We should learn to procrastinate on unimportant things (which most things are) and learn not to procrastinate on important and urgent matters. A person's time may very well be his most valuable possession; it's how you spend your time that matters.

Focusing daily on your top three priorities

Q 10.38 **How should we focus on the most important and urgent things?**

A 10.38 When you arrive at work each day, you should set aside a few minutes to create a to-do list for the day, or you should have already done this at the end of the previous workday. Let's say your list has ten items on it. (Many of you will have more than ten, but let's keep the math simple for purposes of illustration.) Divide the list into your top three priorities and your bottom seven. If when you leave work at the end of the day, you have not worked on your top three priorities but you have crossed off your bottom seven items, do not feel good about your accomplishments that day. You focused on the wrong items. It's the top three priorities that define your career and your overall success—the contribution and value you bring to your job, your project, and your company.

Q 10.39 **If the top three items are so important, then why do you suppose we tend to work on the bottom seven items at the sacrifice of the top three?**

A 10.39 You probably know the answer. The bottom seven items tend to be easier. We get instant gratification from crossing one off the list. Moreover, they tend to be more fun and take less time to complete than a top-three item. At the end of the day, many of us will take comfort in crossing off all of the bottom seven items as we rationalize that surely the seven items are collectively as important as one of our top three items. They don't even come close!

Q 10.40 **Are you saying that we should cross off all of the top three before the day is over?**

A 10.40 Usually, it is not possible to achieve so much in one day. But if at the end of the day, you haven't touched any of the bottom seven items, but have made significant progress in closing one of the top three, you should feel very good about your accomplishments that day.

Q 10.41 Are you saying that it's okay to *not* work on the bottom seven?

A 10.41 I don't care if you do or you don't work on them. If you have five minutes between meetings, and you can cross off one of your bottom-seven items, go for it. However, if you have 30 minutes or more to spare, do not work on a bottom-seven item. Instead, focus on a top-three item.

Something that I did wrong for years early in my career was reserve one hour of time during each workday to work on my "bottom seven." What I should have done when I could find a full hour to concentrate was work toward resolving one of my top three items.

Working on the least important items

Q 10.42 How can I ignore the bottom-seven kind of items? There can be hundreds of these tasks over the course of a project.

A 10.42 Relatively speaking, there will be an infinite number of problems that will come your way in your lifetime, but you only have a finite amount of time to solve them. Therefore, you must pick your battles and take on the problems that have the most value to your job and career. You and I both know that you will find time to solve many of your "bottom seven" problems, but you never, *never* will have time to solve them all.

Q 10.43 So should I just ignore many of the bottom seven?

A 10.43 Yes, but in a responsible way. For example, if someone has requested your time for a task that does not fall within your domain of responsibility, and you have not committed to perform the work, nor do you have the time to do so, then tell that person—in a professionally mature manner—that you are sorry, but you don't have the time. If you can direct her to another person or alternative solution, then do so. If she doesn't think that there is another option, then she can choose to escalate the issue over your head in an attempt to alter your priorities. This is how business works.

Q_{10.44} **But what if doing the work would only take four hours, but an escalation could tie up two full days? If I think that I would probably lose the escalation anyway, then shouldn't I just do the four hours of work in the first place?**

A_{10.44} Not necessarily. Perhaps you are better off spending the four hours doing the work. But perhaps this request is the straw that breaks the proverbial camel's back, and you need to ask someone of higher authority to support your need for help or to change some of your current commitments. The higher the level you reach in an organization, the more often you will be asked to do more work than you can handle. You must make smart choices. You must manage your domain of responsibility; no one else has that duty.

Determining top-three priorities

Q_{10.45} **How can I figure out what my top three priorities are?**

A_{10.45} You probably already have a good idea of what they are, but they should be things that are important or urgent. Top-three priorities often can affect your commitments, your performance rating, your career, or your boss or sponsor.

For example, let's say that you are a PM. You might call a 20- to 30-minute meeting with the appropriate project members to brainstorm top priorities for the project. Say you come up with a list of 15 items. Now prioritize the list.

A method I often employ is the H-M-L technique, in which the group assigns each item a high, medium, or low priority based on its relationship to other items on the list. Let's say you assign eight items a high priority rating. Focusing only on these eight items, decide which are the highest, medium, and lowest priorities. In very short order, the top three items will emerge. (Identifying your top three to five items is fine; however, I would prefer you focus on three at the most.) By the way, because you are a benevolent dictator, it is important that you assert yourself if the group is unable to fully agree on the ordering of priorities.

Q 10.46 **Earlier you referred to the top three priorities as your top three problems. Which are they?**

Priorities = problems

A 10.46 They are both. You should know your top three problems—also called your top three priorities—to solve. Moreover, one or more of the three problems could represent risks. A *risk* is an event or condition—typically a problem—that could occur, but hasn't yet. So one of your top three priorities might be that you work on a problem representing a risk so that you can avoid it or lessen the damage that could be done if it does happen.

Q 10.47 **If I am working on three projects at a time, should I know my top three priorities on each project or the top three priorities overall?**

Managing priorities across multiple projects

A 10.47 Both. You should know your top three priorities on each project, but in this case, that means you could have a total of nine priorities on which to focus. That is too many. Therefore, choose from those nine priorities your top three. They could all come from the same project, or one or more could come from each project.

Q 10.48 **What if I don't know what my top three priorities are? Is this really such a big deal?**

A 10.48 Yes, it is a really big deal! For example, if you are a PM, and I stop you in the hallway at work and ask you to state your top three priorities, and you cannot, you might say, "I have a really tough project with a lot of problems. I can't really say what the top three are." My response would be that you are not an effective PM or effective leader.

You might reply, "You don't know me. I am a very effective PM and leader. How dare you draw that conclusion from such a brief encounter." I would say to you that if you can't immediately articulate your top three priorities, you probably are not primarily focused each day on solving the top three. You are likely spending too much time working on the "bottom seven." Truly effective leaders know that they must stay focused on the items that offer the greatest return on investment—and you are not doing this.

Q10.49 Some days it's a zoo where I work, and I am unable to focus predominantly on my top three priorities. Is this okay?

A10.49 In general, you should focus on your top three items each day, but life happens. If interruptions and noise occasionally leave you unable to focus as planned, that's okay. However, if this inability to focus becomes a pattern, then that is not okay. You are not effectively managing your domain of responsibility. You are the problem.

To-do list

Q10.50 Is creating a to-do list for the week at the start of each week a good idea?

A10.50 It's a great idea! Here's how I do it. At the start of the week, I list the items that I need to work on that week. Then, working mostly off that list, I create a to-do list for that day. Every morning, I review the list of items for the week and modify it based on new events. Then, working off that list, I again create that day's to-do list. I continue this approach throughout the week.

"Problems are our friends"

Q10.51 I don't look forward to the plethora of problems that confront me each day. As a leader, am I in the wrong job?

A 10.51   Perhaps, but if you expect to remain a leader in whatever job you choose, you must learn to like and be comfortable around problems. You should adopt the attitude that "problems are our friends"—without problems, you probably would not have a job. Moreover, your level of salary is likely related to your ability to solve problems.

As a consultant and mentor, if I did not have problems to confront, I would not have a job. I sincerely and enthusiastically look forward to the problems that my clients throw at me. If too many are coming my way, then I will prioritize them, and the most important and urgent problems will be solved first.

The higher you climb career-wise and the more responsibilities you take on, the greater the likelihood that you will be unable to resolve every problem. You will either need to get help from others or accept that some problems take longer to resolve than you'd like. Whatever challenges you must confront, thinking about problems with the right mindset can make all the difference in your effectiveness and enthusiasm.

Q 10.52   Is it best to make quick decisions?

Making good, quick decisions

A 10.52   First and foremost, it is important to make good decisions. But it usually is better to make decisions quickly. If the decision you are making could have serious consequences, make sure that all pertinent information has been considered and that you have consulted key stakeholders who will be affected by the decision. Occasionally, holding off for a little while on making a decision can help ensure that the best decision is made.

Q 10.53   Is making decisions at the end of the day better than doing so at the beginning of the day?

A 10.53   The answer may vary for each of us, and each person must try to understand and work within his own natural cycle.

For example, I find that I tend to be a bit more alert and objective during the first two-thirds of the day than during the last third. If you have a similar cycle and have to make a decision at the end of the day, but doing so can wait until the next day, formulate your position now but revisit the decision the next day, when you may be more alert and have slept on it overnight.

Empowerment

Q 10.54 **What is the real definition of empowerment?**

A 10.54 Empowerment is an overused word these days, but it is an underutilized concept. To me, empowerment comprises three actions: (1) understanding your job, (2) taking ownership of your job, and (3) doing whatever is necessary—within legal and ethical parameters—to accomplish that job.

Q 10.55 **Why do you say that empowerment is an underutilized concept?**

A 10.55 Because the three actions I've listed that lead to empowerment are not often taken. I believe that many people do not truly understand their jobs. If they did, they would be better performers. Although an RM has the duty to ensure that his employee fully understands her job, many RMs fail to do this. Moreover, many employees do not take it upon themselves to define their jobs and negotiate those definitions with their bosses.

Taking ownership

Q 10.56 **How do you take ownership of your job?**

A 10.56 By bringing passion to your job each day and caring about success—your own and that of individuals who rely on the commitments you've made. When you take ownership of your job, you behave as if you own the company and the company is defined by your domain of responsibility.

Q_{10.57} **What do you mean by doing whatever is necessary to accomplish the job?**

A_{10.57} Those of you who do own your own company, or have in the past, know full well what I mean here. Because if you truly believe that *if it is to be, it is up to me* and you cannot pay your mortgage or put food on your table unless your domain of responsibility is taken care of, then you will make things happen—big time!

Q_{10.58} **As a project manager, how much authority do I really have?**

Authority of a PM

A_{10.58} A lot! It's your project. Its success or failure has a lot to do with your leadership. When there is a problem on the project, it is *your* problem. You may not have to be the one to solve it, but you are the person charged with making sure that it gets solved. Remember: *If it is to be, it is up to me.* You will be held accountable for the successful outcome of the project. Your job includes making your boss and the project sponsor look good. You have wide latitude, but not absolute authority.

Other parts of this book discuss the limitations on your authority to change the committed delivery date, for example. But in general, if you need to assume authority yet doubt that it is yours to claim, ask the project sponsor or your boss for guidance. I suggest you err on the side of assuming too much authority rather than too little.

Q_{10.59} **Is it good to challenge the authority of higher management?**

Challenging authority

A_{10.59} Maybe.

- *Yes*, if you are constructively and professionally questioning a decision or directive made by a higher-up that does not seem to be in the best business interest of the project, client, or company. Make sure your argument is fact-based and delivered in a respectful manner, offers specific alternatives, and leaves the impression that you want what's best for the business.

- *Yes*, if the decision or directive appears to be unlawful or unethical.
- *No*, if senior management has concluded the discussion is over and it is time to implement the decision. Your opinion may differ from a higher-up's, but that doesn't necessarily mean that you are right or your superior is wrong.

Begging forgiveness versus asking permission

Q10.60 Do you believe that it is "better to beg forgiveness than to ask permission"?

A10.60 Yes, especially in today's fast-paced, highly competitive world. If you routinely wait for permission to make things happen, you will miss many opportunities. Moreover, if you ask permission and it is declined, you are no longer able to pursue that course of action. If you do, you could be fired for insubordination.

Q10.61 Are you saying that I should not ask management for permission—that I should just strike out on my own every time I want to do something?

A10.61 Of course not. If you sense that you should get permission before moving forward on a task, then act accordingly. If you cannot decide whether to ask for permission, then ask, just to be safe. At the same time, you want to develop a reputation for taking the initiative and making things happen.

Thinking for yourself

Q10.62 Do you believe that most people think for themselves?

A10.62 Absolutely not! Most people allow themselves to be led. The most important lesson to learn from working on projects and within organizations (and from just living life) is to think for yourself—to challenge tradition, authority, and the status quo professionally and maturely, and also to routinely question your own behaviors and actions.

Otherwise, you become enslaved by the past and its outdated and ineffective ideas. You are a willing victim of indifference, mediocrity, narrow-mindedness, and unimaginative thinking. Then you are stuck inside the proverbial box, doomed to repeat past mistakes. Eventually, you and those you lead become grossly ineffective. One of the most important traits of a consistently effective leader is thinking for himself or herself. Remember: *It's not about the ability of those around you to lead; it's about your ability to lead, despite what is happening around you.*

Q10.63 **Can you give some examples of people's failure to think for themselves?**

A10.63 A person who does not think for himself may:

- Blindly follow processes and procedures regardless of their effectiveness
- Retreat from confronting problems that negatively affect his performance
- Constantly allow others to dictate and manage the use of his time
- Consciously do things wrong the first time
- Accept substandard work from others
- Follow "groupthink" regardless of its effectiveness
- Consistently ignore his instincts
- Not take the initiative to challenge questionable decisions made by those in positions of authority
- Not propose a better way to do something
- Bow to the will of others even when he knows it's not the best course of action
- Routinely repeat past mistakes
- Think he cannot make a difference.

Q10.64 **Why is it so hard for people to think for themselves?**

A10.64 Many of us have not been sufficiently trained in or sold on thinking for ourselves. We are encouraged to conform, even if conformity will harm our well-being or the well-being of our project, organization, or company. Not thinking for ourselves is often the path of least resistance.

Consider an organization with a project management office that has defined, documented processes and procedures. I often hear members of such organizations complain about the rigidity and bureaucracy imposed on them. When I ask for specific examples of the problems caused by having defined procedures, many cannot articulate a problem. Most of those who can identify a legitimate problem still blindly follow the processes and procedures. They don't think for themselves. They allow processes and procedures to "think" for them, instead of trying to alter the system to better suit their business needs.

Q10.65 Can you give an example of how resource managers often don't think for themselves?

A10.65 Consider a case in which an organization has a hiring freeze in effect. A manager or project sponsor needs to hire someone with unique, hard-to-find skills. If he does not, he will not be able to meet his project's delivery or revenue commitments. Because the manager or project sponsor knows about the hiring freeze, he assumes that he will not be allowed to hire anyone, not even the perfect candidate, so he doesn't even try. But if the manager or project sponsor has an approved and funded project and no problems on the project that are spiraling out of control, most executives would support such a hire in order to protect business commitments. In this situation, the manager or project sponsor should have thought for himself, not made an assumption, and pursued management's support in hiring the candidate.

Q10.66 I have made mistakes on past projects, and some of my current project teammates are aware of them. How can I get my peers to see me in a new light?

Letting go of past mistakes

A10.66 You must first stop seeing yourself in the "old light." We all make mistakes. Admit to them, learn from them, and apply those lessons going forward. Eventually, most of your peers will have a positive impression of you, and they will respect you more than they did before you made the mistakes.

Q10.67 What if some of my peers still have a negative impression of me?

A10.67 You do not have control over what others choose to think about you, but you are able to take action to learn and grow from your past. Most peers will respect you for your growth and professional maturity. The few peers that will not let go of the past probably do respect you, but for whatever reason, they don't want to show it. Their behavior suggests professional immaturity, and they are the ones with the problem. You should move on.

Q10.68 Are the best project managers those who have made no big mistakes?

The potential value of making big mistakes

A10.68 Not necessarily. I applaud those few PMs who have made no significant mistakes; you are a minority. However, I think mistakes have great value, as long as you are learning from them and not repeating them. No one intentionally makes big mistakes, nor do they want them in their work history, but adversity can help sharpen one's work habits and character. I have made some big mistakes, and while I would not want to relive any of them, I believe that I have far more to offer others as a consultant and mentor because of them. If a person consistently makes only small mistakes, I question his willingness to take personal risks and stretch himself on behalf of the project and organization.

Being a creative problem solver

Q10.69 To be a consistently good leader, do I need to be a creative problem solver?

A10.69 Yes. But don't overlook asking for help from the talented people around you. You do not have to have all the answers, but you do need to persevere in working toward the best solution.

Determining the proper behavior

Q10.70 How can I best determine how to behave in a certain situation?

A10.70 There are several options to consider.

- Ask yourself how would you want your employee to behave if you owned the company and an employee in your current position was faced with this situation. Looking at things from the owner of the company's viewpoint can make the best course of action more apparent.
- Seek counsel from higher-ups such as your boss or project sponsor. These people likely have more experience to draw from. Always try to learn from others who have "been there" or who have a more objective view of the situation.
- Meet with your team and ask for counsel. You might be surprised at some of the creative and useful solutions that can come from your team—even from those members junior to you.

Saying "we" versus "I"

Q10.71 When is it appropriate to say "we," and when to say "I," in the context of a project or team?

A10.71 Many of us have been conditioned to say "we," such as "We have a problem," "We have a solution," "We think this is the right thing to do," or "We need help." However, when there is a problem or a solution to report, get accustomed to saying "I"—even though the problem or solution affects others, too.

The best leaders are quick to take personal ownership of problems and do not claim that others are responsible for them. Moreover, the best leaders condition themselves to take ownership of a solution even if the solution required others' input. By taking ownership, a leader is far more likely to ensure the best solution is reached, and she stands accountable for that solution. A good leader does not deflect ownership onto others, especially when a solution could turn out to be less than optimal. "We," indicating shared ownership and responsibility, is most appropriate once your team has proven itself successful.

Q10.72 **Should one do the right thing or the popular thing, assuming each will cause a different outcome?**

Doing the right thing versus the popular thing

A10.72 Leadership is not always about doing what's popular; it's about doing what's right. When both choices yield the same result, it's easy. But often the results are different. Remember, it's about doing the right *business* thing, even if doing so causes you to occasionally make decisions that are less popular than you feel comfortable with. In the long run, you will be far more effective—and far more respected.

Q10.73 How important is decisiveness in being a leader?

Decisiveness

A10.73 It's important. It is better to make a decision and occasionally be wrong than to delay a decision excessively or not make one at all. We have all been around leaders who will not make decisions or who make them only after much delay. This behavior can have a crippling effect on the progress and success of a project or organization. I have discussed elsewhere in this book methods that can be used to help ensure the best decisions are made.

Persistence

Q10.74 How important is persistence in being a leader?

A10.74 It's important. Persistence is one of my favorite soft skills. I call it an "equalizer." I'm not the brightest star in the sky, but I am very persistent. Persistence levels the playing field for all of us. Success is not about how smart you are, but more about what you do with what you have. Through persistence and determination, you can accomplish almost anything that is important to you.

> 66 *Great works are performed not by strength, but by perseverance.* 99

> —Dr. Samuel Johnson, English poet, critic, essayist, and lexicographer

---

Courage

Q10.75 How important is courage in being a leader?

A10.75 Especially important. The number-one reason leaders fail is that they are too soft; they have weak backbones. They lack the courage to be as effective as they should be and need to be. These leaders often:

- Place a higher value on being liked than on being effective
- Embrace consensus management rather than take personal accountability
- Take great care to not "rock the boat"
- Sacrifice integrity for approval
- Pass off tough decisions to others
- Wait until the last possible moment to make decisions—then make only safe ones
- Work on the easy things at the expense of the most important things

- Avoid necessary and timely confrontation
- Allow the behavior of others to shape them, rather than taking the initiative to shape the behavior of others.

It's not easy standing up to those around you, be they executives, clients, vendors, contractors, peers, or team members. But if you expect to be consistently successful as a leader, you must demonstrate the courage to lead yourself and your team to success. It's not about effort or lofty intentions; it's about results.

> **❝Life shrinks and expands
> in proportion to one's courage.❞**

—Anaïs Nin, French-born American author and diarist

Q10.76 I am not very courageous, and I wish that I could muster the courage that I respect so much in others. Any advice?

A10.76 Yes. Fake it! As insincere as that may sound, fake it! Why? Because no one can tell the difference. And after a while, you also will believe that you are courageous, because you become what you think you are. Courage is only a thought away. Try it. You can do it. It will begin to feel comfortable.

Q10.77 How important is resolving conflicts in being a leader?

Resolving conflicts

A10.77 It is important. It is natural for people to sometimes disagree. And disagreement does not necessarily mean that either party is wrong. As a leader, your job includes getting past a disagreement and helping the parties reach the best business solution. It's often helpful to ask other people, such as subject matter experts, to meet with the original parties to discuss the issues and move toward the most effective resolution. In most cases, you will achieve satisfactory closure, and everyone will feel good about the outcome. However, although "feeling good" is important, it is not as essential as reaching the best business decision.

Q 10.78 How important is it for a project manager to take a position on project issues, rather than let project members work out problems by themselves?

A 10.78 It is optimal for project members to work out issues by themselves, and quickly. However, problem resolution isn't always congenial or efficient.

Here's an example from my own experience while mentoring a PM. On the way to a meeting, the PM and I came upon two team leaders in the hallway having a loud, heated, and nasty discussion. The PM decided that we should join them; a few minutes later, we headed off to our meeting. Once we were out of earshot, I asked her why she didn't take a position on the issue to help move it to closure. She said that had she taken a position, she would have alienated one of the team leaders. I told her that she actually alienated both of them by not taking a position. They would probably have preferred that she make a decision so they could move on. And it would not be her problem if one of them disagreed with her decision and took it personally. Doing so would indicate the team leader's own professional immaturity.

Never avoid making a decision or taking a position on an issue because you fear alienating someone. As a leader, you must not be a fence-sitter. You must demonstrate enough backbone to help close decisions, when appropriate.

**Delivering bad
news**

Q 10.79 Can you give me some pointers for delivering bad news?

A 10.79 As leaders, we all find ourselves having to deliver bad news from time to time. It's never fun, but it is essential. You should strive to deliver bad news as soon as reasonably possible and with the appropriate level of discretion.

Delivering bad news as soon as reasonably possible means that, in most cases, *you* attempt to resolve the problem before involving higher-ups. If you think that you must inform your leadership about the problem and get their help, do so quickly. The sooner the problem is addressed, the less harm may be done to the project.

Make sure that you do not blindside anyone when relaying bad news. No one wants to be surprised by hearing about a problem from a third party or at an inopportune time.

Q 10.80 **Can you give me an example of how to deliver bad news as soon as possible and with discretion?**

A 10.80 Let's say you have a meeting scheduled with your boss Monday morning at 8:00 a.m. You arrive at work at 7:30 a.m. and discover a really big problem related to your project. At 8:00 a.m. you enter your boss' office and find that your boss' boss is also there. In most cases, you should *not* tell your boss the really bad news in the presence of his boss. Instead, discreetly ask to see your boss outside his office. Then briefly inform him of the really bad news. Your boss will not like hearing the news, but will appreciate your discretion in sharing it. It is now up to your boss to decide whether he wants to share the bad news with his boss. In most cases, he should not.

Q 10.81 **I think the bad news should be shared with the boss' boss. After all, they are all in this together. Why do you disagree?**

A 10.81 First, the boss' boss, upon hearing the bad news, may begin to lose confidence in your boss because your boss was not aware of the news until now. The boss' boss may question his effectiveness as your leader.

The second reason is that we tend to think most problems we encounter are bigger than they turn out to be. Do not develop a reputation for wasting upper management's time by proclaiming that the sky is falling every time a problem arises. They will later learn that you overreacted. Perform due diligence before involving higher management. (By the way, if higher management does become involved, be prepared to be micromanaged.)

Q10.82 Speaking of being micromanaged, I detest it. How can I avoid being micromanaged?

A10.82 Oftentimes, a person is micromanaged because he "asked for it" through his actions or inactions. By demonstrating that you are capable of managing your assignments, those above you are less likely to feel the need to micromanage. Most people do not want to micromanage others—it's too time-consuming and annoying, to say the least.

Q10.83 Can you give me an example of how to avoid being micromanaged?

A10.83 Imagine that you are a PM, and your team is producing a new or enhanced software product. Most of the product's components are ready for a formal test, and its end-to-end performance is measured. A project member tells you that early data indicates that performance is a dismal twenty times slower than expected. There are two possible courses of action:

(1) You immediately call the client and inform her that the performance is twenty times slower than she expects, but add that she should not be concerned because you will do whatever is necessary to resolve the problem. But when she asks you what the problem is, you say you do not yet know. She asks who is assigned to own the problem; you say you haven't yet decided. She asks what your plans are to resolve the problem, and you tell her that because you chose to inform her immediately, you haven't decided what your next step will be. Frustrated and anxious, she says she is heading over to see you. You are about to be micromanaged—and you have earned it.

(2) You ask the project member if the performance problem is related to a particular part of the software, configuration, set of data, or user screens—or if it is pervasive across the entire product. If he doesn't know the answer, you ask him to go back to the test lab and find out as much as he can about the problem in the next three hours. Other project members can help, but you ask him to be discreet and not allow the performance problem to leak out of the lab until the necessary fact-finding can be performed.

The project member returns at the end of the three hours with new information. The problem is not pervasive across the product; it is isolated to a specific sequence of actions using certain data files. You assign the project member to own the problem resolution and ask him to prepare an initial plan by 10:00 a.m. tomorrow that identifies project members who may be required to help.

You then call the client and tell her that there is a performance problem in an isolated part of the product, and it is performing twenty times slower than expected. You add that you've assigned a project member to own the resolution, and he will have a plan on your desk before noon tomorrow. Furthermore, you tell the client that you will call her twice each day—at 11:00 a.m. and 4:00 p.m.—with updates, until the problem is under control.

The client chooses not to micromanage. Why? Because you have demonstrated that you are in control and are managing the issue. There is no need to micromanage.

Q10.84 In your example, why did the project manager tell the project member to be discreet about the performance problem?

A10.84 If the problem leaked out to the client, the PM could lose credibility with the client. Therefore, it is important to move quickly during the initial problem-discovery phase and not allow the problem to drift for days or weeks.

Being accountable for your success

Q10.85 Occasionally I read studies showing that people with certain attributes are more likely to be successful. These attributes include gender, height, ethnicity, body build, and appearance. If I don't fit the "preferred" profile, what can I do?

A10.85 Personally, I don't put any credence in these studies as they relate to the individual. The world is full of people who are very successful but do not have the supposedly favored attributes. Be thankful for whatever gifts you do have, focus your energy on continuing to improve your attitude, performance, and relationships, and work to become the person you want to be. Remember: *If it is to be, it is up to me.*

Learning to say "no"

Q10.86 I have a hard time saying "no" to requests for my time; consequently, my core assignments sometimes suffer, and I find myself working more overtime than I'd like. Any advice?

A10.86 First of all, you must understand your job. If it is your job to say "yes" to all of these requests—but you do not have the time to fulfill them—then you must work with your boss in getting the help you need. Don't just tell your boss that you need help; be specific in describing the work you have, where you need help the most, and how much help you need. First, articulate the problem, then propose the solution, then tell your boss exactly what you need from him.

If it is not your job to say "yes" to every incoming request, then learn to say "no." You might direct requestors to other people who may be able to help. Or you might say "no" today but "yes" if they come back next week or next month. But sometimes, we must rally to protect the business, and we may need to work more overtime than we would like. Later in this book, I discuss working overtime and how much is "too much"; see Chapter 16, "Overtime Work."

You own your domain of responsibility and your workday. No one can manage it for you; you must assert yourself in managing your assigned, committed duties. Not satisfactorily executing your core assignment is professionally immature behavior.

Q10.87 I seem to be a magnet for problems—I always have more on my plate than most of my peers do. Could I be doing something wrong?

Causing problems for yourself

A10.87 Consider that:

- If a person has weak interpersonal skills, then he may experience more problems in his working relationships.
- If a person has an "attitude," that can also cause people to want to avoid her or it can worsen confrontations.
- If a person has a poor record of fulfilling commitments and closing issues, this "baggage" will only increase over time.
- If a person does not manage her time well or takes on too much, then she can easily become overworked and stressed.
- If a person has shown an ability to manage tough situations, then it may be that more difficult issues are intentionally given to him to resolve. (Having this ability is good, but still requires managing each day effectively.)

These are but a few examples of personal qualities that can make a person's life more complicated, messy, and stressful. They can also slow or stop career growth, or even lead to destruction of a career. The good news is that all of us can consciously work to improve ourselves. You are not a victim unless you choose to be.

Managing expectations

Q_{10.88} How important is it to manage expectations?

A_{10.88} It's very important. Whatever your role on a project or in an organization, people react to you based on their expectations of you and what they believe your expectations are of them. If you are not sure what those expectations are, ask—or define, present, and negotiate them. The project management discipline exists in part to define and manage expectations: Requirements, scope, project plans, tracking, and defining roles and responsibilities all help set and manage expectations.

Being a role model

Q_{10.89} To be most effective as a leader, do I need to be a role model?

A_{10.89} If you are a consistently successful leader, you already are a role model for others to emulate. And yes, leaders must be role models. Set an example. It's not enough to tell others what to do and define appropriate behavior; you must also walk the talk. Those around you learn far more from your actions than they do from your words.

I was mentoring a senior vice president of a major corporation, and he asked me how to get his executive staff to stop coming late to his meetings. My answer was simple: Start showing up on time yourself. If you want your team to come to meetings on time, then you must also show up on time. That's being a role model.

Learning to mitigate problems early

Q_{10.90} As a project manager, I find that I tend to take the easy route in decision making. I assume that the worst case will likely *not* happen and that the best case *will* likely happen, and I therefore amble along on the current path. However, many times, much later down the road, I find that the path I chose was weak and led to serious problems. Any ideas on how I can address potential issues earlier and more effectively, before they become major obstacles?

A10.90 You are halfway there, because you recognize that your leadership style is weak. If I am wrestling with an issue and am not sure whether to address it aggressively now so that it will not be a major problem later, I sometimes do the following, with very good results. I imagine that it is x-number of weeks or months from now, and that the worst has happened (or at least something worse than the best-case scenario). I ask myself what I would have done differently if I could turn the clock back. I then apply the "lessons learned" *now*, while I can still make a difference.

Let's say you have a contractor who does not plan sufficiently and gets testy when you attempt to track her progress against her nonexistent plan. (Silly, I know. Stay with me here.) She would rather work at warp speed and just do her best. As a PM, you know how foolish this method is, and how one team member's shortsightedness can bring down an entire project. Still, you take the path of least resistance and give in to the contractor's whims.

But now, taking my advice, you imagine the worst-case scenario happening because there is no plan and not enough tracking. You see how much damage the contractor did and wish that you could go back in time to insist that proven project management methods be used. The good news is that you *can* go back to the "past" (today) and insist on the proper level of discipline now to avoid harm to the project. You pay a price now, aggravating the contractor, so that you can avoid a major price later (lost revenue, low customer satisfaction, disappearing profit margins, and lost jobs).

Q10.91 What's more important: projects or people?

The importance of projects versus people

A 10.91 Of course, the answer can vary depending on the situation. But generally speaking, in a business setting, projects are more important than people. "Whoa!" you might say. But think about it. Without projects, your company's employees need not come to work. Your company needs projects for its survival. People, on the other hand, are disposable and replaceable. There is always someone who can do your job. An individual may be critical at the moment, but eventually, we all can be replaced. It's not a friendly thought, and most people do not want to hear it—but it is a business reality.

Q 10.92 But without people, you can't build products or perform services. Do you agree?

A 10.92 Yes. No debate there. However, people can be replaced.

There are a whole lot of talented people in this world to replace any of us. But before this topic causes too much heartburn, consider this: People are so important that I have reserved a key position in organizations and companies to ensure that people are being nurtured—the resource manager. A primary purpose of resource managers is to nurture employees, to help each employee reach his or her potential in the organization and company. If people weren't important, then their well-being would not be so critical—but it is.

The primary role of a project manager is to be the nurturer of projects. The resource manager and the project manager may have very different roles, but they are both essential in ensuring the continued success of a company.

Q 10.93 If projects are more important than people, how does this affect projects?

A 10.93 Most of the time, knowing that projects are more important than people does not affect the way we work, but occasionally it can. Let's say a critical delivery date for a major client is approaching. If the product is delivered late, then the organization will likely lose a large part of the client's account. This, in turn, will lead to revenue loss—and could cause many employees to lose their jobs. Dottie is an employee in the critical path for the delivery date. She had planned to take a two-week vacation starting one week from now. If she is absent from the project for two weeks, the deliverable will be late, and people will lose their jobs. What should be done? To protect the business, Dottie should be asked to defer her vacation so the product can be delivered on time. The project, in this case, takes precedence over the person.

Q 10.94 Couldn't one also conclude that people are more important than the project because Dottie's deferred vacation saved people's jobs?

A 10.94 We could debate this point, but don't miss the bigger picture–the importance of running a successful business. We are all sometimes required to sacrifice our time and personal interests for our employers. In the business world, when we must weigh the importance of projects versus people, projects usually win.

Q 10.95 Why did you say "projects *usually* win"? When would a project not "win"?

A 10.95 Let's revisit the example in which Dottie is in the critical path, and her absence from the project would cause some employees to lose their jobs. Dottie was expected to defer her vacation. But let's say Dottie is instead suddenly faced with a major family crisis. Dottie tells her boss that she must leave to be with her family in this time of grave need, and she knows she will be gone for at least two weeks. Moreover, she will not be able to perform any work from afar. Dottie's absence will cause some coworkers to lose their jobs and the company to suffer.

What should her boss do? Fire her if she leaves? After all, projects are more important than people. Right? In this case, wrong! Dottie's boss should support Dottie's need to be with her family. Why? As important as Dottie's job is for her financial survival (and for other reasons), it pales in comparison to the importance of her life overall and of her family in this situation. Dottie should run, not walk, to be with her loved ones. All of us will face a "once in a lifetime" situation in which obligations outside of work must take priority.

Note: I added this extreme example to illustrate a case, albeit an atypical one, in which the best interest of the business may not prevail. Some of you reading this may be thinking of ways this situation could have been handled differently or even been avoided (by having back-up personnel, for example). The point is that sometimes the "right" solution is painful, but I believe that in a case like this, life is not part of business; business is part of life. Choose life.

CHAPTER 11

Sharing Power

> **Sharing power between two parties can dilute the commitment and effectiveness of both parties.**

Q11.1 Is sharing power a good thing?

A11.1 No, not if what you mean by *sharing power* is two or more people being held equally accountable for a result, or accountable for separate parts of the result, and neither being accountable for the whole. Sharing power equally goes against human nature. Any time something defies human nature, it should be avoided. When two or more people must work together, one should be designated as the leader. The leader is the person who feels the greatest level of accountability and is considered the primary interface for the team.

Sharing power equally can go against human nature

Q11.2 In my experience, sharing power is very common. Do you agree?

A11.2 Yes. Sharing power is common on projects and across organizations. Project members are often assigned to co-own activities and tasks; projects often have more than one project manager; even steering committees made up of executives from across many organizations often give each member an equal vote, yet no one has the final vote. So-called leaders who assign people to share power risk jeopardizing outcomes and creating problems that could have been avoided. These "leaders" are either inexperienced, too soft to make tough decisions, or incompetent. These

Sharing power is common

are harsh words, but the nearly unworkable situations that sharing power creates call for this stern assessment.

Q11.3   What are the disadvantages of sharing power?

A11.3   There are at least eight reasons why sharing power should be avoided.

1. **No one is accountable.** No individual has a personal stake in the project's outcome. There is no single point of focus for the entire endeavor. Instead, each person focuses predominantly on his own tasks, with little interest in the other person's progress.

2. **Personal commitment is lower.** Personal commitments will always be of higher priority than shared commitments. This means that a person's passion for the job is considerably weakened by sharing an assignment with another.

3. **Gray areas emerge.** Each person sharing the power has a designated domain of responsibility. These domains will overlap, creating a gray area—or no-man's land—that will be ignored by both parties. Neither party feels full responsibility for gray-area tasks and events.

4. **Accountability for problems is confused.** When a problem or issue arises, it is not always clear who to take it to and who will own it, especially for issues falling into the gray area.

5. **There is no final arbiter.** No one has the power to resolve a dispute—especially not with the sense of urgency required. This can cause issues to drift and emotions to fester.

6. **Differences in personality and work habits can cause friction.** The power-sharing parties will have different styles. These differences can be in organization, discipline, efficiency, follow-through, people skills,

dedication, politics, and a whole lot more—and they can cause conflict.

7. ***Personal animosity can lead to conflict.*** When two people share power, it is inevitable that one person will expend more energy and effort than the other—or at least believe this to be true. For many, this can cause resentment and bitterness toward the party not pulling her weight or toward the leader who divided the power.

8. ***Recognition is problematic.*** It is difficult to single out one person over the other for special recognition, even if appropriate, when both were assigned to share the work necessary to achieve the outcome.

Q_{11.4} As a project member, I think that I can work fine while sharing accountability for a commitment with another project member. Can you give me a specific example of why this doesn't work?

An example of the downside of sharing power

A_{11.4} It can work, but it typically doesn't work well. Let's imagine that you and I are assigned by our boss, Jen, to resolve a problem. We do so over the next several weeks, but you contribute 90 percent of the effort, while I contribute 10 percent.

A short time after we resolve the problem, our organization has a meeting for all staff. In that meeting, Jen proudly announces that we have resolved the problem. Everyone applauds and shows their respect for a job well done. How does this make you feel? We receive equal credit, but you did most of the work. Most people in your position would feel as if they had been cheated, not given the recognition they deserve. They might even feel resentful or bitter.

Q_{11.5} I don't have a problem with receiving equal recognition, even if I put in more work. After all, I am paid to do my job, and I did it. Isn't it about duty, not recognition?

A sign of professional maturity

A_{11.5} You certainly are noble to think that way. Moreover, you demonstrate an unusual sense of professional maturity. But based on my experience, you are in a very, very small minority who think that way.

Introducing emotions into the mix

Q_{11.6} Don't you think we should all strive to think that way?

A_{11.6} Not necessarily. Working on projects is challenging enough; why introduce negative emotions that can be avoided? Most people put in a position to equally share a new commitment with another person will make all of their other commitments a higher priority. Why? Because those other commitments are not shared; there is no question as to who will be held accountable. We bring the most passion to our work when we have committed to something that is all ours and we alone receive the recognition for completing it.

When there is an assigned lead person, she will see the commitment as more personal. Another person can be the follower. He might be assigned a little or a lot of the work; however, he is more likely to think of his assignment as a personal commitment and be more passionate about its outcome than if he were sharing power with the lead person. Of course, if the follower does most of the work, it is expected that the leader will acknowledge this and give recognition where it is due.

Two or more PMs on a project

Q_{11.7} You mentioned earlier that there should not be two or more project managers on a project. Why is this a problem?

A_{11.7} I commonly see projects that have two or more PMs. The PMs can come from a marketing unit, a business unit, an information technology shop, a development or build team, a client, or other sources. Having more than one PM is bad because it dilutes accountability, creating "gray areas," among other reasons noted earlier.

Q11.8 Can you talk more about the "gray area" in the scenario where there are two project managers, one from an external client's organization and one from the company developing the product or providing the service?

A11.8 Each PM has a domain of responsibility. Figure 11.1(a) depicts each domain as a circle surrounding each PM. There will be some overlap, or a gray area, between the two circles. Many or few duties may overlap, but no matter how many fall into the gray area, the project is in danger because neither PM feels fully accountable for responsibilities in the gray area. Worse, neither PM feels accountable for the entire project. To avoid this, there should be only one PM who is accountable for everything.

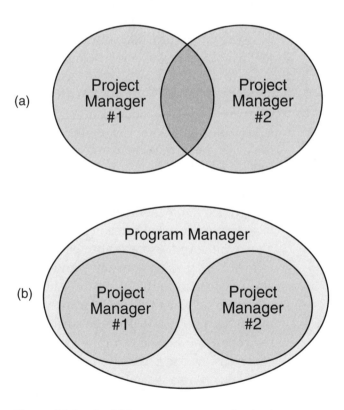

Figure 11.1. Avoid two or more people sharing power

PM in name only

Q11.9   What if the project manager from the company is chosen as the overall project manager, but the client insists on his project manager being called "project manager" as well. How do you handle that?

A11.9   First of all, the client must be convinced that having a single leader who is personally accountable for the project is really in his best interest. Whether that person is a PM from the client's side or from the company's side is not the issue. If the client's PM still insists on being called a PM, then the true PM can be called the *program manager* and the client's PM called a *project manager*. Of course, in reality, the client's PM serves as a team leader.

Figure 11.1(b) shows a possible outcome where a program manager is assigned to be accountable for the entire project and the two project managers are within her domain of responsibility. The program manager and project manager #1 could be the same person. Notice, for purposes of illustration, that the domains of both PMs are smaller now that a program manager is heading up the project.

Committees lacking a person with final authority

Q11.10   If a committee does not have a designated leader who can make the final decision on controversial issues, how can it resolve them?

A11.10   It is common in many companies for a project to affect many different organizations. If this is the case, a committee—commonly called a *steering committee*—made up of a representative from each affected organization is often formed. The steering committee resolves issues that can affect more than one of the organizations represented. Often, these steering committees have no formal leader with the authority to resolve issues between members. Instead, the committee is expected to work together to reach a consensus. As discussed earlier, making decisions through consensus is a bad idea in a business or project environment; it tends to yield a less-than-optimal solution. But a committee may work well if it has a designated leader who has the necessary authority to make the final call on controversial issues.

Q11.11 What do you think of the increasingly common practice of "job sharing"?

A11.11 Job sharing is a variation of sharing power. It is two people working on the same task with the same responsibilities, but at different times. Often this sharing arrangement leaves both individuals equally accountable, but they are also both ultimately accountable. Job sharing is popular in some organizations, but does it typically work successfully?

Job sharing, like power sharing, is fraught with the eight downsides I mentioned in Q&A 11.3. It also challenges human nature. But my experience suggests that job sharing may be slightly more successful than other forms of power sharing. There are two primary reasons for this. The first is that in job sharing, each person typically has a defined scope of responsibility, yet each person feels accountable for the whole job when he is on "active duty." So, for half the time, each member feels ownership of the full tasks.

The second reason why job sharing may have a higher success rate is that through job sharing, employees are better able to accommodate their personal needs while still meeting their organization's business needs. Their gratitude for the arrangement can lead to a strong positive attitude, which will help job sharing work.

"Job sharing" versus sharing power

Q11.12 Any last thoughts on sharing power?

A11.12 Sharing power between two parties can dilute the commitment and effectiveness from both parties—and the overall project can suffer. By making one person accountable—in charge and driving the endeavor—so many prob-

Bringing the best out in each of us

lems, such as the eight listed in Q&A 11.3, go away or are significantly diminished. Work and life get easier. We gain more control over our destiny and are far more motivated to excel. Focused responsibility and accountability bring out the best in each of us.

CHAPTER 12

Interpersonal Communications

> **❝** *People will forget what you said, people will forget what you did, but people will never forget how you made them feel.* **❞**

— Maya Angelou, poet, author, historian, and actress

Q₁₂.₁   Is it okay to complain?

A₁₂.₁   No, not if you're asking if it is okay for Ahmed to complain to Rajesh about something that Stephanie can resolve. This is what I call whining or moaning, and it suggests professional immaturity. It is negative energy. Nobody wants to be around a whiner. But if Ahmed "complains" directly to Stephanie about something that Stephanie can resolve, that is *not* what I call complaining. Ahmed is taking the first step in fixing the problem. Taking a problem directly to the person who can either resolve it or influence its resolution is demonstrating professionally mature behavior.

Q₁₂.₂   You say that complaining is a sign of professional immaturity, but it is pervasive in my organization. Are you saying that most people in my organization are professionally immature?

A₁₂.₂   Bingo! It is my experience that *most* people in the workforce often demonstrate professionally immature behavior. Most don't mean to, nor do they even realize that they are doing so. Professional immaturity is behavior that is disruptive, destructive, or otherwise void of benefit in a business environment. It often manifests itself in weak personal initiative, weak accountability, self-absorption, and having little awareness of how one's own behavior affects others.

**Professional
immaturity**

Q12.3   What is another example of professional immaturity?

A12.3   Here are several indicators of professional immaturity. I could easily list scores more.

- You discover that you are likely to miss a commitment but do not tell those who are dependent upon your deliverable.
- You do not ask for help, without which you will miss a commitment.
- You believe that you are not responsible for commitments that are delivered late to you.
- You believe that you are ready for a promotion because "enough" time has elapsed since your last promotion.
- You have to be asked to work overtime to fulfill your commitments.
- You say that you will get back to someone—and you fail to do so.
- You cause a problem, yet do not apologize or offer to help remedy the situation.
- You believe that you deserve an award for fulfilling the requirements of your job without doing any more than is expected from someone at your level.
- You believe that you have no accountability for that which affects your domain of responsibility.
- You surprise someone by escalating an issue without first attempting to resolve the matter with him.

Q12.4   I see similar signs of professional immaturity frequently in others and sometimes in myself. What can be done?

A12.4   Reading this book will help you learn behavioral best practices, enhancing your professional maturity. Also, your boss should teach professionally mature behaviors to his employees. Culture-training classes (Chapter 27, "Project Culture") are yet another tool for training the members of a project in the behaviors expected of them.

Q_{12.5} Why are so many people in the workplace professionally immature?

A_{12.5} They never learned to be otherwise. Most of us did not grow up discussing professional maturity at the dinner table. School systems and universities give it light treatment. When an employee is hired, whether she is just out of college or is coming from another job—she is expected to already know about professionally mature behavior. Of course, this is an unreasonable expectation.

Resource managers are charged with teaching professional maturity to their employees. But in companies that have a large ratio of employees to managers and little face time between them, managers do not perform enough employee coaching and counseling.

Managers are charged with teaching professional maturity

Q_{12.6} Why is not asking for help a sign of professional immaturity?

A_{12.6} Many project members resist asking for help for so long that the project is harmed. Everyone loses in this scenario. There are many reasons we may not ask for help in a timely manner: pride, ego, and intimidation, as well as fear that our reputations, promotability, and job opportunities may suffer. But if you worked for me, none of these reasons would be sufficient to justify not asking for help. Asking for help is a sign of the project member's strength, not weakness.

Asking for help

> **❝Asking for help does not mean we are weak or incompetent. It usually indicates an advanced level of honesty and intelligence.❞**
>
> —Anne Wilson Schaef, psychotherapist and writer

Q_{12.7} Aren't you concerned that individuals will ask for help too often, putting unnecessary burdens on fellow project members?

A12.7 I am not advocating letting someone else do your job, instead of you rising to the occasion. I am advocating tapping into the wealth of knowledge, skill, and experience surrounding you. I believe that the sum of the parts—the project team as a whole—far exceeds the value and power of the individual parts. A team that helps its members is more fulfilling to work with and is likely far more productive.

But keep in mind that project members will not long tolerate (nor should they) a project member that dumps his responsibilities on others.

Helping others when there is no direct benefit to you

Q12.8 Should I help others when doing so does not affect my domain of responsibility or benefit me directly?

A12.8 Yes, but do so with a level head. For example, if someone asks for your help, and the task might require up to two hours of your time, always say "yes." You cannot convince me that you can't find up to two hours of time to help a fellow project member. However, if someone requests days' or weeks' worth of help—and saying "yes" will cause you to break your commitments—then you must say "no." You do not have the authority to break your commitments; only the person that you have made the commitment to or a higher authority can make that call. We all need help from time to time. Do what you reasonably can to help others. You will eventually need help too.

Positive attitude

Q12.9 How will having a positive attitude help me?

A12.9 There is a saying: *You can change your life by changing your attitude.* Everyone wants to work around people with great attitudes. No one wants to be around party poopers. Having a good attitude helps us see life as a great opportunity—an adventure—that we are blessed to experience. We all have our obstacles and burdens, but these are not what define us. We are, instead, defined by our dreams and hopes and the actions we take to achieve them. Our greatest obstacles are almost always ourselves. Dare to be different. Dare to be bold. Dare to reach for your dreams, despite everything that is going on around you.

Q 12.10 How can I maintain a positive attitude when I work around negative people?

A 12.10 Don't allow others to define you. You choose your own attitude; nobody chooses it for you. A positive attitude can be contagious (so can a negative one). People will look forward to being around and working with you if you have a positive attitude. If others' negative behavior is undermining your ability to achieve your commitments, then you must take action. If you worked for me, saying that you missed a commitment or provided a low-quality deliverable because someone within your domain of responsibility has a poor attitude would not be a valid excuse. You still remain accountable.

If the person with the negative attitude has no influence within your domain of responsibility, then you can choose to do nothing. If you are around the person frequently, you may choose to encourage a change in her attitude or at least try to better understand what is behind it . . . but that is your choice.

❝*Attitude: It is our best friend or our worst enemy.***❞**

—John C. Maxwell, leadership expert

Q 12.11 Is there ever a time when it is okay to speak ill of others?

Speaking ill of others

A 12.11 No, not in the conventional sense. Putting others down does not raise our status or help our character; the opposite occurs. Moreover, speaking ill of others only worsens a bad situation. We now become part of the problem, instead of being part of the solution.

It is good to speak "ill" of someone if you have a sincere interest in understanding him so that you can improve your working relationship with him. For example, you tell your boss that your relationship with Miguel, a peer, has problems you seem unable to get past. You note that your boss appears to have a good working relationship with Miguel, and you ask her for advice in better understanding Miguel and what you can do to improve your relationship with him.

Supporting other peoples' ideas

Q12.12 Should I support other people's ideas?

A12.12 Make sure that you understand others' ideas before passing judgment. Many of us resist new or different ideas, so be open to their potential benefits, but also realistic about any potential downsides. Listen to the creative ideas of others with the same attention and openness with which you would want others to listen to your ideas. Business *always* needs new and different ideas.

Random acts of kindness

Q12.13 Do you believe that "random acts of kindness" can benefit an entire project or organization?

A12.13 Absolutely yes! I am a big fan of "random acts of kindness." The workplace is made better when members of a project strive to do something beneficial for someone else.

For example, you are heading to a shared fax machine to pick up a fax sent to you. When you arrive, there also is a fax for someone else, and that person's office is in the opposite direction from your office. Consider walking out of your way to deliver the fax. If you enter the person's office and she is not there, leave the fax on her chair . . . without a note to say who left it.

Performing such a random act of kindness without seeking recognition makes me feel best about who I am and who I choose to be. Of course, performing random acts of kindness *and* receiving recognition for them is also a great feeling.

> **66** *Sometimes when we are generous in small, barely detectable ways, it can change someone else's life forever.* **99**

—Margaret Cho, American comedian and actress

Q 12.14 How quickly should I respond to an e-mail or a telephone call?

A 12.14 You should respond with the sense of importance and urgency that it requires. Generally, you'll know how urgent the message or call is, but if you do not, find out. If you cannot find the time to respond promptly and fully to an e-mail, then quickly reply with the date (and time of day, if appropriate) you will respond. The e-mail sender may not like being "put off," but your immediate response and honesty will be appreciated. If the sender cannot wait for your full response, then he can urge you to respond more quickly. If that fails, he can pursue an escalation in an attempt to shift your priorities.

Response time to e-mails and phone calls

Q 12.15 What can I do if I cannot get someone to respond to my e-mail or telephone call?

A 12.15 Make sure the other party understands the importance and urgency of the request. Include a date and time by which you need a response, if appropriate. Depending on the importance and urgency, you may need to escalate your request to a higher authority—often the person's boss—in order to get the attention you need. Try not to surprise the person by escalating over his head. Make sure he has been reasonably informed of your need and has had a chance to address it.

Q_{12.16} But what if escalating over the person's head upsets him and endangers our relationship?

A_{12.16} You must successfully complete the tasks in your domain of responsibility. An escalation may be required in order for you to fulfill your responsibilities. It is an action of last resort, but if it is required, it must be pursued. It's not personal; it's business. Don't make an escalation personal through your attitude or approach. If the other party makes it personal, that's his problem.

"Please" and "thank you"

Q_{12.17} Should I say "please" and "thank you"?

A_{12.17} When you believe that the occasion calls for these words, then use them. Most people appreciate hearing them. Your use of them can also set an example for others. Kindness and courtesy can be contagious.

Q_{12.18} When I do things for others, I expect a "please" and "thank you." Should I expect this?

A_{12.18} No. It is asking too much to expect this in the business world. I agree that these words are expected in general and are much appreciated; however, they are not required for success, nor are they always necessary.

For example, say a person working under your direction is sending you, via e-mail, a dozen different pieces of information that you requested. Should you thank her by e-mail for each message she sends? No. After she has sent them all? Perhaps, but possibly no.

Do not allow your relationship with an otherwise excellent and reliable project member to sour because she did not say "thank you." Customs vary among project members. Just because you were raised to expect these words does not mean that you are right to expect them from others. Do not fixate on hearing, or not hearing, "please" and "thank you." There are far bigger obstacles on which to focus. (And if you don't expect to hear these words, but you do, what a nice surprise!)

Q12.19 I work with a person who occasionally makes mistakes, but will never admit to them. Do you believe that a person should "fess up" to mistakes?

Admitting to mistakes

A12.19 Yes. It is a sign of professional maturity to accept responsibility for mistakes we make. When a person makes a mistake and will not admit it, it's very likely that others are aware of the mistake. This can cause tension in the working environment and can cause others to lose respect for the person who will not admit to his mistake.

Admitting mistakes can improve communications between people. And my experience shows that the respect people have for someone actually *increases* when that person admits to making a mistake. When you make a mistake, (1) admit it, (2) apologize, if appropriate, (3) initiate the needed restitution, and then (4) move on. We all make mistakes.

Q12.20 I sometimes get so angry about things that happen at work and have come close to losing my temper. Any advice?

Losing your temper

A12.20 For starters, *don't lose your temper!* If you do, you will damage relationships and lose opportunities. Work on not taking things so personally, and strive to show tolerance for others. It could be helpful to talk about this with someone you respect or even seek professional help. Your boss should be able to help you or suggest someone else who can. However, think first before telling your boss that you have trouble managing your anger. Many bosses will help you and look out for your best interest; a few might use your admission against you.

Q 12.21 What should I do if I am personally threatened?

A 12.21 Don't make it worse. Do not do anything that would encourage violence. You may be able to defuse the situation
verbally and restore calm, but this is a risky approach and
might not work.

In most cases, you should immediately report the incident
to your boss. Your boss then has the duty to inform his
boss, the human resources department, and perhaps others. If the threat is immediate, security should be called in.
You want to distance yourself as best you can from the
incident and allow others to pursue an appropriate resolution. Threats are very serious and should be considered so
by everyone involved.

Q 12.22 What if my boss has threatened me?

A 12.22 Run, don't walk, to your human resources department. Do
not tolerate abuse from anyone—including your boss. But
be prepared for the whole affair to get ugly. Unfortunately,
there are no "win-win" options. Doing nothing is almost
never acceptable. If you are uncomfortable reporting the
threat to HR, consider discussing the situation and your
options with a trusted authority or friend before you take
any action.

Q 12.23 What can I do if someone else gets credit for my work or
achievements?

A 12.23 The standard and reasonable approach should always be
to take the issue to your boss to get support and an appropriate resolution. Obviously, this situation should never
be tolerated. Depending on how severe the situation is,
you could choose to confront the person and expose the
wrong; however, not everyone feels comfortable with this

approach. If the violation is severe, I suggest you first inform your boss and obtain his support before considering other actions.

Q 12.24 **What can I do about someone who repeatedly spreads lies and undermines my reputation behind my back?**

Undermining a person's reputation

A 12.24 Probably not much. For starters, you should inform your boss. She may take some action, including discussing the issue with the other person's boss. You can also confront the person and attempt to win him over, but in my experience, this does not often work. Why? Such a professionally immature person probably has a pattern of underhanded behavior and is not likely to be easily rehabilitated. If the situation is serious enough, and especially if the person has a history of this type of behavior, I believe the person should either be placed on notice or fired immediately. This bad behavior doesn't just hurt one individual; it can undermine an entire project or organization. It should not be tolerated! If you are a project manager, you may want to have the person removed from the team—at a minimum.

Q 12.25 **What can or should I do if I don't like someone with whom I'll be working?**

Not liking a coworker

A 12.25 First of all, sometimes we must meet someone more than halfway. We tend to judge the actions of others more harshly than we judge our own. We are often unwilling to exercise empathy for others, without which it can be nearly impossible to understand them.

You have the power and ability to let your dislike of the person go. Make it a personal project to focus on the person's admirable qualities, and do your best to genuinely win him over. A team of two is far more powerful than two teams of one. I believe that three of the most important things that we can do in this world are *forgive others*, *give to others,* and *love others*. It's not easy to always live by these tenets, but it is satisfying when we do.

Working together doesn't require you to be friends, but it certainly requires civility. You don't have to become "best buds," but if you allow your dislike of the person to interfere, you are hurting yourself. Is it really worth that?

If your feelings about the person are rooted especially deeply, for serious reasons that I do not address in this book, then you might choose to seek professional help or ask your resource manager to assign you duties that will help you avoid contact with that person.

A coworker not liking you

Q12.26 What can I do if I work with someone who doesn't like me?

A12.26 The good news is that you likely don't need that person to like you in order to function fully as an adult and as a professional. It would be great if everyone always liked you, but that's not going to happen—for anyone! You aren't facing reality if you expect otherwise. So don't give someone else so much power over you that they can negatively affect your hour, day, or week. Be civil. Treat others with respect and dignity. Don't intentionally give others reasons to dislike you, but beyond that, let it go. You have dreams to fulfill.

> ❝ *I was always looking outside myself for strength and confidence, but it comes from within. It is there all the time.* ❞
>
> —Anna Freud, Austrian-born British psychoanalyst and psychologist

Hanging out with your ethnic group

Q12.27 Is it wrong for a person to hang out at work with only people of his own ethnicity?

A_{12.27} A person should be free to choose the people he wishes to spend time with at work as long as his choices do not interfere with anyone's performance and commitments to a project or organization. But there is an exception for managers. For example, if a manager has lunch with or chats with only people of her own ethnicity, yet she has people of other ethnicities reporting to her, then there can be a *perception* of impropriety. That is, her other employees may believe, correctly or not, that she may be discriminating against them, and that they are at a disadvantage for opportunities, promotions, awards, and salary increases compared to the *chosen* group. Managers must play by different rules because of their power and influence in the organization and company.

Q_{12.28} How can I *not* make things personal, or take them personally?

Making and taking things personally

A_{12.28} Most of us wrestle with this issue sometimes. It can help to look at your job as strictly business—not personal. At work, the objective is to have a successful business outcome. It's not about you. It's not about your ego. It's not about winning or losing. It's about the success of your assignments, your project, your organization, and your company. It's about the satisfaction of your clients. It's about everything that helps us achieve business success. You should care about success. You should work with passion and take ownership of everything that can affect your domain of responsibility. But in the end, when the dust has settled, it's all about what is best for the business.

Some people have a tendency to make situations seem personal, and some people have a tendency to take things personally. Doing so is a sign of professional immaturity; professional immaturity harms successful business outcomes. Resist allowing others to draw you into a personal conflict versus a business conflict. Do things because they are the right business thing to do, not because you or someone else takes things personally.

CHAPTER 13

Resolving Conflict through Escalations

❝You can't please everybody if you are going to make a difference in this world.❞

—Melvin Chapman, educator

Definition of an escalation

Q13.1   What do you mean by an escalation?

A13.1   When two affected parties are unable to agree on the resolution of an issue after they have made a sincere attempt to negotiate one, an *escalation* is pursued to resolve the problem. Escalating is the act of calling upon higher levels of project leadership or management to resolve an issue.

Definition of an issue

Q13.2   What do you mean by an issue?

A13.2   An *issue* is a situation that arises when two parties are unable to agree on the resolution of a problem that, if left unresolved, can have a significant impact on the project.

Determining which party initiates the escalation

Q13.3   Which party should initiate the escalation?

A13.3   Typically, the party who is not in the power position should do so. For example, say you have a document that is distributed to a list of approvers and reviewers. If an approver will not approve your document, then you must initiate the escalation to obtain her approval. Why? Because she is in a power position; you need her approval. However, if a reviewer of the document does not approve it, you don't "care" because you do not require his approval. The reviewer must initiate the escalation. Typically, the party in the power position does not need to initiate the escalation. The party who needs to close the issue typically is the one who must initiate the escalation.

Q13.4 When should I begin an escalation?

Beginning an escalation

A13.4 Begin an escalation only after a reasonable attempt to re-solve the conflict with the person. About 95 percent of the time, both parties can work things out between them-selves. When they cannot, assistance from higher up is needed. You should initiate the escalation as soon as rea-sonably possible, but within *two workdays* of the time you realize you are at an impasse in resolving the issue.

Q13.5 As a project member, who should I escalate to?

Determining the person to escalate to

A13.5 Organizational cultures vary, but two common approaches are to escalate to your PM (team leader first, if appropri-ate), or to the other person's resource manager. I accept either approach, but prefer the approach in which the re-source manager is involved.

Q13.6 Usually, you seem to advocate doing things independently of management so that decisions can be made more quickly and politics can be kept out. Why do you think management should be involved here?

A13.6 I do generally advocate independent thinking, not an overreliance on management. But for escalations, I believe management involvement:

1. ***Helps employees reach their potential in an orga-nization and company.*** Escalating to an RM forces the RM to stay involved with and nurture the employee

and the relevant issues. Too many managers dump their employees on the doorsteps of PMs and then disappear, instead of sticking around to help their employees meet their commitments and reach their potential in the organization and company.

2. ***Allows RMs to fairly evaluate the performance of their employees.*** If RMs are to evaluate the performance of their employees, then they must stay connected to them in order to understand issues that arise and to assess their performance.

3. ***Keeps RMs abreast of relevant issues.*** In organizations where PMs have a lot of power (which I favor), weak RMs tend to become weaker and remove themselves from the day-to-day issues their employees and the organization face. Employees, projects, and organizations need RMs who are knowledgeable about what is going on around them.

Involving the PM

Q13.7   Are you saying that I should not involve my project manager in escalations?

A13.7   A PM can help resolve many conflicts that might arise between project members. If you decide to initiate an escalation to management, you should still keep the PM apprised of the escalation and its outcome. In many cases, the PM should be involved in the escalation because he will want the outcome to be in the project's best interest.

Q13.8   What if the project manager disagrees with the outcome of an escalation I have initiated without his participation? Does he have any recourse?

A13.8   Yes. The PM can reopen the issue and take it up the management chain, independent of the outcome of your escalation.

Q_{13.9} How high up the project leadership chain or management chain should I escalate?

A_{13.9} You should escalate until one of four things occurs:

- You obtain a resolution that you feel is satisfactory.
- Your management chain and the other person's management chain meet, and the highest authority makes a decision.
- Your boss or some boss within your management chain says "stop."
- Your project sponsor makes a decision.

Q_{13.10} What recourse do I have if I don't like the decision someone in my management chain or the project sponsor makes?

A_{13.10} You have little or no recourse. Before the final decision is made on the escalated issue, make sure your position has been fully presented and understood. You should define the effects, both positive and negative, should you win or lose the escalation. Once the decision has been made by the final authorities, live with that decision and make the best of it.

If there is a legal or ethical problem with the decision, and integrity is being trampled upon, run—don't walk—to buck the management that made the final call. Do not ever support illegal or unethical behavior, or you will eventually go down with it! (See Chapter 18, "Ethics and Integrity.")

Q_{13.11} If I do not like the outcome of the escalation, when is it okay to ask that the issue be revisited?

A_{13.11} Only in cases in which significant new news that you think can tip the decision to the other side becomes available. Always consult your boss beforehand.

Q13.12 As a project member, do I need my resource manager's approval to escalate an issue over someone's head?

A13.12 Yes, unless your boss has told you otherwise. When you approach your boss for support, he has four choices:

1. *Agree with you, give you the go-ahead to escalate, and offer to help if asked.* This is usually the best choice a boss can make, because the accountability for closing the issue rests squarely on your shoulders.

2. *Agree with you, give you the go-ahead to escalate, but choose to participate with you.* A boss might do this to support your position because you are new to the escalation process, easily intimidated, or potentially outnumbered—or management on the other party's side owes him a favor—just to name a few possible reasons.

3. *Disagree with you and direct you to stop the escalation.* Do not escalate. If you cannot negotiate the outcome you seek, then move on.

4. *Direct you to "give" the issue to him; he will close it by working with the other party's management.* Unfortunately, this choice is common, but it is typically the worst option because it takes the accountability away from you. Moreover, you get stuck with the negotiated outcome—whether you like it or not. Also, how can your boss fairly evaluate your performance when he is performing for you?

Q13.13 If the fourth option is so bad, why do managers take this approach?

A13.13 Because they don't know better. Managers mean well and typically think they are doing the best thing for you. But by taking over your issue, your resource manager undermines your respect in the organization and your performance.

Q 13.14 I worry that escalating situations will cause some folks to not want to work with me. What do you think?

A 13.14 If you worked for me, I would hold you accountable for the success of your project assignments. If you have any obstacles, you must do what is in the best interest of the business to resolve the problems—no matter what others will think. If you are a team leader or PM, your team relies on you to demonstrate the leadership necessary to help the whole team be successful.

Concern over harming relationships with others

Q 13.15 How can I be certain that escalating is the right thing to do? I fear burning bridges and losing friends.

A 13.15 For a moment, imagine you own the company and you have an employee faced with the same decision: to escalate or not to escalate. Would you, as the owner of the company, prefer that the issue continue to drift unresolved, or would you want it to be escalated to higher levels of project leadership or management so that it can be resolved and everyone can move on?

The answer is simple: Get it resolved! It's business. Don't make it personal. If someone chooses to make it personal, then that is that person's problem, not yours!

Q 13.16 If the issue is between me and my boss, is it okay to escalate over my boss' head?

A 13.16 No, not in most cases. Your boss has the authority to make decisions that affect his domain of responsibility—and you are likely within that domain. However, if you are a project member and your resource manager has made a decision that affects your project, you must inform your PM of the outcome of that decision. The PM can then choose to escalate over your boss' head to change that decision.

Escalating over your boss' head

Q 13.17 As a project manager, is it okay for me to escalate an issue over my boss' head?

A13.17 The answer is still *no*. However, as the project manager, you have the duty to inform the project sponsor of your boss' decision. The project sponsor can then choose to escalate the issue higher.

Q13.18 When is it okay to escalate over my boss' head?

A13.18 If the issue pertains to an illegal or unethical matter, then you can go to a higher authority. Your boss may not like it, but you should consider doing so anyway. (See Chapter 18, "Ethics and Integrity.")

Q13.19 My company has an "open-door policy" whereby we are encouraged to go over our boss' head or over anyone in our management chain if we feel we are being treated unfairly or we disagree with a decision. Moreover, we are told that there will not be any negative repercussions. Do you support this policy?

A13.19 Yes, but with caution. Most companies have a policy like this as a safety net to help prevent problems from festering and becoming much bigger problems. If you owned your own company, you probably would have such a policy, too.

Having this policy is sound business practice, but it may not always be implemented as advertised. You cannot be certain that there will be no negative recourse. Why? Because the policy is being carried out by humans (yes, managers are humans, too!). Some resource managers may take an escalation personally and plan to "pay you back." For example, you may have been slated for a 5 percent salary increase, but you only receive 2 percent. Or your boss claims she's pursuing a new opportunity for you, but is actually doing nothing. There are subtle ways for a boss to "get even."

Now don't misunderstand: Most managers will take the high road and will implement the open-door policy as it was intended. However, there are a few who will not, and it may not always be easy to tell the difference between those who will implement the policy fairly and those who will not. If you choose to take advantage of the open-door policy, know that it could negatively affect you, so do so carefully.

Q 13.20 Do you think that when there is an escalation, there is almost always one party who is clearly wrong?

Escalating doesn't mean either party is wrong

A 13.20 On the contrary. In most escalations, neither party is wrong. Each is simply looking out for his domain of responsibility—as he should! Someone at a higher level, who sees the issue more objectively from a larger business perspective, must intervene. If you never or rarely find yourself escalating issues, then I question how effective you are in making the best business decisions.

Q 13.21 Many of the Q&As in this chapter seem to be written mostly for project members. I am a project manager. Does your advice apply to me?

PM's behavior with escalations

A 13.21 Yes, for the most part. A key difference is that your boss may not require you to obtain her permission to escalate issues to closure as long as they do not go beyond an organizational level you and she have previously agreed upon. If you need to escalate an issue above that level, you will need your boss' permission and perhaps the project sponsor's permission, too.

Q 13.22 I am a project manager who works in a relatively small company with few layers of management. If I escalate issues, before long I could wind up in the CEO's office. Is that okay?

Escalating to the CEO

A 13.22 If there are issues that must be resolved, and the only way that they will be properly addressed is to take them to the

CEO, then that may be the correct approach. Or the CEO may designate his senior VPs to work on the issues.

Yet another approach is to lobby for the formation of a steering committee made up of representatives with authority from each area of the company. The steering committee would decide the outcome of the escalated issue. For this to work most effectively, one person on the committee must have the final say if the group cannot agree on a decision that is in the best business interest of the company.

If you need help in determining how best to proceed with an escalation, consult your boss or project sponsor.

CHAPTER 14

Meetings

*❝When planning a project, we often overlook
the large number of meetings that will be necessary to attend—
and those necessary to avoid.❞*

Q_{14.1} Meetings are a big problem where I work. There are too many, they are usually run poorly, and they take too long. Any advice?

**Too many
meetings**

A_{14.1} Most of us waste a lot of time on meetings. Only attend meetings that you *need* to attend—that is, if you need something as a result of the meeting, or someone else needs something from you during the meeting. Be sensitive to the needs of those who require information from you or require your participation and discussion in order for their meeting to be successful. Don't attend meetings out of habit or because you are curious about something.

Q_{14.2} It seems that I rarely need to attend meetings for myself; I almost always go so that I can share information or participate in discussion. But these meetings are taking up too much of my time. What can I do?

**Managing
demands
of covering
meetings**

A_{14.2} Can you give the same information to others outside of meetings so that you do not have to attend them? If not, ask those inviting you to meetings if you can arrive at a certain time and stay only for a specific portion of the meeting

Note: This section focuses on general meetings. It does not specifically discuss project tracking meetings, although many of the Q&As in the chapter may also apply to those meetings. The subject of project tracking meetings is addressed in Chapter 29, "Project Tracking."

so that you are not "killing time" waiting for your turn to present. If appropriate, say that you will not be able to attend at all if you are required to attend the full meeting.

If, no matter what you do to remedy your situation, you are still required to attend meetings for which you don't have time, take ownership of the problem. Work with your manager to get help. Perhaps you can offload some of your work to one or more other team members, or you can acquire an assistant to help you with your workload. Whatever you do, do not simply dump the problem on your boss; be active in determining the appropriate solution. Doing nothing is not acceptable and is an indicator of professional immaturity.

Calling a meeting

Q 14.3   What should I keep in mind when I call a meeting?

A 14.3   Schedule the meeting with sufficient advance notice for the attendees—preferably at least one or two days—so that they can plan for the meeting and plan other events around the meeting. Make the objective for the meeting available ahead of time so that attendees know what to expect.

Best times of day to schedule meetings

Q 14.4   What are the best times of day to hold a meeting?

A 14.4   Schedule meetings when people are most likely to be available—during the "safety zone." Avoid, if possible, scheduling meetings before 9:00 a.m. or after 4:00 p.m. Why? Because many people arrive at work "late" or leave work "early." It is also a good idea to avoid scheduling meetings during typical lunch times. Of course, the "safety zone" shrinks or can comprise a different set of times if meeting attendees are in different time zones.

Q14.5 Are you saying that there are only five or six "safe" hours in the day to hold a meeting?

A14.5 Depending on the importance and urgency of the meeting, it *can* be scheduled outside the "safety zone," but doing so makes it less convenient, maybe even a hardship, for invitees. However, if you're holding a meeting with few invitees, whom you already know are likely to be available, scheduling it outside the "safety zone" should not present a problem.

Q14.6 How can I stop meeting invitees from arriving late and leaving early?

Attendees arriving late or leaving early

A14.6 I have addressed this problem by scheduling all meetings to begin at 10 minutes after the hour so that attendees can arrive on time from their last meeting. Allowing 10 minutes between meetings gives attendees time to travel, make calls or check e-mail, and relax. Furthermore, all of my meetings end 10 minutes before the hour (or earlier) so that attendees have time to get to their next meeting if it starts on the hour.

It is amazing that we attempt to do what physics has said we cannot: be in two places at the same time. People don't hesitate to schedule a meeting from 9:00-10:00 and another from 10:00-11:00. This never works, but it doesn't stop us from doing it. The 10-minute buffer between meetings sets attendees up for success, not failure.

Q14.7 After scheduling a 10-minute buffer between meetings, what can I do if I continue to have a problem with attendees arriving late or leaving early?

A14.7 If the meeting is routine, then tell everyone in attendance that it is essential for them to arrive on time because late arrivals cause problems for other attendees, the person who owns the meeting, and the business. Productivity can fall when people waste time by being late. Discuss the need to demonstrate respect for others by abiding by meeting times. Note that arriving to a meeting late or leaving early can be a sign of professional immaturity—unless, of course, there is a valid reason for doing so. Ask attendees for their support to help make these meetings successful.

Q14.8 I've had this talk with attendees, but there are still a couple of people who will not cooperate. What can I do? (Should I lock late arrivers out of the meeting?)

A14.8 Resorting to locking the door is childish. So is embarrassing late arrivers and early departers in front of the group. These are all demeaning and professionally immature behaviors.

Some meeting leaders assess a monetary fine, perhaps a dollar, for every minute that an attendee is late. When enough money has been collected, the team uses it for refreshments or a celebration event. This is cute, but it is hardly an effective deterrent, especially for those with money to spare and who like to be the center of attention. Still others note the names of latecomers at the top of the meeting minutes. This is not a bad idea, but its effectiveness is limited. There are a lot of gimmicks that can be employed, but I don't play these games. I expect those who attend my meetings to be professionals who care about doing the right thing.

Q14.9 Are you naïve or what?

A14.9 My experience shows that the vast majority of attendees will play fair as long as I play fair with them. As I said earlier, I schedule meetings to allow 10 minutes of travel and free time between sessions, and I act as a role model by arriving at my own meetings on time.

Do not tolerate attendees who won't play fair

Q14.10 What do you do with attendees who won't "play fair"?

A 14.10 I sit down with the individual to tell her that I need her participation. If she still does not cooperate, I ask her boss for help, but before I do so, I tell her that I am about to meet with her boss. I have found that this technique almost always works. I will not tolerate repeated lateness to routine meetings. All eyes are on me as the leader to ensure that the team or project is successful. The goal is not to be popular. It is to be effective and to ensure success for the group.

Q 14.11 Should I take minutes for my own meetings?

A 14.11 Only if the meeting is short and has few attendees; otherwise, a scribe is needed. When meeting leaders take the minutes, they slow down the meeting and lose concentration, and the meeting is less effective. Having a scribe will free the meeting owner to drive the meeting.

Recording minutes

Q 14.12 Should another meeting attendee be the scribe?

A 14.12 It's possible, but preferably not. The scribe can be a person in the organization whose job includes supporting projects and teams. Some organizations call this a project analyst. (See Chapter 5, "The Project Analyst," for more about the role of this stakeholder.) I suggest that whoever acts as scribe also write and distribute the minutes—after they are reviewed and approved by the meeting owner. This encourages good note taking and ensures that the minutes will be thorough. Alternatively, the meeting owner can write the minutes from the notes taken by the scribe (and credit the note taker at the beginning of the minutes). This technique can also encourage good note taking.

Selecting a scribe

Q 14.13 How do you feel about the meeting owner electronically recording the meeting and transcribing the minutes from the recording?

Electronic recording

A 14.13 Although this technique can be a viable alternative, there are two possible problems. Some members may not be comfortable being recorded and therefore may participate less in the meeting. (This downside could also be positive: It could encourage attendees to speak only if they have something meaningful to contribute.) Get attendees' support for this approach before adopting it.

The other problem with recording the meeting is that it forces the meeting owner to spend twice as much time on the meeting—attending it *and* listening to it. You probably do not have this much time to spare. If you really want to use an electronic recorder, consider turning it on during a meeting only to capture key pieces of information that are likely to be included in the meeting minutes. This approach will waste some of the attendees' time, but will waste less time than physically writing the notes during the meeting.

Distributing minutes

Q 14.14 How quickly should meeting minutes be written and distributed after a meeting?

A 14.14 Within one workday for general meetings; two workdays for project tracking meetings.

A required attendee is a no-show

Q 14.15 What if a key person does not show up for my meeting?

A 14.15 Cancel the meeting. It can be a big waste of time to hold two meetings, one without the required person and another with the required person. When the meeting is called, the key attendees must know that their presence is essential and that the meeting will be postponed if they do not attend.

Q_{14.16} Any tips on conducting meetings in which everyone is in the same meeting room?

A_{14.16} Here are several tips for the meeting owner to follow:

- Begin the meeting with a declaration of the meeting's objective. This will help the attendees stay focused and will also keep the meeting as brief as possible. When the objectives have been reached, end the meeting—unless it would be helpful to discuss follow-up issues now.
- If more than one topic will be addressed, the meeting owner should have an agenda for all to follow.
- As key agreements are reached or attendees are assigned to action items, record these results where all attendees can see them (e.g., on a white board or flip chart).
- Give everyone a fair chance to be heard, and consider their points. The person who talks the loudest or is the most assertive does not have a monopoly on ideas. Many times, attendees who are reserved and quiet are among those with the best ideas.
- Do not allow any attendee to take the meeting off on a tangent.
- If an item is raised that has merit for follow-up at a later meeting, then "park" the item on a list to be revisited at the end of the meeting. The meeting owner will distribute the items on this list to the appropriate people (who may or may not be at this meeting).
- Before the meeting is over, briefly review the key agreements reached and the work items assigned.

Tips on conducting local meetings

Q_{14.17} I often conduct remote meetings. Do you have any tips?

A_{14.17} In addition to the tips for conducting local meetings, here are several tips for the meeting owner to follow when running a remote meeting:

Tips on conducting remote meetings

- Be sensitive to time zone differences. If this call is not convenient for remote attendees, then accommodate them on the next call and incur the hardship locally.
- Be sensitive to differences in organizational culture regarding working overtime, the manner of inoffensively directing work (such as asking participants to take on tasks rather than directing them to do so), gender- and boss-related issues (demonstrate respect for all participants), and the use of language.
- Have attendees announce that they are entering and exiting the meeting so that remote attendees will know who is present.
- Consider using PowerPoint® or Visio® presentations so that everyone on the call can easily follow along (everyone should be seeing the same information at the same time) and remain focused on the discussion.
- Occasionally ask remote attendees questions to ensure that they are following the meeting discussion and are not distracted by other work or socializing.

Posting meeting guidelines

Q14.18 Do you find that organizations with meeting guidelines posted in their meeting rooms tend to conduct more effective meetings?

A14.18 Yes. Meeting guidelines remind all attendees of elements that can help the meeting be more effective. Also, it seems that every meeting has one or more attendees who act as the "conscience" of the meeting; these folks tend to remind others when the meeting is off-focus and is losing effectiveness.

Meetings used to communicate solutions— versus working on problems

Q14.19 Should I call a meeting to resolve a problem if I have already resolved it and am satisfied with my decision?

A14.19 Yes, if you believe that the issue should be discussed to get others to "buy in," or if calling a meeting is an effective way to communicate the resolution.

Q14.20 What should I do if my boss occasionally attends my meetings, and when she does, she has a bad habit of taking the meeting off on tangents?

Boss takes meetings on tangents

A14.20 You have two choices: You can immediately note that the discussion has gone off on a tangent, and get the meeting back on track. Do this professionally and tactfully—not because she is your boss, but because she is a person who should be treated with respect and dignity. Or, after the meeting, you can discreetly ask your boss not to take meetings off on tangents. Appeal to her to help you conduct effective meetings.

I favor the first approach because it addresses the problem immediately and saves valuable meeting time, but the second approach is fine for those who feel the need to be especially sensitive with their bosses.

If you as a meeting owner do not take control of meetings, it is likely that during your next performance evaluation, your boss will criticize you for running poor meetings. She will say that whenever she attends your meetings, she observes that they frequently go off on tangents—not realizing that she is the problem.

CHAPTER 15

Celebrations

66 Gratitude is not only the greatest of virtues,
but the parent of all others. 99

—Cicero, Roman philosopher, orator, and statesman

Project celebrations are important

Q15.1 Do you believe that project-related celebrations are important?

A15.1 Absolutely! Project milestones and events should be planned to happen at least every three months and should be challenging but achievable. Celebrating the successful completion of a milestone is motivating, exciting, and helps the team to bond. It's a great way to promote a culture that encourages the best from people and shows its appreciation for their contributions. Celebrating the first milestone on a project is especially important so that the team feels appreciated for achieving it. This is great motivation to reach the remaining milestones.

Celebrating late achievements

Q15.2 Should a celebration occur if the special milestone or event was delayed, but eventually achieved?

A15.2 Yes. The team still achieved the event through hard work and persistence and despite difficult obstacles. A team that finished late yet achieved the goal may savor and appreciate the celebration even more.

Initiating celebrations

Q15.3 Who has the duty to initiate celebrations?

A_{15.3} Typically, the project manager does. The PM has the best understanding of the major milestones and has the most to gain by creating and ensuring a productive work environment where morale is high.

Q_{15.4} What is an appropriate form of celebration?

Types of celebration

A_{15.4} It doesn't have to be big or costly. It could be lunch, an afternoon off, tickets to a movie, or an after-work get together. Perhaps the team should be given the opportunity to brainstorm celebration ideas. Just the act of stopping to celebrate—to recognize and thank the team—can go a long way. Managers might need to be involved to approve the celebration if it involves giving project members time off, conducting an off-site event, or activities that require funding.

Q_{15.5} What if some project members are not pleased with the method of celebration?

Disinterested project members

A_{15.5} If the choice of celebration does not please or interest everyone, then vary the kinds of celebrations from milestone to milestone or from team member to team member, so that everyone can enjoy themselves and feel special. Do not forgo celebratory events because you fear that some may be uninterested or unenthused.

CHAPTER 16

Overtime Work

*❝It's not about the need for working overtime;
it's about the need for achieving specific business results
while balancing the need for personal time.❞*

The business of working overtime

Q16.1 From a business perspective, how should overtime work be viewed?

A16.1 Overtime work is often thought of as a safety net to ensure that work—especially committed work—gets done with the sense of urgency required so that the business thrives. Rather than temporarily hiring employees during peak work periods and laying them off when the workload subsides, businesses usually prefer that core employees meet the business need by working overtime.

Organizations' overtime policies vary

Q16.2 Do most organizations or companies view overtime similarly?

A16.2 Every organization has its own culture. Some organizations don't want their employees to work any overtime except in rare cases—and some of those cases would require approval from the employee's boss. Some organizations pay their employees for overtime work. Some organizations are subject to union rules. In my experience, most organizations rely on and expect some overtime from their employees in order to meet their business objectives.

How much overtime is required?

Q16.3 How much overtime is a project member expected to work?

A_{16.3} The short answer is: However much it takes, within reason, to get the job done. Understand, however, that the point is not to work more hours, it's to get *results*. These results can be related to fulfilling your commitments or to meeting business needs that might surpass your commitments.

Q_{16.4} **What do you mean by "whatever it takes—within reason"?**

How much overtime is too much?

A_{16.4} The answer will vary from company to company and depending on the situation. But in general, an employee may work as much as 10 hours a week of overtime—sometimes for many weeks or months at a time. However, if you are working *more* than 10 hours per week of sustained overtime, something may be amiss. You might be overloaded, you might require additional training, you might have unproductive work habits, you might be in the wrong job, or you might want to work the extra time because you love your job. Talk with your boss and PM if you feel you are working too much overtime.

Q_{16.5} **Are you saying that I should never have to work more than 10 hours of overtime in any given week?**

Avoiding "burnout"

A_{16.5} No, I am not saying that. In fact, sometimes your overtime may exceed 10 hours in a given week, depending on the importance and urgency of the issue at hand. However, long-term, it is strongly preferable that a project member not be required to work more than 10 extra hours on average per week. Doing so could contribute to "burnout," personal hardship, and other negative outcomes.

Q_{16.6} **What if someone wants to work more than 10 hours of overtime each week? Would you allow it?**

Voluntary high levels of overtime

A_{16.6} Probably, as long as no government or company rules are being broken and there are no safety, health, or security concerns. An employee who's eager to make progress may get passionately caught up in a project. I respect that and can relate. If there were insufficient funding available to pay for the additional work, then I would work with the employee to find some other means of showing my appreciation. Examples might include giving her time off, funding to attend a relevant trade show or conference, an award, special training, a highly visible position, or a quicker promotion.

Impact on productivity and quality

Q 16.7 I have heard that working overtime causes a person's productivity and quality to suffer. Has this been your experience?

A 16.7 It depends. Some people might be less productive and might make more mistakes while working overtime if they are distracted by non-work-related thoughts. On the flip side, I believe many people who are highly motivated and focused are capable of excellent productivity and quality while working overtime. For one thing, they might get "on a roll" because they are able to concentrate on their work with fewer distractions than they would experience during normal work hours. Of course, working excessive overtime for a sustained period can negatively affect almost anyone's performance.

Link between overtime and career

Q 16.8 I am quite productive and can almost always get my job done within the standard work week. Do you believe that not working overtime is hurting my career?

A 16.8 Perhaps. You may be achieving the expected results based on your job level, but working overtime can help move the business further than it would go if no one worked overtime. And project members who are willing to go the extra mile are more likely to open doors to greater opportunities and promotions.

Q16.9   Then are you saying that I am wrong to avoid overtime—even though I am able to get my job done within the standard work week?

A16.9   It is not a matter of being right or wrong; it is a matter of choice. I cannot overstate the importance of an employee achieving what he believes is a healthy balance between his personal and professional lives. Naturally, the more we dedicate ourselves to something, the likelier we are to receive the recognition and rewards that go along with those achievements. It is a matter of personal choice.

Q16.10   Then are you saying that working overtime is good for my career?

A16.10   It depends on why you are working overtime. If you are working overtime because you made a mistake or are unproductive, then doing so might help you save your job. If you are working overtime to achieve more than is expected of you or because you volunteered to "save the day," then, clearly, it will help your career.

Q16.11   Should overtime be planned into projects?

A16.11   On longer-term projects, no. On very short projects with a sense of urgency for the deliverable, yes, if overtime is appropriate to meet the business needs. Overtime is one form of buffer contingency. If overtime is planned into long-term projects, then those projects are at greater risk of failure to meet commitments. But for an urgent project that might be only days or weeks long, all project stakeholders might be asked to rise to the business need.

Q16.12   When there is overtime on a project, is it a sign that one or more people have "messed up"?

A16.12 Not necessarily. Projects can be quite complex and every project is unique in terms of technology, interpersonal relationships, budgets, business needs, client expectations, and so many other factors. Even on a "typical" project, overtime may be required as project members approach a major milestone and scurry to achieve the date on time. Of course, overtime can also be the consequence of having overzealous sales and marketing folks, inadequate or misunderstood requirements, poor estimates, weak planning and tracking, weak leadership, and a host of other ills.

The best-run projects, by the way, are not necessarily those that finished without overtime being required. Businesses should strive to constructively and consistently get employees to achieve a healthy level of productivity. Some overtime may be inevitable.

CHAPTER 17

Mentoring

> **Mentor: someone whose hindsight can become your foresight.**
>
> —Anonymous

Q17.1 Is having a mentor really helpful?

A17.1 If you have an interest in learning and mastering a profession—project management or any other—then there is no better way to learn the craft than by having a mentor by your side. A *mentor* is a trusted counselor and subject-matter expert whose primary objective is to help a mentee be more effective in a specific area of interest by helping develop the mentee's potential.

Q17.2 How should I go about finding a mentor?

A17.2 There are many methods to consider. Here are a few:

- *Get help from your boss.* Because your boss likely has more contacts within the organization or company than you do, he may be able to find a qualified person who is willing to take the time to mentor you.
- *Look around your work environment* and identify people you respect and who have mastered the knowledge and skills you seek. These individuals are potential mentors.
- *Go into the community* and talk with practitioners, university professors, or family and friends to find a mentor.

- *Join professional organizations.* Project Management Institute chapters, for example, often have mentoring programs for their members.

Your boss as your mentor

Q17.3 Why couldn't my boss be a potential mentor?

A17.3 Your boss likely has good mentoring skills, but a person's boss often is not the best mentor for that person. Why? Because for a mentee to benefit the most from a mentorship, the mentee must be totally open and honest with the mentor. There are no stupid questions in a mentor-mentee relationship.

It's not unusual for a person being mentored by his boss to find that his next performance review yields a lower-than-expected rating. When a boss evaluates the performance of an employee, that boss must give the benefit of doubt to the employee if certain concerns or observations cannot be proven. But in the case of an employee who is mentored by his boss, the boss has all the data needed to show that the employee is weak in certain areas—*because he told him!*

If this happened to you, how likely would you be to continue using your boss as your mentor? Not very! Always be cautious if you are considering choosing a mentor who has power over your salary, promotions, awards, and job opportunities. This applies to your immediate boss or someone up your direct management chain.

Q17.4 Are you saying that I should never use my boss as my mentor?

A17.4 No, I am saying that your boss typically is not the best choice of mentor, but there are exceptions. I have seen cases in which bosses, as well as managers directly up their mentees' management chain, are great mentors for their employees. Just be sure you understand how the mentoring relationship will affect salary increases, promotions, and other elements of a successful career.

By the way, whether or not your boss becomes your mentor, it is essential that you and your boss have a great working relationship. You need each other. Your boss has the duty to coach and counsel you—to help you reach your potential in the organization and company.

Q 17.5 If I were to approach someone and ask him to be a mentor, what should I say?

A 17.5 You would be specific about your expectations of the person. Be sure you:

- ***Specifically state the knowledge and skills that you are hoping to acquire and hone as a result of the mentorship.*** Are you only looking for brief, occasional discussions or for a more substantial relationship, such as a mentor who will review documents you have produced or a project plan that you have created, or who will participate in a review of your entire project?
- ***Estimate the time commitment you think may be required.*** For example, is it two to four hours a week, two hours a month, or occasional full days?
- ***Propose a way to schedule time with the mentor.*** Should you have pre-allocated time slots, go through his admin person, directly call him, or walk into his office?

If the person agrees to be your mentor, consider creating a brief "document of understanding" that defines the mentoring relationship and agreed-to goals.

Initial conversation with a potential mentor

Q 17.6 What if a potential mentor said "no" to my request to be my mentor? I would have a hard time dealing with that rejection while continuing to work with that person.

A 17.6 Expect a "no." The people that you would naturally seek out as a mentor are typically well-respected and very busy people in the organization. It is very possible that they do

Rejection from a potential mentor

not have the time to help you. They may feel as bad about saying "no" as you do hearing it. Understand, however, that these folks are honored and flattered by your request. Do not take "no" as a personal rejection; they are just being honest about their limited time.

If you have a difficult time personally working with or around a colleague after hearing a "no," then you are the problem. You are exhibiting professionally immature behavior. Instead, be friendly and show by your actions that you continue to respect and admire the person. Over time, you may find that your colleague will make time to work with you because he really wants to.

> 66 *The fear of rejection ... is even more dangerous than rejection itself. That fear can prevent you from taking the necessary risks that could lead you to true success.* 99
>
> —Jack Perry, American insurance executive, author, and motivational speaker

Good chemistry between mentor and mentee

Q17.7 Any tips on what to look for in a mentor?

A17.7 A mentor should, of course, have the knowledge, experience, and skills that you are seeking. It's also essential to have good chemistry with a potential mentor. You must be comfortable with your mentor's demeanor and feel that he is approachable and that you can trust him when you tell him about mistakes you've made or ask him "stupid" questions. The mentor's teaching approach should be tactful and his criticism of your work constructive. Every time you seek his advice and counsel, you should feel as if you have been helped.

Q17.8 Is there an advantage to having a mentor from within my company rather than one from the outside?

Accessibility of mentor

A17.8 All things being equal, you want a mentor who is accessible when you need him—preferably someone who is just down the hallway. I mentor up to a dozen people at any given time, in about as many companies. But as good as my mentoring skills may be, I don't always make the best mentor because I am not necessarily accessible. When a mentee calls me, I might be in the middle of conducting a seminar or consulting or traveling. I may not be able to return the call until late in the day. Most of the time, it is okay for a mentee to wait for a return call until later in the day, but there are also times when a mentee would like, and perhaps need, instant accessibility.

Q17.9 Is it okay to have more than one mentor?

Multiple mentors

A17.9 Yes. You could have a different mentor for each skill area you wish to develop. For example, you might have a mentor who is superb in the hard skills of project management, such as gathering requirements, developing project plans, implementing earned value management, assessing risk, and performing project reviews. You could have a mentor who has great leadership and soft skills such as negotiating, communicating, working with others individually as well as bringing them together as an effective team, and helping people reach their potential. You could have a mentor who has "street smarts" and will show you how to be politically savvy in a corporate environment.

You could also have more than one mentor for one skill area. You might choose to consult all of your mentors when difficult, controversial, or very important issues come up.

Q17.10 As the resource manager of an employee being mentored, is it okay for me to request information

Boss' access to mentor's information

from the mentor regarding my employee? She has a performance review coming up.

A17.10 Yes, if you are seeking "good news" that benefits the employee. No, if you are seeking "bad news" that could harm the employee's performance review. The mentor is less valuable to the employee if the mentor violates the trust inherent to the mentor-mentee relationship. The point of having a mentor is to help the employee, and trust is fundamental.

Benefits of being a mentor

Q17.11 I am interested in becoming a mentor. What are the benefits?

A17.11 There are many. Here are some of the most noteworthy:

- *Mentoring is highly satisfying.* If you enjoy helping others, mentoring is a great way of helping others to learn and grow. Mentees are typically folks who truly want to learn, and they soak up your knowledge and the wisdom your experiences have given you. I personally feel that there is no greater satisfaction than giving to others in a way that helps them to help themselves— and then they turn around to help others.
- *You learn so much from others.* I may have learned more from teaching others than I have from doing things myself. When you do things yourself, there is only so much you can learn from the limited environments within which you work. But when you are teaching others, many more challenges can emerge, which helps a mentor sharpen his own skills.
- *You make many friends.* You develop closer business relationships and meet people with whom you otherwise would not have had contact.
- *Your stock value grows.* The respect people have for you will likely increase, as will your overall worth to the organization, company, or community.

Q17.12 What are the downsides of being a mentor?

A17.12 There aren't many, and they are not as significant as the benefits. Here are two worthy of mention:

1. ***Mentoring can demand a lot of your time.*** You may find yourself wanting to give more of yourself than you have time to give, especially because mentoring is likely only a small portion of your job.

2. ***It can be hard to say "no."*** When you see great potential in people, you may wish that you could work with all of them. You don't want to turn anyone away.

Q17.13 As an aspiring mentor, how can I best work with mentees?

A17.13 First and foremost, you are there to help those you are mentoring. It's not about you; it's about them. Depending on what skills mentees want you to teach them, you may want to attend some of their meetings and meet some of the people they frequently work with. I often perform what I call "day shadowing." I spend a full day with the mentee and attend all of her meetings. At the end of the day, we retire to her office to discuss the events of the day. I note all of the good things the mentee said and did and offer suggestions for improvement where applicable. If there is time throughout the day to reflect on events and meetings immediately after they occur, do so. However, I have found that many of the people I mentor are so busy that little time is available until the end of the day.

Q17.14 Did you encounter any surprises as a mentor?

A17.14 Yes, two big ones. Many years ago, I began teaching project management skills to mentees. Of course, project management skills can comprise many skill areas, but I expected most of the calls and contact time with mentees would be about the project management hard skills of planning and tracking projects, applying earned value techniques, and so on. What I discovered was that most of my time—at least 80 percent—was spent talking about leadership, soft skills, and relationships, not the hard skills. Now, I spend about 95 percent of my mentoring time talking about soft skills.

The second surprise I encountered: When a mentee contacts me with a problem, I often ask her what she thinks is the right thing to do. More than 80 percent of the time, the mentee says the right thing. This means that the greatest value I often bring to the mentor-mentee relationship is *validation* that the mentee has the right idea and is planning the right approach. In other words, we often know what the right thing to do is in a certain situation, but having a trusted confidant as a check and balance—a sounding board—can really boost a mentee's confidence to move forward with that approach.

Choosing not to obtain a mentor

Q 17.15 Any more thoughts on mentoring?

A 17.15 Yes. I have found that many people who are given the opportunity to work with a mentor choose not to. Even though these folks understand the benefits of having a mentor by their side, many people will not pursue this great personal and career opportunity.

Q 17.16 Why do people choose not to have mentors?

A 17.16 These people may:

- *Be bashful.* Some people are fearful of approaching a potential mentor and "bothering" him; moreover, rejection by a potential mentor can cut too deep.
- *Have low self-esteem.* Some people feel they are not worthy of extra attention, especially from others gifted in their craft.

- **Be complacent.** Some people are okay with their current position and stature in their organization and do not feel the need or desire to obtain help.
- **Be too proud.** Some people think that having a mentor is an admission that they do not know it all or are not the best at what they do. What others think about them is more important than what they think of themselves and their personal development.
- **Have limited time.** Some people are already stretched in their jobs and do not feel that they have time to add anything else to their already full plates.

Q17.17 What's the bottom line on mentoring?

A17.17 The bottom line is that having a mentor can greatly benefit a person's skill development and effectiveness, increase his value to his organization, and enrich his satisfaction with his chosen craft. Whatever your craft and skills, there is always more to learn from others. In the long run, you're likely to be very pleased that you did reach out to accelerate and raise the bar on your personal growth. We are far more effective when we ask for help from, and stand on the shoulders of, those who have gone before us.

The benefit of being mentored

CHAPTER 18

Ethics and Integrity

**❝ Right is right, even if everyone is against it;
and wrong is wrong, even if everyone is for it. ❞**

—William Penn, founder of the U.S. state of Pennsylvania

**Integrity is not
an option**

Q18.1 Is integrity an option?

A18.1 No. More than ever, the business world needs leaders who routinely practice integrity. Simply put, *integrity* is knowing the difference between right and wrong and choosing the right action. As a leader, your integrity is indicative of your character. Use it to build your success and the success of those you lead. If you find yourself unable to decide what the right thing to do in a particular situation is, sometimes it can help to discuss the issue with a trusted third party to ensure that you are not too close to the issue and can see it for what it really is.

**❝ Listen to the whispers of your conscience
as if they were shouts. ❞**

—Anonymous

**Integrity
appears to be
in short supply**

Q18.2 Why do you believe there appears to be such a lack of integrity in the business world?

A18.2 All leaders must model integrity. Most of us have a great internal mechanism that helps us immediately recognize the difference between right and wrong. But our consciences can be compromised when we find ourselves looking for a competitive edge that will help us, our products, and our companies be as successful as possible. What may begin as dabbling in behaviors we know are wrong can turn into a wholesale belief that integrity is for others to practice and that it no longer applies to our situation. Wrong! Integrity applies to all of us all of the time.

Q18.3 **What should I do if I encounter illegal or unethical behavior?**

A18.3 First of all, distinguishing right from wrong may not always be easy; sometimes we encounter gray areas. Don't always assume purposeful wrongdoing. When you encounter a suspicious situation, you can (quietly) research it and ask questions. Seek help from a corporate ombudsman, legal counsel, or other trusted sources.

Second, never support someone who engages in illegal or unethical behavior. If you do, expect to go down with it. And if you think that the wrongdoer will protect you, think again. People who commit illegal or unethical activities are notorious for selling out those who are loyal to them. If you encounter illegal or unethical behavior, you have several choices: do nothing, mitigate the situation before it develops into something much more serious, distance yourself from the behavior by leaving the organization or company, or be a whistle-blower.

Q18.4 **What do you mean by mitigating the situation?**

A18.4 If another person or group is considering doing something that is illegal or unethical, you might be able to convince them to stop before any real harm has occurred. Sometimes a rational voice can expose a bad idea for what it is.

Q18.5 **What if some harm has already occurred? Should I still intervene and attempt to rectify the situation?**

A18.5 Perhaps, but this is a personal choice, and you should consider the situation carefully. Keep in mind that intervening

Encountering illegal or unethical behavior

Mitigating the situation

potentially puts you in harm's way. You may be able to do some good, or your involvement may backfire and you might be seen as a threat. Moreover, your knowing about the situation may draw you more deeply into the mess. Some companies have defined specific steps for their employees to take if they suspect or know of illegal or unethical behavior. As stated earlier, it may be wise to consult a trusted third party for advice and counsel. Although we may wish for these decisions to be easy, they typically are not.

Doing nothing

Q18.6 Which of the other options you mentioned are best?

A18.6 There is no simple answer. Some people would say to stick your head in the sand and do nothing. The danger of this approach is that by doing nothing, you are supporting and condoning the behavior. You may even be considered an accomplice to the misdeeds. Moreover, you might find yourself consumed with anxiety, constantly looking over your shoulder for fear that something or someone is "gaining on you." Not a good way to live a happy and quality life.

Leaving the organization

Q18.7 What about the option of leaving the organization or company?

A18.7 Leaving is not always so easy. There may not be another job for you in another organization of the same company. And if there is, it could require you to move from one location to another, which is expensive and difficult. Quitting the company and finding another job, of course, also can be a great hardship. Moreover, the job that you are leaving could be a job that you have worked hard for many years to obtain. You might like your job a whole lot. Distancing yourself might be worthwhile, but it can be a mighty heavy price to pay.

Becoming a whistle-blower

Q18.8 And the option of being a whistle-blower?

A₁₈.₈ To many people, whistle-blowing could be considered the high road. You are exposing illegal or unethical behavior and working within the system to improve your workplace. Unfortunately, not everyone holds whistle-blowers in such high esteem—particularly not those who have condoned or supported the poor behavior or have friends whose poor behavior is being exposed. Whistle-blowing can help you clear your conscience, but it can also be a lonely road. Because illegal and unethical behavior can take a long time to expose and reach closure, you may have to continue to work with people you've helped expose. Some folks more loosely connected to the poor behavior may never be punished, yet you must still work with them, too.

Q₁₈.₉ What about being an anonymous whistle-blower?

A₁₈.₉ That's an option. But be prepared for the worst-case scenario, in which your anonymity is eventually lost as you become more involved in exposing the behavior.

Becoming an anonymous whistle-blower

Q₁₈.₁₀ I don't like these options. What should I do?

A₁₈.₁₀ Nobody likes these options. That's why I say that there is no simple answer. Any difficulties you may be having in your personal or professional life, or both, could make your decision even more difficult. Each of us must choose the option that seems right for us. Again, confiding in a trusted third party and talking through the options can be helpful. Most of us will likely be exposed to illegal or unethical behavior sometime during our careers. As I said earlier, whatever you do, *do not* become a part of the behavior, or you will surely go down with it.

Confer with a trusted third party

Q₁₈.₁₁ If my boss directs me to do something illegal or unethical, what should I do?

A₁₈.₁₁ If the request is not in keeping with your boss' typical behavior, consider discussing the issue with your boss. Per-

Bad behavior requested by your boss

haps you can persuade him to avoid any underhanded behavior. Sometimes a person is so close to a situation that he doesn't realize the potential for improper behavior until someone else raises the issue.

If your boss is well aware of what he is asking, then run—don't walk—to avoid becoming part of the illegal or unethical activity. Your options include those already discussed. Remember, your boss' attempt to pull you into a web of illegal or unethical behavior will only hurt you. What makes this scenario so much more difficult is that your boss should be the first person you can confide in if you come across illegal or unethical behavior. However, as I stated earlier, most companies have a designated person or department for employees to go to should they encounter such behavior, such as a corporate ombudsman, legal counsel, or other trusted sources.

As a PM, performing questionable work

Q18.12 As a project manager, if I am asked to, should I produce work that I believe has no business value or represents a poor business choice, even if it is not illegal or unethical?

A18.12 In general, if you believe that the project you are being asked to manage is a poor business choice, first consider discussing your views with the project sponsor. The sponsor will likely have more information about the purpose of the project than you have been made aware of. If you still disagree with the sponsor's decision and are unable to persuade him otherwise, consider telling your boss what you think. Your boss can decide to take the issue higher up the management chain. You can also consider discussing your views with a respected power player within the organization who might be able to influence the sponsor without it being viewed as a formal escalation.

Escalating over the project sponsor

Q18.13 But what if I am very passionate about my views? Should I escalate over the sponsor's head?

A 18.13 The simple answer is *no*. Why? Because you can read an organizational chart, and the sponsor has the right to make such a decision—just as you have the right to make some decisions about how you will run your project. You could ask the sponsor if he would mind including his boss in a friendly, informal discussion of this issue. This could work. Your sponsor might say, "Interesting. Frankly, I am curious about what my boss would say about this issue. Let's have that informal chat." Or your request could backfire—the sponsor could say, "Not just no, but heck no. I made the decision, and I do not want to hear any more about it."

Remember, your job is to manage projects. When you are asked by higher-ups to manage a project, that's what you do. (See Chapter 13, "Resolving Conflict through Escalations," for more about escalating issues.)

Q 18.14 As a project member—not a project manager—should I perform work that I believe has no business value or represents a poor business choice? Again, the work is not illegal or unethical.

As a project member, performing questionable work

A 18.14 Discuss the issue with the PM. If you are not pleased with the outcome of your talk, then discuss the issue with your boss to explore other options. Whatever your boss decides to pursue, do not stop working the plan of record. You have commitments to fulfill while this issue is potentially being resolved.

Q 18.15 Are you saying that if I don't like something about a project, I should go to the project manager before I approach my boss?

A 18.15 In most cases, yes. You are a member of a team, and the PM is the head of that team. You want to be a responsible team member who strives to resolve such issues with your PM. One exception: You might go to your boss is if you believe there will be benefit in first discussing your views with him. Your boss might defuse the issue or give you more confidence to pursue it further with the PM.

Lying and distorting information

Q18.16   Is lying, exaggerating, or distorting information considered a breach of integrity?

A18.16   Big time. Don't ever be a party to such behavior. It will damage your reputation—and you could lose your job.

Q18.17   I work in a marketing organization, and my boss has instructed me to lowball bids to increase the odds of winning contracts. Once we have the contract, we will add in costs throughout the life of the contract to make up for the low bid. Do you think that lying can sometimes be justified in order to win new business and save jobs?

A18.17   No! Not only is this clearly unethical, it is illegal as well.

Q18.18   But don't you agree that if you don't play this way, you and your company will lose out in the long run?

A18.18   Short-term, I may lose a contract or two. But long-term I likely will win far more business as my reputation for honesty and delivering on commitments spreads around the business community. Illegal and unethical behavior undermines the entire business community, and everyone suffers.

Performing questionable work requested by your boss

Q18.19   If my boss directs me to do something, and I disagree with what she is asking me to do, should I do it anyway? It is not an illegal or unethical activity.

A18.19   Yes, assuming that you have the appropriate authority to do what you've been directed to do. But first discuss the issue with your boss so that she has all the relevant information to make the best decision.

Q 18.20 What if I do what my boss tells me to, but other people who are equal to or of higher standing than my boss tell me that they disagree with what I did? Is it okay to tell the truth and say that I only did what I did because my boss insisted?

Avoid being overtly transparent

A 18.20 In general, avoid being overtly transparent. You want to support your boss. However, in a case in which your actions can harm your reputation or career, I would not take blame for a decision that was thrust upon you—*provided that you clearly presented your position to your boss*. If you did not, then you are just as much at fault as your boss.

Q 18.21 Is it good to place one's own interests above the interests of the organization or company?

Company's interests versus personal interests

A 18.21 No. It's not about you. It's about coming to work each day and helping to move the business forward. That's why you were hired, that's what you committed to do, and that's your duty. But you and your company should both benefit from your working there. If you believe that your company is benefiting more than you are and that you are always getting the short end of the stick, then work to turn this situation around. Your boss should want to listen to and work with you. However, understand that in any organization there may be situations that appear to require unreasonable sacrifice and dedication. Do not judge your situation based on what's going on in the short term. Step back and take the long-term view.

Q 18.22 I plan to leave the company. When should I tell my boss that I am leaving?

Informing your boss that you are leaving the company

A 18.22 There is an oft-quoted unwritten rule stating that you should give two weeks' notice. Perhaps your company even mandates two weeks'—or more—notice. If you don't know, then find out. But regardless of the "rule," written or implied, I am more interested in your doing the right thing: *demonstrating integrity*.

Two weeks is almost never enough time for others to appropriately prepare for your replacement so that your longer-term commitments can still be met. Ask yourself: If you owned the company and an employee in your position was planning to leave, how much notice would you hope for? The answer should influence your actions. You might not necessarily fully support the company owner—after all, she likely will be biased in favor of the business—but at least ask yourself this question to make sure that your actions are in the realm of being reasonable.

CHAPTER 19

Telecommuting/ Working from Home

66 In increasingly more cases, telecommuting is a win-win for all parties involved—provided there is flexibility when the business requires it. 99

Q_{19.1} As a project member, should I be able to work from home if I want to?

A_{19.1} It's not your decision. That decision typically rests with your resource manager or management higher than your boss.

The choice to work from home

Q_{19.2} What are the factors that are commonly considered before a project member is permitted to work from home?

A_{19.2} Here are some examples:

- *Cost.* Do the benefits to the company outweigh the cost to set up a productive home office environment?
- *Security.* Does the home office provide sufficient security for company-sensitive information? What precautions can be made to safeguard data? Is the data too sensitive to be allowed outside a standard in-office secured work area?
- *Availability.* Will the project member be accessible when needed?
- *Team bonding.* Can the team communicate frequently and fully enough? Will the project member make the necessary extra effort to reach out to her coworkers?

Factors that affect working from home

- *Productivity.* Will the project member be able to be productive while working in a home environment?
- *Personal restrictions and commitments.* In order to accept or keep the job, does the project member require a home office to accommodate a physical or health restriction, to meet personal obligations (such as caring for an infirm family member), or to save hours of commuting time (especially for those who have young children)?
- *Trust.* Can the project member be trusted to dedicate at least the minimum amount of time to her work? Does she have sufficient organizational skills and discipline, and does she work well with little to no supervision? A slacker in a company office will likely be a slacker in a home office.
- *Fairness.* Will other employees think that it is fair or appropriate for one employee to work from home if others cannot?

**Obtaining
your boss'
permission**

Q_{19.3} How should I approach my boss for permission to work from home?

A_{19.3} Here are some ideas:

- Put a business case together that shows the benefits to your project, boss, company, and you. List the disadvantages of your working from home, too, and what you would do to mitigate them.
- Address factors such as costs, security, and your availability.
- If working from home is new or rare in your organization, you might propose taking "baby steps" at first: You will work from home on a trial basis only one or two days a week to show that it can work well. Then, after a set period of time—perhaps one to three months—you will work at home full-time. Be prepared to discuss how you will measure the effectiveness of working at home.

- Talk about how you will help ensure that working from home will be an acceptable alternative. For example, tell your boss that you will provide frequent progress reports, increase telephone communications, attend occasional in-office meetings, and solicit periodic feedback from project members—to name a few.
- Be prepared to shoulder some of the costs.

Q_{19.4} As a project manager, what changes might I have to make on my project to support one or more members who telecommute?

Accommodating telecommuters on a project

A_{19.4} The first priority is to not put the project at risk. Project success is never something that can be compromised. This is why the team is employed. Telecommuting can be allowed only if it will not interfere with the project meeting its business objectives.

To support a project with members who telecommute, try the following:

- Include the entire project team (or representatives) in a discussion about how telecommuting can work.
- Set expectations for all project members—both telecommuters and company-office members.
- Ensure that work rules are defined, such as setting typical start and end times for the workday, notifying project members when out of office, and providing emergency contact numbers or another mechanism for emergency contact.
- Employ technology such as video conferencing and instant messaging to mitigate having limited face-to-face contact.
- Consider having a socializing-like tool on your company Intranet that project members can use to easily ask questions or post project status and information.
- Start slowly and make adjustments as needed. For example, require telecommuters to come in for face-to-

face weekly tracking meetings, even if they do not need
to attend other meetings in person.

- Verify that telecommuters are fulfilling their duties by
monitoring productivity, requiring them to provide proof
of work they've completed, and noting responsiveness
to e-mails and phone calls.

- Increase the frequency of communications so that the
telecommuting members stay connected and bonded
with you and other dependent members.

- Avoid the "I don't want to bother the telecommuters at
home" mentality.

- Include all project members in celebrations when major
milestones or events are achieved.

- Be willing to be flexible and open to ideas that can help
telecommuting work.

**Business
decisions drive
telecommuting
decisions**

Q19.5 As a resource manager, why should I allow employees
to work from home? It is far more convenient and
controllable to have them all in a single location.

A19.5 Perhaps you should *not* allow them to work from home—
maybe the work they do is not conducive to being done
offsite. However, telecommuting can often save a business
money and create happier workers. Some studies show
that allowing some employees to work from home can
reduce real estate and overhead costs. Productivity can
also increase: Telecommuters often face fewer unnecessary interruptions and, of course, they save time by not
commuting to the office. In some cases, allowing employees to work from home can mean the difference between
retaining them or losing them.

**Working
"extra" hours
from home**

Q19.6 As a telecommuter, should I feel duty-bound to work
more hours than I would in the office because I have the
great convenience of a home office, and I am saving a
bunch of time and money by not commuting?

A_{19.6} I do not believe that you have the duty to work more hours; after all, your productivity is probably measurably higher than it would be in an in-office environment. But it is good to appreciate this great opportunity, and you should occasionally show your gratitude for it. If you choose to work extra hours beyond those you are required to or must, you may gain more respect from co-workers and from management. Moreover, it can be wise to demonstrate to management how your telecommuting is helping the company. Doing so might help you retain the telecommuting opportunity—maybe even your job.

CHAPTER 20

Awards and Recognition

" The deepest craving of human nature
is the need to feel appreciated. "

—William James, American psychologist
and philosopher

**Identifying
award
candidates**

Q20.1 Who is responsible for ensuring that the right members
of a project receive awards?

A20.1 Resource managers must ensure that the appropriate
project members are identified and receive awards. It is
expected that the project manager—and possibly other
project stakeholders—will be consulted to ensure that the
right candidates are selected. Alternatively, the PM can discreetly initiate the identification of the award candidates
and make a proposal to management.

Q20.2 Why don't you think the project manager has the duty to
identify and distribute the awards?

A20.2 Typically, PMs are not trained to know who is deserving
of an award. The PM would likely nominate the "most
valuable players" on the project. It is very possible that
these MVPs are also the highest-level employees who earn
the most money. Even if these MVPs performed very well
on the project, their contributions might not be award-
able—they might only have done what was already expected of employees at that job level. Usually, an award is
given to someone who has achieved results beyond what
is expected from him at his job level. Resource managers
are expected to give their employees recognition.

Q_{20.3} As a project member, I want to perform at a level that qualifies me for an award. Should I work with my resource manager to better understand the award process?

A_{20.3} Yes. There are many ways an employee can earn an award for exceptional performance. Your boss is the best person to explain these methods. It is also a good idea for you to talk with your boss about your desire to perform at a high level so that he pays more attention to your performance and provides appropriate feedback.

Q_{20.4} What are some ways an employee might be recognized?

A_{20.4} Rewards might include a certificate of recognition, cash, a gift certificate, time off, permission and funding to attend a conference or trade show, a special training opportunity, assignment to a special project, or achieving visibility to company bigwigs—to name a few. Salary increases, bonuses, and promotions can also be given.

Q_{20.5} What if a project just completed successfully, and management gave the project manager and team a fixed amount of cash and told the group to determine how best to divide the award money among its members? Is this a good idea?

A_{20.5} This is usually a bad idea. First of all, as I mentioned earlier, the PM and team likely will focus on who contributed the most to the project regardless of their position level in the organization. Project members at a higher job level are, of course, expected to contribute more than lower-level project members. Second, this approach suggests that management have weak backbones—they're not doing their job to determine who is most deserving of an award.

| **Insufficient awards** | **Q**20.6 | Do you believe that in general, organizations and companies sufficiently recognize and award their project members? |

A20.6 Most companies perform weakly in this area. It is far better to err on the side of giving too many awards of too-high value than too few awards of too-little value. Awards don't just reward top performers; they also encourage others to stretch themselves and perform at their best. The number-one reason why organizations and companies lose employees is that the employees do not feel appreciated. Awards are a great way to show that management cares about its employees.

Q20.7 If the benefits of providing generous awards are so great, then why don't more organizations and companies do a better job of administering an effective awards program?

A20.7 The simple answer: These companies have weak and ineffective management. The three major reasons why so many organizations do so little to reward employees are: (1) they do not have a well-defined awards program; (2) they claim to have insufficient funds for awards; and (3) they have weakly implemented an awards program.

| **Insufficient funds for awards** | **Q**20.8 | Isn't *claiming to have insufficient funds for awards* a legitimate argument? |

A20.8 In most cases, no. This is a common excuse. I believe that a resource manager should set aside at least $2,000 per year per employee for awards. This doesn't mean that every employee will receive an award; in fact, many will not. They have to earn the award. Perhaps one employee might receive an award of $300. Another person might receive several similar small awards. Still another might receive a large award of $5,000.

Q20.9 But $2,000 per employee adds up to a lot of money. Many organizations don't have that kind of money.

A20.9 Most organizations have the money. Two thousand dollars per employee is pocket change—lint in the dryer trap—for most organizations. Don't tell me that $2,000 per employee is not available, especially in companies in which senior executives get multi-million-dollar bonuses. Keep in mind that the cost to an organization of losing an employee can easily be $75,000 or more. The investment of at least $2,000 per employee as one effective way to show appreciation can indeed be a great investment in promoting high morale and reducing employee attrition.

Q20.10 What do you mean by *weak implementation of an awards program*?

Weak backbone, weak awards implementation

A20.10 It is easy for many in management to lose focus on an awards program. Without oversight by middle and senior management, many lower-level managers will perform weakly in this area.

For example, it is relatively common for managers to talk themselves out of issuing any awards for fear that some employees will feel that they have been overlooked or, if they do receive an award, it will be seen as too little, too late. There will almost always be some controversy when awards are administered. It is the duty of management to demonstrate a backbone and enforce an effective and consistent awards program.

Q20.11 I have done the math: There doesn't seem to be a sufficient return on investment if I work extra hard to achieve an award, particularly if overtime is required. If I continue to do what I am doing now, I will continue to see salary increases and job promotions—although maybe not as quickly as those with more ambition will. So why should I care about "extra" recognition?

Are awards worth it?

A_{20.11} It's your choice. Many people derive a deep sense of satisfaction from their dedication to helping projects and organizations be more successful. Life is an adventure. I would not be as self-fulfilled if I woke up each morning just wanting to get by. Many people want to make a difference—leave their mark. I do what I do for the inner me. Ask yourself: If you owned the company, which type of employee would you want to attract—those who do only what is required, or those who put in extra time and effort?

Envy of another's recognition

Q_{20.12} A peer has received an award, and I am envious that I did not also receive one. I feel bitter. Should I congratulate my peer?

A_{20.12} I would. The peer did nothing wrong. Others recognized your peer for doing an especially good job. I believe you should try to feel good for the recognized person—allow him his fifteen minutes of fame, and share in his special moment. After all, when your time comes, you would greatly appreciate others being happy for you. If you feel you are being overlooked, don't sit and stew about it. Find out what the criteria are to get recognition, and constructively work toward achieving those results.

I don't feel appreciated

Q_{20.13} I feel that I am not appreciated for the value that I bring to the project or for the many little extra things I do. What can I do to gain more appreciation?

A_{20.13} Most of us think that we are not appreciated as much as we would like—whether it be for the many small things we do throughout the week or for the challenging job we must perform. Our natural tendency is to focus on ourselves and our own deeds, not on the merits or deeds of others.

Focusing so much on obtaining the appreciation of others is not productive. Doing so can make you feel bitter and resentful. Instead, choose to be a person who does things for others. Do not expect "thank yous" and signs of appreciation, but when you do get them, enjoy and appreciate them. If project members and peers do not seem to appreciate your skills and the value you bring to the job, let it go. Just focus on doing the best you can and making sure that you bring value to whatever you are assigned.

Q20.14 Should I discuss with my boss others' lack of appreciation for me?

A20.14 You need to work through this issue, so perhaps your boss can be helpful. But know that saying you feel unappreciated can be interpreted as a sign of professional immaturity or weak social skills. If you have a trusting, productive relationship with your boss, then go for it; otherwise, seek professional help or help from sources who have less influence on your career.

Q20.15 Should the members of a project be subject to bonus or penalty incentives?

A20.15 Yes, whenever possible and practical. Bonus and penalty incentives can be tricky to administer, but the performance of project members can be so positively affected that having these incentives can be very worthwhile. Some organizations and companies approach this by offering profit-sharing plans, which are often easier to implement.

Offering bonus and penalty incentives

CHAPTER 21

Personal Development, Job, and Career

66At the end of the day, you should play back the tape of your performance. The results should either applaud you or prod you.99

—Jim Rohn, American motivational speaker and personal development coach

Your boss and your career

Q21.1 Is my boss responsible for my career growth in the organization and company?

A21.1 No, you are. However, your boss has the duty to work with you to help you reach your potential in the company. Your boss should open doors to training and opportunities for you. He has access to funding and contacts that you may not be aware of or are unable to make happen on your own.

Q21.2 Should I approach my boss about my career growth or wait for him to approach me?

A21.2 Take the initiative to open a dialog with your boss about your career. If you take action, your boss is likely to act more quickly than he would if you waited for him to approach you.

Unsure of your career interests

Q21.3 What if I am not sure what I want to do in the future?

A21.3 Caution! If you don't know where you want to go, don't expect your boss to magically figure it out for you. However, your boss likely will have some ideas and options for your consideration. He might tell you to talk with others in the company to expand your understanding of the options that are, or can be made, available.

Q21.4 **What do you mean by "options that *can* be made available" ?**

A21.4 Just because a job doesn't exist in your organization or company today doesn't mean that it can't be created. Many jobs that exist in an organization today did not exist five or ten years ago. Every day, unique jobs are being created in companies just like yours.

Q21.5 **If I approach my boss for a new assignment or job, should I expect that job to quickly be made available?**

A21.5 No. First and foremost, you have a duty to complete your current assignments and help fulfill the current commitments in your organization. However, I expect your boss to work with you in helping you reach your goals in a reasonable amount of time. If you have a special interest in moving into a new job, be part of the solution—that is, prepare a plan to phase yourself out of your current roles and responsibilities. That plan might include teaching another person the skills needed to help take over your duties.

Seeking a new assignment or job

Q21.6 **Is there a certain time frame my boss should stick to when moving me into a new job?**

A21.6 The time frame can depend on how skilled a replacement for you must be, the availability of those skills, the commitments that have been made, the funding available, the business need, and many more factors. However, in general, resource managers should be working for the move to take place within six months to a year.

Q21.7 **Isn't that a long time to wait?**

A_{21.7} It's not about you. It's about protecting business needs first. You are employed to help fulfill commitments that are required to sustain a successful enterprise.

Unsure of your job duties

Q_{21.8} What if I am not sure of what is expected of me in my job? Should I ask my boss?

A_{21.8} No. Even though your boss is responsible for making your duties clear to you, do not ask. By asking, you shift the problem to your boss. Instead, be part of the solution and approach your boss from a position of strength. List on only one sheet of paper the primary duties that you believe make up your job. Meet with your boss and tell her that your list represents what you view to be the essence of your job. Then ask your boss for her agreement and discuss the details associated with each listed item. When the meeting has concluded, both you and your boss should agree on what is expected of you.

Position of strength

Q_{21.9} What do you mean by "approaching your boss from a *position of strength*"?

A_{21.9} If your boss creates a list of your primary duties, you might not like her list. There may be parts of your assignment that you would prefer not to do. But if you take the initiative to create the list, you are more likely to influence the outcome of the discussion with your boss; you are approaching your boss from a *position of strength*.

We all are required to perform tasks that might not be among our favorites. We need to do what the business needs require; however, I want you to take the initiative and define your job in a way that allows you to perform more tasks that you enjoy and fewer that you dislike.

More important: career or project?

Q_{21.10} What's more important: my career or the project's success?

A21.10 From whose point of view? From your company's viewpoint, your project's success—whether you are a PM or not—is the most important. After all, that's why you have a job. However, from your perspective, I would argue that your project's success is still the most important. Surprised? Think about it. Your own success is dependent upon the success you bring to all of your assignments. If you leave behind a trail of successful performances for your company, you are also blazing the path to a successful career. However, keep in mind that you still have the duty to initiate talks about the direction of your career with your boss and to ensure that your boss is working with you on behalf of your career interests.

Q21.11 **What if I don't want to be on the project to which I am assigned?**

Dislike project to which you are assigned

A21.11 Discuss the situation with your boss. If you have a valid concern—for example, you do not have the prerequisite skills or you believe the job will not help you in achieving your objectives within the organization—your boss should listen and work with you for the benefit of both you and the organization. Keep in mind, though, that you come to work to perform for your boss and organization. You presumably have the necessary skills, and your organization has the work to assign you. You do what you can to help promote the success of the organization.

In the short term, business needs will almost always come first; however, long-term, the intent is for both you and your company to benefit from your business relationship. Whatever you do, genuinely maintain a great attitude and put your best face forward. In the long run, you will be glad you did.

Dislike job

Q_{21.12} What if I don't like my job and I don't look forward to going to work?

A_{21.12} Then do something about it. Don't wait for someone else to do something. No one else cares as much as you do about your job—so you must take the initiative. Remember: *If it is to be, it is up to me!* Obviously, something must change if you are unhappy with your job. It might be as "simple" as changing your attitude, or as demanding as being retrained for a different vocation. Or the needed change might be something in between.

Q_{21.13} But don't my managers owe it to me to place me in a job I really like?

A_{21.13} What are you smoking? Your company's primary objective is to utilize your knowledge and skills for the greater good of the business. No one owes you anything. We both know that it is in your boss' best interest to work with you in moving you into a job in which you have a genuine interest. But do not leave this to chance. Take the initiative to either move toward the job types that you prefer or expand your current job in ways that make the work more challenging, interesting, and fun.

Trolling your resume outside your company

Q_{21.14} Is it a good idea to always be trolling my resume outside my company?

A_{21.14} Generally speaking, no. You do your best work when you remain focused, disciplined, dedicated, and loyal. Floating a resume can distract you from performing your best at your current company: You are not fully committed and are not likely to reach your peak efficiency as a professional or a contributor.

Perhaps it is a good idea to float your resume if you believe your company cannot help you achieve your current objectives, whether they be personal or professional.

Q_{21.15} Why do you say perhaps it is a good idea to float my resume?

A_{21.15} Because I cannot know your inner reason for doing so. Many people believe in the proverbial notion that the grass is greener in another company than in their own. These folks are often wrong. If they are running from problems—such as working with a difficult person, facing the same issues on project after project, new opportunities seeming hard to come by, and slow advancement, to name a few, most of the same problems will be waiting for them at the next company—and may even be *worse*.

The grass is typically only as green as you make it. If you are not willing to dig your heels in at your current company and make what differences you can, then you are not likely to do that at your next company, either. You will be waiting for others to do it, as you are in your current company. If this is the case, you may be waiting for hell to freeze over. The result is that many of these problems will follow you wherever you go.

Most of us are better off making our current situation and company work more effectively than we would be if we ran to another company and hoped for the best. Having said all this, there are, of course, cases in which an employee can perform better in a different company. However, I suggest careful thought be given to understanding your objectives and whether or not they can be achieved where you now work.

Q_{21.16} Do I need to seek training or can I learn sufficiently through on-the-job training?

On-the-job versus formal training

A_{21.16} Seeking appropriate formal training can be far more beneficial if you want to improve your performance. If your training is only on the job, then you may not be learning new skills and behaviors, and you are missing out on guidance from outside experts. In addition to getting formal training, you can benefit greatly by working with a mentor. There is no better way to learn a craft than from a qualified mentor. (See Chapter 17, "Mentoring.")

Paying the costs for professional memberships/ certifications

Q21.17 I want to join a professional organization related to my job and seek a corresponding certification, but my boss will not pay for it. Is this fair or reasonable?

A21.17 Although refusing to pay for your membership and certification might be shortsighted on the part of your boss, it may be both fair and reasonable for several reasons. Some organizations have limited financial resources and budget to work with and must fund only those employee requests that address a direct, important, and perhaps urgent need for the organization. Some nonprofit, governmental, or academic organizations may have other restrictions that may prevent their funding such an activity. The rejection of your request may be all about business, so don't take it personally. But if you think that the benefits of joining a professional organization can benefit your career and organization, then consider paying for all or part of the membership fee yourself. For example, if your boss will fund your joining the professional organization, but not the certification exam, negotiate with your boss. Perhaps he will pay the exam expenses only if you pass the exam; otherwise, you will pay.

Q21.18 Why did you say that "it might be shortsighted on the part of your boss" to not fund an employee who has a desire to join a professional organization related to his job?

A21.18 Managers have the duty to help their employees reach their potential in the organization and company. This includes ensuring that they are appropriately trained and are growing in their chosen professions. It is almost always a win-win to support such an employee's request. Doing so also helps to foster a positive culture of support and improvement. Not supporting such requests can encourage employees to seek employment elsewhere, in organizations that provide more opportunity for growth.

Q21.19 What if my boss won't pay for a book related to my job duties or pick up the expense for a relevant class?

Paying for
books or
classes

A21.19 Again, I would expect most organizations to cover expenses that are considered reasonable and would have a direct benefit on your job performance. However, don't expect your company to pony up for every book or magazine you want to purchase that is related to your field. As a professional, you have some responsibility to maintain your knowledge and skills independent of your company's willingness to cover these expenses. And training classes away from the company can be very expensive. It may be that your organization's budget can support only a limited number of employees taking training courses during a specific period of time.

Again, as a career professional, be willing to contribute to your training. For example, perhaps your boss is willing to pay for class tuition if you pay for the travel expenses. Be creative. It's your career.

Q21.20 How much training is it reasonable for me to expect per year from my organization? One week? Four weeks?

Amount of
training to
expect from
organization

A21.20 The answer is not that straightforward; it depends on a number of factors, such as the industry you serve, the level of skill you already have, the importance and urgency of the training to the business needs, the funds available, and your availability. Most organizations recognize that training their employees is necessary and beneficial, but it can be a challenge to implement training programs. Ask yourself how much training you *need* to be sufficiently productive.

Q21.21 Should I expect my boss to identify the training I need, then locate and register me for that training?

A21.21 No. Although a boss' job is to help his employees reach their potential in the organization and company, many managers are weak in doing so. You should personally take the initiative when it comes to your career growth. Work closely with your boss, but do some homework beforehand and be prepared to propose training that would help you be more proficient in your projects and organization. You are far more likely to get training if you play an active role in making it happen.

Volunteering for new work

Q21.22 Should I volunteer for new work?

A21.22 Yes, as long as taking on more work will not mean underperforming in your current domain of responsibility. You first have the duty to fulfill your commitments. If your commitments are under control, then volunteering for new work can greatly benefit your organization, your value to the organization, and your personal growth.

Creating a job

Q21.23 Can I create a job that doesn't exist?

A21.23 Yes. This is being done nearly every day in most companies. The more knowledge, skills, and experience you accumulate, the more likely you will see opportunities to fill niches across your organization or company. Many of my most fulfilling roles were jobs that I volunteered for or created.

Q21.24 What if a job I want to create is outside of my domain of responsibility?

A21.24 Most jobs created are likely outside of a person's direct domain of responsibility. Obtain support from your boss if you want to expand outside of your domain of responsibility, especially if your interest goes beyond your boss' domain of responsibility. Your boss may need to obtain support further up the management chain to help you achieve your goals.

Q21.25 Should I care more about my strengths or my weaknesses?

A21.25 This can be a controversial subject, but my experience favors focusing on your strengths. You are defined far more by your strengths throughout your career and life than by your weaknesses. Don't misunderstand—you want to know your weaknesses and improve them. However, my experience shows that most people will not significantly improve in areas in which they have low aptitude or interest—even though they have the ability to change in those areas. Areas in which you are naturally gifted will serve you far more in your career and life if you work to continually develop and build upon them.

Focus: your strengths or your weaknesses?

Q21.26 How can I find out what I am most gifted in?

A21.26 Most of us have a good idea of what many of our strengths are. We have been told about our strengths by many people, such as our family, friends, teachers, peers, and bosses. If you remain uncertain about your gifts, then you must seek counsel. Be candid and ask for an assessment from people you respect and trust to be truthful. Also, taking aptitude tests might highlight your strengths. Finally, a mentor who can work very closely with you and observe you firsthand in your work environment can be of special value. I believe that everyone—with no exceptions—is a genius in something. A person's genius may not lie in areas that we commonly focus upon in our culture, but she can still gain great benefit and satisfaction from focusing on her natural gifts.

Discovering your talents

Q_{21.27} Do I have to do something out of the ordinary to discover some of my gifts?

A_{21.27} Yes. Although you likely know what many of your gifts are, you may not know the limits of your gifts—and you will never know those limits unless they are tested. I will use myself as an example. I have known most of my life that I am an exceptionally good communicator when I am one-on-one with people or with small groups of people. However, I doubted that I could be as good a communicator with large audiences—say, in the hundreds—especially because I thought I would probably freeze up if I spoke to a large group. But unless I sought opportunities to perform in front of large audiences, I would never really know if my knack for communicating with others also extended to these bigger groups.

What I found was that I certainly had some rough edges to overcome, but I was far more effective than I had expected. With a bit more practice and experience, I discovered I was notably effective with large audiences. This is a gift that I could not easily have known about had I not stretched myself to perform in new situations. Again, what I am saying here is that you already know of many of your gifts, but unless you reach out and experiment with new situations and opportunities, you cannot know their limits.

Q_{21.28} Do you believe I have a duty to help others find their "gifts"?

A_{21.28} No, not necessarily, unless you are a teacher, boss, or mentor. However, as a leader, it will benefit everyone if you help others understand their gifts and help them maximize their contributions and value to a project or organization by assigning tasks and activities that will make the best use of their gifts.

Q_{21.29} At what age do you believe people begin to be less creative, less enthusiastic, and less effective and contribute less to a project, organization, or company?

Age and one's ability to achieve

A_{21.29} *There is no such age!* However, my observations indicate that many people believe that they have peaked in terms of job level, salary, and overall value to their organization or company somewhere in their mid-40s. They feel that their careers have topped out. This is only true if you believe it to be. As Henry Ford said, "Whether you think you can or whether you think you can't, you're right."

History demonstrates that age is not a negative factor in determining ability or achievement—in fact, it is seen as an advantage to have more years of experience and wisdom. In accomplishing my dreams and goals, I fully expect this year to be better than last year, next year better than this year, and so on. And I am well past my mid-40s!

Q_{21.30} How important is it to balance one's personal and professional lives?

Balancing personal and professional lives

A_{21.30} Absolutely essential! But what is a good balance for one person may be a poor balance for another. It's highly personal, and the level of balance can change throughout your career and life.

For example, if you spend a huge amount of time at your job, then you are sacrificing your personal life, which might include relationships, hobbies, and spiritual needs. On the other hand, if you spend only a minimal amount of time and energy at work and are passive in developing your career-related skills, then your career will likely be negatively affected—although your personal relationships may flourish.

It's all about choice, and you get to decide. But whatever you decide to focus on will take away from something else. Also understand that you can choose to change your mind and the balance along the way.

Q21.31 If I have a family, am I wrong to consistently be working overtime?

A21.31 It is not a question of being right or wrong; it is mostly a question of choice. What do you want *for* your career and life, and what do you want *from* them? Most jobs require "some" overtime, as we discussed in Chapter 16, "Overtime Work." Putting in some overtime is the responsible career choice. The extra time you are putting in at work is likely helping your career and, therefore, your long-term financial success.

We are all complex beings. We typically want it all, but this is not realistic. Some people are quite content with multitasking across dozens of focus areas, while others are far more content to focus on a small handful of priorities and savor each one in depth.

Progress report for your boss

Q21.32 Should I periodically submit a progress or status report to my boss even if it has not been requested?

A21.32 Yes. These reports are one means of communication with your boss. They are not a substitute for frequent face-to-face, verbal, or even electronic communications, but they keep your boss informed of your activities and accomplishments. They can refresh your boss's memory when it's time for you to receive your performance review. And these reports offer you a window into your performance by revealing what you have accomplished and what your plans are for the coming reporting period. You can assess your performance more objectively and make appropriate adjustments.

Q21.33 What should I put in these reports?

A21.33 The answer can vary. It is a good idea to propose to your boss a short list of topics that should be covered in the report. Your boss will have his own ideas, too. The resulting discussion should be valuable for both of you. Topics can include: (1) accomplishments from the reporting period, (2) plans for the upcoming reporting period, including your top three priorities, and (3) special items of note.

Q21.34 **How frequently should I provide these reports?**

A21.34 If you are relatively new to a job or organization, you could create one every week. Otherwise, in most cases, monthly reports are fine, but do not provide them less frequently than once a month. Of course, depending on your type of job and the relationship you have with your boss, these reports might need to be provided weekly—even for very experienced employees. Consult your boss to be on the safe side.

Q21.35 **How long should the reports be?**

A21.35 Typically, one or two pages for weekly reports and up to three pages for monthly reports. Strive to create reports that are too short rather than too long.

Q21.36 **How can I learn from my mistakes as well as from my successes?**

Continuous personal improvement

A21.36 Here's a simple yet effective technique that can help you grow your leadership skills and become more effective to-day than you were yesterday—and even more effective tomorrow than you are today.

Set aside 10 minutes or so of quiet time first thing each morning to do three things.

1. Think back on yesterday. List the top three things you did that were noteworthy achievements—actions that made a difference for the better. The items on your list could be actions that led to:

   • Resolving a problem

- Meeting a commitment
- Protecting schedules
- Reducing costs
- Improving quality
- Improving the client relationship
- Improving morale
- Improving the image of your boss or project sponsor
- Improving your relationship with a coworker
- Making a timely decision.

Reflect on these moments to reinforce the behavior you want to repeat.

2. Now list the top three things you did—or didn't do—that led to missed opportunities; that is, things you should have done differently in order to have been more effective. Items on this list could be actions that led to:

- Missing an opportunity to resolve a problem, or causing a new problem
- Missing a commitment
- Harming schedules
- Increasing costs
- Lowering quality
- Harming the client relationship
- Lowering morale
- Damaging the image of your boss or project sponsor
- Hurting your relationship with a coworker
- Failing to make a timely decision.

Now imagine yourself performing or behaving more effectively so that you know what to do when similar situations arise.

3. Think about the most important things that you need to focus on today and, drawing on what you have learned from yesterday's events, imagine the most appropriate behavior to adopt so that you are more effective to-

day than you were yesterday. If you do this relatively short exercise each day—week after week, month after month—you will be pleasantly surprised at your rate of growth.

Q_{21.37} This technique reminds me of post-project reviews, only this is performed daily. It will give me the opportunity to learn yesterday's lessons and immediately apply them to today. But how can I muster the discipline to do what you've suggested daily?

A_{21.37} Doing this immediate self-assessment can help you recover from missteps quickly, while you can still take effective action to repair damage done. We often avoid self-assessments, especially if they are routine, because we prefer to avoid any reminders of our so-called failures. But for professionals, these self-assessments of our actions are essential for our continued growth, maturity, and effectiveness.

> **66** *Nothing so conclusively proves a man's ability*
> *to lead others as what he does*
> *from day to day to lead himself.* **99**

—Thomas J. Watson, American industrialist,
entrepreneur, and former chairman of IBM

CHAPTER 22

Promoting Change in Your Organization

It is not the strongest of the species that survive, nor the most intelligent, but the ones most responsive to change.

—Charles Darwin, English naturalist

Bringing ideas back to your team and organization

Q22.1 I occasionally attend project management conferences, classes, and seminars. Do I have a duty to bring ideas back to the office?

A22.1 Your company is probably paying for your attendance, so yes, at a minimum, you have the responsibility to bring noteworthy ideas back to your personal domain of responsibility so that you and your company benefit from the investment in sending you to the event. Arguably, you also have the duty to bring ideas back to your organization for areas that may be outside your immediate domain of responsibility.

Q22.2 Can you suggest a process for bringing ideas back to benefit my domain of responsibility?

A22.2 Before the event and again at the start of the event, pause for a few moments to ask yourself what your objective is for attending the event—what are the goals you hope to achieve? It can help to write a paragraph (or less) outlining your goals. You can periodically review what you've written to remind you of what you're hoping to get out of the event. This information should also help you choose sessions to attend (if the event is a conference or organized like one). Including your boss in this planning exercise can help ensure that you maximize the investment for yourself and for your organization. It's important for you—and your employer—to receive a reasonable return on the investment of your valuable time.

After each session throughout the day or at the end of a day-long session, pause to write down, perhaps as bullet points, the key ideas that you want to remember and revisit later. If the event is spread across several days, do this at the end of each day. Just before you leave the conference or within hours of returning to the office, pause to reflect on the full experience and on all the information that you recorded for review. Sift through the list and identify the ideas that you believe have merit for further study and adaptation into your work duties. Don't spend a lot of time sifting through the list. The most noteworthy ideas should readily come to you.

After some reflection time—say somewhere between 15 to 60 minutes, depending on the event you attended and its duration—begin to prioritize your edited list. Although you may have identified a dozen or more worthwhile ideas, I suggest you reduce the list to the top three. (Q&A 10.45, Chapter 10, "Leadership Styles, Attributes, and Behaviors," offers an effective approach to prioritizing a list.) My experience is that if you keep more than three to five items, you will likely become overwhelmed and will not implement any of the items well. Keep in mind that you invested hours or days in the event; make sure that you receive an appropriate return on that investment.

Q₂₂.₃ **What criteria should I use in prioritizing the list? In other words, how do I determine which items carry more weight than others?**

A₂₂.₃ The simple answer is to select those items that will most significantly improve the performance of your assigned duties. A priority item could be one that:

- Is simple to implement and can be used often—say, an item that will help you run more effective meetings

- Will not be used often—such as a method to help develop a work breakdown structure—but when used can have a significant positive effect on a project
- Will improve your people skills, which you use every day when communicating with others.

Q₂₂.₄ What did you mean when you said, "Arguably, you also have the duty to bring ideas back to your organization . . ."?

A₂₂.₄ Not everyone in an organization who would like to attend an event has the time or funding to do so. Consequently, the leadership of an organization often expects those who do attend events to bring back ideas that can help the organization, not just the individuals who attended. These ideas can be communicated to others in the organization through trip reports, group meetings, classroom training and discussion, and various proposals to peers and management.

It's good that you have the opportunity to improve your skills, but it's great that you can also promote improvement across your team or organization. The benefits to the organization are obvious, but there are also many benefits for you—such as recognition, development of your leadership skills, and the satisfaction of knowing that your impact can extend beyond your immediate domain of responsibility.

Initiating change at the top of an organization

Q₂₂.₅ I have been told more than once that if I want to really make a change for the better in my organization, I should sell that change at the top—that top-down support and implementation of an idea is the best way to effect change. Do you agree?

A₂₂.₅ The simple answer is "yes," with a big **BUT**. I say "yes" because selling the top person in your organization on your ideas and having that person champion the change as it cascades down the management chain and into day-to-day operations can be an effective approach—when it works. Unfortunately, my experience shows that it may work only about 5 percent of the time. Why? Here are some reasons:

- You may not have done a good job of selling the idea because you did not do enough research beforehand.
- You did a "dump and run"—you dumped an idea on a senior manager but didn't stick around to help implement it.
- As important as your idea is to you, it may have paled in comparison to the top items on the senior manager's plate.
- You may have a weak senior manager who is ineffective in actually implementing ideas.
- The senior manager may have embraced your idea, but it lost momentum as it filtered down.

Q_{22.6} If changes proposed to a senior manager typically stick only about 5 percent of the time, what can a person do to help proposed changes stick more often?

Being a catalyst to make proposed changes stick

A_{22.6} The key is to champion the change—that is, be willing to be part of the solution and nurture the change through its implementation. When you propose a change to a senior manager, understand that he is extremely busy and cannot find the time to take on most new proposals. So inform the senior manager that you are volunteering yourself to champion the change and lead the work required. Let him know what support you need from him. Be specific: Do you need approval to proceed, a memo to others with his signature, a telephone call to an involved party, or a specific funding amount? Let the senior manager know your specific plan to implement the proposal and how you will keep him updated on the progress being made and the problems requiring his help.

Q_{22.7} Are you saying that when a proposal sticks, it is almost always because someone championed the proposal and drove it through to completion?

A$_{22.7}$ Absolutely! Things don't happen by themselves. They happen because someone chose to make them happen.

<table>
<tr><td>Management's
role in
promoting
change</td><td>

Q$_{22.8}$ Do you believe that most changes that have some positive effect across an organization are only possible because management directed the changes?

A$_{22.8}$ No. It is a myth that management is required to direct most positive changes in an organization. Recall my definition of leadership: *Leadership is not about the ability of those leaders around you to lead; it's about your ability to lead despite what is happening around you.* If the members of an organization realize the power and influence each of them has in promoting change across their organization, then look out—the pace of positive change will significantly increase.

</td></tr>
</table>

Management's role in promoting change

Q$_{22.8}$ Do you believe that most changes that have some positive effect across an organization are only possible because management directed the changes?

A$_{22.8}$ No. It is a myth that management is required to direct most positive changes in an organization. Recall my definition of leadership: *Leadership is not about the ability of those leaders around you to lead; it's about your ability to lead despite what is happening around you.* If the members of an organization realize the power and influence each of them has in promoting change across their organization, then look out—the pace of positive change will significantly increase.

Non-management's influence in promoting change

Q$_{22.9}$ I am a bit skeptical (to say the least) that non-management can have such a dramatic effect on positive change in an organization. Can you give me examples of situations in which non-management employees can be a catalyst for change?

A$_{22.9}$ There are actions management need not initiate in order for the actions to succeed (although these actions are often initiated by management). Of course, if an action requires funding, then management will likely need to be included in the equation. But most actions do not require funding or require only minimal funding. They include:

- Defining the methodologies to be used across an organization
- Creating and implementing a process for the continuous improvement of methodologies
- Defining, documenting, and distributing procedures that others can benefit from
- Setting up and implementing a mentoring program
- Identifying and initiating the training required to improve the skills of the members of the organization

- Implementing post-project reviews immediately after projects have completed
- Implementing a lessons-learned process to be incorporated at the start of new projects so that members of new projects learn from past mistakes and past noteworthy actions
- Identifying and continuously improving on the tools and technologies used throughout an organization
- Defining the roles and responsibilities of your job.

Q_{22.10} It seems to me that many of the items that you listed should include management somewhere in the process. Do you agree?

A_{22.10} I do, but these are items that non-managers can champion for the benefit of a project, department, or organization. Management buy-in and support is important for many of these items, but not having it does not necessarily mean that these actions cannot be successful. Most managers will willingly support employees who care enough about improving the work environment that they personally take the initiative to do so.

Q_{22.11} I have a manager who will not support me in a proposal that would benefit her department and the larger organization. Some funding is required, but the obstacle seems to be my boss' unwillingness to support changes proposed by me (and others) and champion them up the management chain. How can I break through this stubborn obstacle?

Obtaining stubborn management's buy-in

A_{22.11} First, make sure that your proposal is well-thought-out. Next, present the proposal in terms that your boss and higher levels of management can relate to. For example, list the benefits in terms of cost savings, increased revenue, productivity improvements, increased market share, improved quality, improved time to market, improved performance or usability, and increased customer satisfaction.

Obtaining peer support for your ideas

Q$_{22.12}$ I think I did everything you just suggested, but I haven't succeeded in convincing my boss. Any other ideas?

A$_{22.12}$ Here's an idea often used by senior managers when they are attempting to sell change to their bosses. First, sell your peers (the key opinion leaders) on the idea. Then, with your peers present, meet with your boss and explain your case. The enthusiasm and support from your peers can help influence your boss' thinking. Many managers are far more likely to be receptive if several of their staff also believe the proposal is the right thing to do.

Q$_{22.13}$ If that doesn't work, is it okay to take the idea over my boss's head?

A$_{22.13}$ Careful! That depends on the boss. If you do take the proposal over your boss's head, do not sneak around. Be open with your intentions, and preferably get your boss' permission. Ideally, I would like you to have a close working relationship with your boss, in which you do not feel intimidated, and she does not feel threatened in any way. Both of you should feel comfortable bouncing the idea off your boss' boss together. When you are trying to decide how to proceed, ask yourself what you would want your employee to do if the situation was reversed and you were the boss.

Another person receiving credit for my rejected idea

Q$_{22.14}$ What should I do if someone promotes and sells an idea and gets all the accompanying credit, but I tried selling the same idea months or years earlier to no avail?

A$_{22.14}$ Get over it! Don't waste your time and energy by being upset with the other person or angry at management for supporting it. Get off your duff and do a better job selling future proposals. It is likely that your due diligence, persistence, and communication skills need (or needed) improvement. (By the way, if years have passed since you last tried to sell your idea—get real! You don't have squatter's rights on ideas forever.)

Q22.15 Is it a good idea to team up with other companies to improve the best practices of my organization?

A22.15 It's an excellent idea! You can learn from each other. But most companies are not interested in helping others unless they also receive some benefit. You will likely have more success in finding a willing partner company if that company is not a competitor. Before you approach a company with a partnership proposal, make sure that you have the support of your boss and legal counsel within your company. Also, make sure that you have clearly defined objectives so that you and your potential partner know what you are looking for and so that you will know when your objectives have been achieved.

Q22.16 There is little respect in my organization from the top down for the project management craft and its corresponding processes. What can I do to turn this situation around?

A22.16 There is a lot you can do. But first and foremost, you must present a convincing reason why a stronger focus on project management will benefit the senior managers and the organization. Talk in terms that appeal to the senior managers and their measurements, such as reducing the duration of projects, cutting costs, decreasing maintenance costs, creating higher-quality products, increasing customer satisfaction, and continuously improving on key organizational metrics.

Q22.17 If I can get management's attention and initial support, what do I do next?

A22.17 Begin your journey by taking baby steps for now. You can define a simple, but flexible, starter project-management methodology that can help achieve the business goals for the organization. Consider getting support for your ideas from your peers first, then present the proposal to the key decision-makers. With their support, pilot your proposal with a project or two—all the while keeping the decision-makers informed of your progress. Once you have some demonstrated successes, champion the adoption of the project-management methodology for new projects. Don't forget to have a procedure defined for continuous improvement of the methodology. Don't expect to launch a PM methodology that covers every possible project and situation. Start small. You can grow it over time. If needed, enlist help in defining and documenting the PM methodology from other members of the organization.

CHAPTER 23

Mergers and Acquisitions

"An organization is built on meeting commitments, not on distractions of uncertainty and speculation."

Q_{23.1} Our company has just been bought out by another. It will likely take several months for the legal documentation and final approvals to be completed. I am a project manager, and my team members have all but stopped their work, based on anxiety over the future of the project, organization, and their jobs. What can I do to get them refocused on the project?

Anxiety harming project progress

A_{23.1} Consult the project sponsor or your boss for help. They might even recommend that an executive come talk with your team (or the entire organization) to tell them what the changes will mean. However, part of the discussion must be about getting back to business and meeting project commitments. The bottom line? If you worked for me, I would still hold you accountable for the outcome of the project, even in the midst of a buyout. Therefore, drive the project as you normally would. If anyone refuses to participate, handle the situation as required.

Q_{23.2} If a senior manager or executive is planning to talk with my team, should there be any homework for the team beforehand?

Team homework in preparation for executive discussion

A_{23.2} You can assemble team members for a brief meeting and ask them to identify their most important questions. You can then forward these questions to the executive so she can be prepared. Keep the list relatively short, including only those questions that are most important to the team.

Limiting discussion to team members only

$Q_{23.3}$ What if I call a meeting of just team members—no senior management—and give them the opportunity to vent for an hour or two? Will this be helpful and productive?

$A_{23.3}$ The meeting will likely be appreciated by the team as they share thoughts and anxieties, but without an authoritative figure, such as a senior manager, to address the concerns, the meeting can backfire and raise the level of anxiety felt by the team. This meeting could, however, be used as a means to collect questions for a senior manager to answer in a later meeting with the team.

Process-improvement initiatives halted

$Q_{23.4}$ The organization in which I work had many process-improvement initiatives that were underway, such as the creation of a project management organization (PMO). However, when news spread that our company was being acquired by a larger company, many of those initiatives were halted. Was this the right thing to do?

$A_{23.4}$ It depends on the initiatives and their importance and urgency. However, because takeovers can take many months to fully implement, it is likely that some of those initiatives should have been continued.

For example, many organizations can greatly benefit from an effective PMO. If a PMO is being created when the news of a takeover breaks, the person in charge of creating the PMO should consult the new company to find out if continuing to develop it is appropriate. At a minimum, there may be best practices that your organization and the acquiring company can share for the benefit of one or both companies.

My attitude is not: "Well, the new company probably already has a PMO and best practices in place—practices we better get used to." My attitude is: "Well, we are going to create the most efficient PMO. The takeover company will want to adopt our practices." When companies are taken over, the business of running the business should not skip a beat.

Q_{23.5} Any last words of advice for dealing with the uncertainty that often accompanies mergers and acquisitions?

A_{23.5} Yes. Times of uncertainty are also times of opportunity. Use these events as an opportunity to demonstrate leadership and the ability to focus and get things done. Doing this now will likely help you down the road. Remember, *it's not about the ability of those around you to lead; it's about your ability to lead, despite what is happening around you.* Go do your job!

Times of uncertainty are times of opportunity

PART THREE

The Project Side

The ten chapters in Part Three focus on the process and procedural side of projects. Some of the topics and issues addressed in each of these chapters are listed below.

CHAPTER 24: THE PROJECT MANAGEMENT INSTITUTE (PMI) AND *A GUIDE TO THE PROJECT MANAGEMENT BODY OF KNOWLEDGE (PMBOK® GUIDE)*

Membership in the project management professional organization; effectiveness of a project manager certified as a Project Management Professional (PMP); following the *PMBOK® Guide*.

CHAPTER 25: METHODOLOGIES AND PROCESSES

Bureaucratic and inefficient methodologies; incomplete processes; method to implement new methodologies; dealing with resistant project members; applying new process ideas to a project.

CHAPTER 26: PROJECT MANAGEMENT ORGANIZATION (PMO)

Purpose of a PMO; respect for a PMO; project managers reporting to a PMO; the durability of PMOs.

CHAPTER 27: PROJECT CULTURE

Accountability for project culture; importance of project culture; culture-training class; topics in a culture-training class; addressing topics from this book; upsides and downsides of classes; changing the organizational culture; cultural differences of a national or ethnic nature.

CHAPTER 28: PROJECT PLANS, SCHEDULES, AND BUDGETS

Getting in control; setting project end date; dealing with unrealistic project end date; changing a project's baseline plan; rolling-wave commitment model; avoiding working overtime early; using project management tools; importance of schedules versus budgets; completing a project early and under budget; obtaining people resources for the project; applying a contingency buffer.

The Project Management Institute (PMI) and *A Guide to the Project Management Body of Knowledge* (*PMBOK® Guide*)

❝PMI and the PMBOK® Guide are about leadership and making choices that are in the best business interest of the organization or company—not about following a canned set of processes and procedures. ❞

Q_{24.1} I have an interest in developing a career in the project management field. Should I become a member of a project management organization, such as the Project Management Institute (PMI)?

Membership in a project management professional organization

A_{24.1} I would. I have been a member of PMI and certified as a Project Management Professional (PMP) since 1992. At the time I became a member, there was no requirement by the company that employed me to become a member or to become certified. I chose to associate with this type of organization because of my interest in improving my PM skills and to get new ideas on how to advance the state of project management within an area of my company.

PMI exposed me to a much broader view of project management and to many people who are helping to advance the PM profession. The networking available today among PM professionals—as well as the great mentoring opportunities that many PMI chapters offer—are invaluable to the new PM person as well as seasoned veterans of the profession. Moreover, the PM profession is continuing to thrive and mature, and it is in your best career interests to be a part of that evolution. As you may know, many companies seeking to hire PM types look for the PMP® certification. Some even require it.

Effectiveness of a PM certified as a PMP

Q24.2 If a person is PMP®-certified, does that mean that she is a good project manager?

A24.2 No. It means that she meets specific requirements for academic education, work experience, and formal project management education. It also indicates willingness to sign and abide by a professional code of ethics, satisfaction of continuing education and professional development requirements, and that she has passed a multiple-choice examination on project management. I know some highly effective project managers who are not PMP® certified. I also know some ineffective project managers who are PMP® certified. However, the PMP® certification does mean that the person has at least a certain level of knowledge and skill and has experience in some aspects of the profession. There is an expectation that the certified person is competent to perform the craft.

Following the *PMBOK®* Guide

Q24.3 PMI has a document called *A Guide to the Project Management Body of Knowledge*—also known as the *PMBOK® Guide*. As a project manager, should I follow this guide through and through?

A24.3 No. Many organizations with good intentions, eager to embrace project management best practices, initially adopt nearly every plan, document, and process described by the *PMBOK® Guide*. The result? An organization may double the time and cost to get a product to market. The *PMBOK® Guide* is an excellent reference source if used as intended. I will repeat here two excerpts from the *PMBOK® Guide* that address your question:

(1) *The primary purpose of the* PMBOK® Guide *is to identify that subset of the Project Management Body of Knowledge that is generally recognized as good practice. "Identify" means to provide a general overview as opposed to an exhaustive description. "Generally recognized" means that the knowledge and practices described are applicable to most projects most of the time, and that there is widespread consensus about their value and usefulness. "Good practice" means that there is general agreement that the correct application of these skills, tools, and techniques can enhance the chances of success over a wide range of different projects. Good practice does not mean that the knowledge described should always be applied uniformly on all projects;* **the project management team is responsible for determining what is appropriate for any given project**.[1]

(2) *Anyone using this document should rely on his or her own independent judgment or, as appropriate, seek the advice of a competent professional in determining the exercise of reasonable care in any given circumstances. Information and other standards on the topic covered by this publication may be available from other sources, which the user may wish to consult for additional views or information not covered by this publication.*[2]

Q24.4   Are PMI and the *PMBOK® Guide* mostly about producing successful projects?

A24.4   Arguably, yes; however, I view them to be about more. They're also about leadership and making choices that are in the best business interest of the organization or com-

Leadership and good business decisions

---

[1]*A Guide to the Project Management Body of Knowledge* (*PMBOK® Guide*), Third Edition, ©2004 Project Management Institute, Newtown Square, PA, p. 3.
    [2]Ibid., Notice.

pany. I believe project management is about building products, performing services, and creating results—all of which are integral in supporting
the objectives of a *business*. It's not about following a canned set of
processes and procedures. There's no cookbook. It's about using good
business judgment and ethically leading a team in achieving whatever is
in the best *business interest* of the enterprise.

CHAPTER 25

Methodologies and Processes

66Methodologies and processes must be flexible to support the business needs; they are in place to serve you—not you to serve them.99

Q_{25.1} The project management methodologies that I am expected to follow in my organization are too bureaucratic and inefficient. What should I do?

Bureaucratic and inefficient methodologies

A_{25.1} Overall, structure and discipline on a project are good things. However, no project management methodology satisfies all the needs of all its users. Therefore, you must think for yourself and tailor the methodology to best fit the needs of your project. But make sure you understand the bigger picture. Although you might not see the benefit of a specific "bureaucratic" requirement, there may be a valid reason for its existence. That reason may go beyond your own immediate interest and benefit the entire organization.

Q_{25.2} But what if I'm not allowed to deviate from the methodology unless I have obtained the proper approval?

Approval to deviate

A_{25.2} Put a case together to win the approval you seek. Play by the rules, but be persistent if you believe you have a better way that will benefit the business.

Q_{25.3} What if a specific process that I need to follow to be successful with my project has not been well defined or implemented? How can I get it properly addressed?

Incomplete process

A_{25.3} You can go to the perceived owner of the process-related problem, do your best to convince him of your needs, and try to get him to agree to remedy the problem within a time frame that is acceptable to you. If this person will not meet your needs, you can escalate to that person's manager. If you cannot identify the likely owner of the process-related problem, or the owner cannot or will not satisfy your needs on a timely basis, then you may have to be creative and solve the problem yourself.

Defining processes to benefit other projects

Q_{25.4} If I define and implement a specific process for my project that could also benefit other projects, do I have the duty to define it for use beyond my project?

A_{25.4} Typically, no. Your mission is first to satisfy the duties that fall within your domain of responsibility—your assigned project(s). You should not take on more work if it means you won't be as effective within your own domain of responsibility. However, if you are able to take on the additional work—even if it is outside your domain of responsibility and will only count as "extra credit"—you might want to consider doing so. Why? Because it can benefit your organization and your career. Your value to the organization increases. But remember, only go after extra credit if you have first taken care of your own domain of responsibility.

Implementing new methodologies

Q_{25.5} If an organization has weak or no methodologies defined but new methodologies are in the process of being defined, is it best to implement them in phases or all at once?

A_{25.5} If weak or no methodologies are currently in place, an organization will likely benefit from phased-in improvements to start. Preferably, those designing the methodology can outline the big picture first. They should then explain when and why each component will be rolled out so that all members of the organization know what to expect and can work in concert with the master plan. (By the way, it is almost always better to have weak methodologies that everyone can build upon than to have no methodologies at all.)

Q25.6 As a project manager, what should I do if some members of my project refuse to follow the methodologies defined by the organization?

Dealing with resistant project members

A25.6 If the project members have reasons for not following the methodologies that you think are valid, work to satisfy their interests as long as the best interests of the project are also satisfied. If you do not support the members' positions, work to find middle ground that is acceptable to all parties and also serves the best interests of the project. If you are unable to work the issue to an acceptable conclusion, assert your authority as the project manager and insist on the adoption of the appropriate methodologies. If one or more members still refuse to adopt the correct methodologies, you must escalate the issue until it is resolved. Begin the escalation with the project member's resource manager, but be upfront with the project member about your intentions and actions.

Q25.7 Who is responsible for ensuring that a reasonable project management methodology is in place on a project?

Responsibility for a project's PM methodology

A25.7 The project manager. Management and the project management organization share some accountability, but the buck stops with the PM.

Q25.8 What responsibility does the PM have if there is a weak or nonexistent methodology within the organization, and the organization isn't interested in developing a stronger one?

A_{25.8} The PM is still responsible for ensuring that a reasonable project management methodology is defined and followed on his project. However, the PM is not responsible for defining a methodology that extends beyond his project—unless, of course, his boss assigns him to do so.

Applying new
process ideas
to a project

Q_{25.9} As the project manager, if I discover a better way to do something on the project, should I immediately apply the new process or technique to the project?

A_{25.9} Not necessarily. It depends on the overall return on investment. Looking at a simple example, if your idea would require two weeks of time to rework the project plan and appears to save one week of schedule time, then do not apply the idea. Don't implement ideas just because they have some merit. Implement them because they make good business sense.

Q_{25.10} What if I often think of ways to make small, incremental improvements that relate to project tracking, metrics, communications, and the like? Should I implement these changes?

A_{25.10} As the project manager, it is your call. Small but continuous improvements can have a profound, long-term benefit to a project and can affect all aspects of a project—not just scope, schedules, and costs, but also quality, morale, and communications. Do your best to implement items that can have a measurable benefit, not just ones that are "nice things to do."

CHAPTER 26

Project Management Organization (PMO)

*66 PMOs serve two primary objectives:
to manage the portfolio of projects in a manner that best
supports the business, and
to help project managers be successful.99*

Q₍26.1₎ Is a project management organization (PMO) a good thing for an organization?

Purpose of PMO

A₍26.1₎ For the right organization, it can be. In my view, the two most important reasons to have a PMO are to (1) manage the portfolio of projects in a manner that best supports the business, and (2) help project managers be successful. A PMO is not about bureaucracy, overhead, and slowing down the business, nor is it about creating attractive charts and catering to senior managers. A PMO is serious about business and exists to help an organization be more successful.

(By the way, a PMO can be known by many names, such as a project office or a project support office.)

Q₍26.2₎ You say that a PMO can be good for an organization. The PMO in my organization doesn't seem to be well respected. Why not?

Respect for PMO

A₍26.2₎ If a PMO focuses predominantly on managing the portfolio of projects and helping project managers be successful, then respect for it within the organization should develop as its value becomes apparent. When a PMO loses sight of its purpose, the organization it serves starts to see it as a black hole where funds are wasted and there is not sufficient return on investment.

When a PMO provides services that directly benefit an organization and its projects, it will gain a good reputation. Look at the following list of services that a PMO can provide, and ask yourself if such a PMO would be welcome in your organization:

- Determining the priority of projects to be funded and worked
- Providing well-trained and competent project managers
- Developing, documenting, and maintaining project management best practices
- Reviewing contract proposals from vendors or from within the organization
- Sponsoring project management education seminars and classes
- Conducting project culture-training classes
- Performing project reviews
- Performing post-project reviews
- Ensuring that new projects apply lessons learned from past projects.

PMs reporting to a PMO

Q26.3 Should the project managers across an organization all report to the PMO, or should they report to various managers dispersed throughout the organization?

A26.3 The project managers should report to a central location. When reporting is dispersed, fewer lessons are learned, and the PMs' growth is significantly handicapped. Moreover, PMs in this situation tend to follow what their bosses tell them to do on their projects rather than (1) exercise good judgment, (2) follow project management best practices, and (3) remain focused on doing the right thing. It is too easy for them to get swept up in local politics.

But project managers who are managed from a single point, the PMO, can learn from each other, grow exponentially, support one another, and work together to continually improve on best practices. The department in which they work specializes in project management, and their training is more frequent and deliberate. As the pooled project managers are "contracted out" across the organization, they tend to be more focused on doing the right thing, because that's what their common manager expects of them and evaluates their performance against.

Q_{26.4} As a PM, I see the wisdom in having all project managers report to a central location, but that's not how it works in my organization. How can I help sell this change in my organization?

Promoting change in your organization

A_{26.4} Depending on your organization's culture, you could take one of several approaches, but here's a solid approach that can be used in most organizations. First, prepare a proposal that briefly explains:

(1) How things are today

(2) What the new organizational structure would look like

(3) The benefits of the new proposal over the existing structure and operation

(4) The steps that must be taken to implement the new proposal.

List the negatives of the new proposal, too—don't attempt to hide anything. Propose your approach to your peers and seek their approval. This exercise will likely yield some additional good ideas that you can incorporate. Then discuss the proposal with your boss and seek her support. From there, your boss should help you get "face time" with the appropriate power players. Make sure that you are not just dumping a problem on senior management. Be willing to be part of the solution to minimize the burden on them and on others.

Durability of $Q_{26.5}$ If PMOs are such a good idea, then why aren't there more
PMOs   of them? Also, why are they often one of the first things
                      to be abandoned when new senior management comes
                      into an organization or when budgets are cut?

$A_{26.5}$ Don't judge the potential of PMOs by their success rates. If
they fail, it's typically because the PMO is poorly led or because of naïve or misinformed senior management. (More
often, it's the former.) For most organizations, disbanding
the PMO is a shortsighted move. Doing so usually reflects
a lack of knowledge and experience regarding the great
benefits a PMO can bring to an organization. However, if
a PMO is poorly formed and implemented, and its value is
questionable at best, then it is a typical target for downsizing or removal. I would rather see a weak PMO turned
around to become a significant benefit to an organization
than see it disbanded altogether.

By the way, I know of many, many organizations with successful PMOs.

CHAPTER 27

Project Culture

❝Once people know what is expected of them, they will rise to the occasion.❞

Q_{27.1} I often hear debates on who has the most control over the culture of a project: the project manager or management. Do you have a definitive answer?

A_{27.1} Yes. The PM has the most control. Although an organization may have processes and procedures in place for the members of a project to follow, the interpretation and execution of these processes and procedures is within the domain of the PM. Ultimately, the PM will decide how to plan, execute, and track a project, mitigate its problems, and encourage good working relationships among the project's stakeholders.

It is a common mistake for an organization to place too much emphasis on process and procedures and too little emphasis on leadership and making effective business decisions. A project can have what appears to be thorough and well-articulated processes to follow, yet have a weak PM as its leader and thus fail miserably in meeting its objectives. On the flip side, a project can start with weak processes, but have a strong, effective PM as its leader and thus be a resounding success. Leadership is by far a more potent ingredient for success. The leadership the PM brings to the project—along with thoughtful use of an organization's processes and procedures—is a powerful force in shaping a project's culture.

Q_{27.2} But it is my experience that a project manager can do only so much in shaping the project's culture—that management defines most of the elements of the project. Do you agree?

A27.2 It may be that way in your organization, but it is definitely not the way it should be—or could be. What PM wants to blindly follow a script that could cause the project to get bogged down by actions that don't yield effective outcomes? Also, an organization's employees need instruction in leadership, independent thought, accountability, and good business judgment. Processes and procedures or directives from a higher authority cannot adequately address these attributes.

Importance of project culture

Q27.3 How important is project culture?

A27.3 Extremely important! Project culture has a lot to do with morale, productivity, team camaraderie, making and meeting commitments, customer satisfaction, quality, and a host of other factors that can positively affect a project's outcome.

PM typically the problem— and solution

Q27.4 Would you say that most projects have a positive culture for members to embrace?

A27.4 In my experience, no. PMs often fail to implement a positive culture. But this is good news for PMs. Because they are at fault, they also have significant control over the solution. I would rather be the problem, because that gives me the power to create a solution.

The need to manage expectations

Q27.5 Why is it so common for organizations to have ineffective project cultures?

A27.5 Because we typically assume so much about others and base our expectations on those assumptions. People cannot truly understand what you expect from them, or know what to expect from you, unless those expectations are defined, discussed, nurtured, and enforced.

Look around you on your current or next project. Note that the members may differ in terms of gender, nationality, age, and physical size, to name a few. But as different as we appear, we are far more different in terms of experiences, habits, traditions, and expectations of others. Even if all of your project members looked alike and lived in the same community, on the same street, in dwellings that looked exactly alike, once those project members entered their homes, their cultures would be radically different from one another. For this reason, we should not assume that everyone on a project thinks alike or has the same expectations of one another. We must set those expectations up-front—at the beginning of the project. The culture a project member is part of outside work is not the PM's business, but the culture that is embraced at work within the PM's project is his business.

Q27.6 **How can a project manager go about defining the desired culture on his or her project?**

Culture-training class

A27.6 The project manager can organize a *culture-training class* for the project. This is the formal training of all project members in key hard skills, soft skills, and processes that are essential in helping ensure a successful project. It provides all project members with a common understanding of how the project will be run and the role that each team member is expected to play. It's about setting expectations. When a project is getting started, its members should attend this class.

Q27.7 **What do you mean by "hard skills" and "soft skills"?**

A27.7 Hard skills are mostly process- and procedure-oriented, such as the mechanics of the development life cycle, planning, tracking, performing risk assessments, escalating, and performing project reviews. Hard skills are easier for most people to learn and apply than soft skills.

Soft skills are more people- and behavior-oriented and include leading, directing, nurturing, enabling, communicating, negotiating, and mitigating. Soft skills are key in helping leaders make things happen.

Topics of culture-training class

Q_{27.8} Can you list the typical topics covered in a culture-training class?

A_{27.8} These topics are usually addressed:

- Roles and responsibilities of project members
- Process methodology
- Project planning process
- Project tracking process
- Escalation process
- Project reviews
- Post-project review
- Communications with people
- Soft skills
- Professional maturity
- Lessons learned.

The subject of culture-training classes is treated in more detail in *Neal Whitten's No-Nonsense Advice for Successful Projects*, Chapter 19, "Create the Desired Culture for Your Project."

Duration of class

Q_{27.9} How long does a culture-training class last?

A_{27.9} It can vary from a few hours to two days, depending on the size and duration of the project and the professional maturity of the project members. It is held near the start of the project and is repeated infrequently throughout the project life cycle for new project members.

Q27.10 Is the culture-training class a good forum to discuss some of the topics discussed in this book?

A27.10 Yes, up to a point. There is limited time to delve into topics that are as broad as those discussed in this book. Do not expect the class to cover a lot of topics, but do expect to cover some key subjects common to all projects, such as accountability, dependencies, roles and responsibilities, and escalations.

Q27.11 Should the project manager conduct the culture-training class?

A27.11 Typically, no. The instructor should be someone within the organization who has significant PM experience and preferably some RM experience as well. The person may come out of the organization's project management organization (PMO). This person should teach the class for all projects so that a uniform culture is being promoted for all projects within the organization.

Q27.12 What's the project manager's role related to culture-training classes?

A27.12 The PM should initiate and schedule the class. The PM works closely with the class instructor to ensure that the teachings support the direction of the project. For example, when "process methodology" is discussed, the PM may have ideas on how to tailor the processes to best support the business needs. The PM may also want to share her ideas on how the project plan should be developed or how project tracking meetings should be conducted. She will likely take the floor from time to time to discuss issues unique to the project.

Q27.13 Who has the final say if the project manager and the class instructor differ on an issue?

A27.13 In most cases, the PM has the final say, because it is the PM who is on the front lines and is held accountable for the project's outcome. In organizations that have weak process maturity and weak professional maturity, then the instructor may have the authority to overrule the PM on certain issues.

Class participants

Q27.14 Who attends these classes?

A27.14 All project stakeholders should attend, including core project members, vendors, contractors, management, the client, and the project sponsor. Some management and the project sponsor may only attend a portion of the training or none at all because of scheduling difficulties. Project members who have a very small role in the project may not be required to attend.

Upside and downside of classes

Q27.15 Earlier in the book (Q&A 10.14) you said that you would mandate culture-training classes for projects of a given size or budget. Have all of your experiences with project-training classes been positive?

A27.15 These classes have definitely saved days or weeks on smaller projects and weeks or months on larger projects. When project members understand what is expected of them and their work environment encourages productivity, significant benefit can come from these classes. But the benefits are negligible if PMs require their project members to sit through the same class over and over, project after project, instead of altering the classes to match the professional maturity of the participants and the unique business needs of each project. These classes must be tailored to the participants.

Q27.16 It seems that these classes can change the culture of an organization—project by project. Do you agree?

A27.16 Yes. The classes are a means of changing the culture of an organization from the bottom up rather than the top down. Most of us reading this book have no or little ability to change the culture in an organization from the top down, but we all have some ability to change the culture on our projects—project by project.

Changing the organization's culture

Q27.17 How do you feel about conducting culture-training classes for all the members of an organization—not just for particular projects?

A27.17 This is a great idea! I have done this many times for organizations and have observed organizations doing this for themselves. It can be most helpful to have all members of an organization hear the same words and participate in the same discussions. This approach also can help shorten the duration of project-level culture-training classes.

Q27.18 Do project members have any duties beyond building a product or providing a service or result? What other duties can be taught in a culture-training class?

A27.18 Yes. Below is a starter list of duties that each project member is also responsible for while building a product or providing a service or result:

- Understanding his job and obtaining agreement from his boss
- Resolving problems with the importance and urgency needed
- Reaching out to help others as long as doing so does not interfere with his own commitments
- Continuously seeking to improve his own work performance

Ongoing duties of project members

- Continuously improving relationships with those around him
- Asking for help on a timely basis
- Helping make his leaders look good
- Demonstrating integrity by engaging in only legal and ethical behaviors
- Learning from past projects and applying the most important lessons going forward.

Cultural differences of a national or ethnic nature

Q27.19 I agree with you that it is important to establish a project culture so that all members have the same mindset. But what if cultural differences that are rooted in some team members' national or ethnic backgrounds could actually harm the project? Should these differences be honored?

A27.19 The goal should be for the project outcome not to suffer. If it were to suffer, then all stakeholders would be harmed. To avoid harm, solutions that are acceptable to all involved parties should be developed. Some give and take may be required. The parties whose behavior is causing problems should suggest viable workarounds to mitigate conflict, but other involved parties should do their best to reasonably accommodate the cultural differences. Depending on who is affected by the conflict, the project manager, and possibly the relevant resource managers, should be included in the discussions. The PM has the ultimate responsibility to ensure the conflict is satisfactorily resolved. As stated earlier, the culture that project members embrace outside work is not the business of other project stakeholders, but the culture of the project team is designed to yield a successful outcome and is vitally relevant.

CHAPTER 28

Project Plans, Schedules, and Budgets

❝ *The beginning is the most important part of the work.* ❞

—Plato, Greek philosopher

Q28.1 Why do we develop project plans?

A28.1 Simply put: Project planning is all about *getting in control*. For example, if a project has no project plan with which to track progress, then no one can say with any certainty whether or not the project is on schedule or when it will complete. The project plan is the foundation for everything that happens during the project. It defines the relationships among scope, time, budgets, and project members.

Project tracking, by the way, is all about *staying in control*.

Q28.2 Is it bad for my boss, project sponsor, or client to set the project end date?

A28.2 No, not as a general rule. These folks typically have information you don't have that is vital in determining the end date. For example, they may be striving to raise revenue by the end of the fiscal year, meet a deadline in implementing a new government regulation, race a product to market to beat out a competitor, meet a contract-set date, or you fill in the blank. If I were your boss, I would often set the project end date.

Forcing the proverbial ten pounds into a five-pound sack

Q28.3 When is it not a good idea to have someone set the end date?

A28.3 When you evaluate the requested end date and determine that it is not achievable, but a higher authority says you must complete the project by then, regardless. Trying to force the proverbial ten pounds into a five-pound sack will make things far worse than first expected. Why? Because the project team will begin to cut corners in an effort to achieve the overaggressive date. These cut corners will almost always harm the quality of the deliverables, so an excessive amount of time is spent trying to recover. You might deliver on time, but a high price is paid in unfinished or weak product features, low quality, high after-delivery maintenance, low customer satisfaction ratings, low project team morale, or project member burnout, for example.

Dealing with an unrealistic project end date

Q28.4 What can I do if faced with an unreasonable project end date?

A28.4 First, do your best to put an achievable plan in place to satisfy the requested project end date. If that course of action is not workable, then negotiate with the requester (for example, the project sponsor) for an alternative approach, such as delivering reduced features or function, increasing cost, outsourcing a portion of the work, or changing the design to accommodate using off-the-shelf components. Your mission is to offer solutions that can help the project sponsor successfully meet his business objectives. Look at multiple alternative solutions, but advocate the specific solution that you feel best serves the business interests.

Q28.5 What can I do if I am still told to deliver by the requested project end date, even though I have done my best to explain why the date is unreasonable and have offered alternative approaches?

A28.5 Having done due diligence unsuccessfully (and because you can read an org chart), proceed with the unreasonable plan. You should also consider doing the following:

- ***Consider the end date a project risk.*** Include the overly aggressive plan as a project risk. Evaluate the project in accordance with your organization's definitions of high, medium, and low risks.
- ***Solicit a review of your project plan.*** Have someone who is well respected within the organization conduct a review of your plan. If that person agrees that your plan is too aggressive and therefore too risky, then you might win an ally in promoting a better plan. (This approach will not help you if the reviewer doesn't think the plan is overly aggressive.)
- ***Establish and track metrics.*** Immediately monitor progress of the execution of the overly aggressive project plan so that early warning signs of a weak plan can be spotted before the project goes too far.
- ***Establish a major milestone to pause and evaluate the progress.*** Identify a major milestone that will take place one or two months from now to use as a benchmark of progress. Once the milestone is achieved, reevaluate the project plan based on the lessons learned to date. Repeat this technique every one or two months. Include these major milestone points in the project plan.
- ***Schedule a project review.*** Insert into the project plan a project review that is to occur in three or four months. The review will be an audit by one or more "outside" folks who are charged with assessing the health of the project. The outside folks are not project team members, but they are typically not outside the company.

Q28.6 Do you believe that project end dates are cast in stone?

A28.6 No, not in most cases. Project end dates should be aggressive, but they must be achievable. If a date has been set but is totally unrealistic, then you are almost always better

Viewing a project end date with flexibility

off moving the date. Otherwise, a bad situation can be made far worse.

For example, if a contract calls for a major penalty if the end date is missed, then tremendous pressure will be placed on the project team to succeed. If we leave an overly aggressive end date alone and foolishly think that we should simply persevere, we might miss the contract date by a year. But if we perform due diligence and reevaluate the project plan, we may miss the contract end date by only four months. Either way, the end date will be missed and a heavy penalty will be levied, but the collateral damage can be reduced by *doing the right thing* and not blindly thinking that the original date is cast in stone.

Dealing with an inflexible project end date

Q28.7 What if you're working on a project, such as a New Year's celebration or an Olympics opening ceremony, that really must meet an end date—and that end date is too aggressive?

A28.7 Remember what I said: You cannot change the laws of physics and put ten pounds in a five-pound sack—even if a country's government or world body says you must. When faced with these situations—and some of you reading this have already faced or will someday face such a challenge—you must be responsible and rework the plan, knowing full well that some items may not get completed in time. Prioritize the work ahead of you, and make conscious decisions so that you achieve the best possible outcome. Whatever you do, make sure that your new plan executing only a portion of the original plan is sound and achieves its limited—but deliberate—objectives.

Limiting the replanning of a project

Q28.8 I often see projects in trouble be repeatedly replanned, with the client and project sponsor becoming more frustrated and the core project team enduring increasing hardship. How many times can a project manager get away with replanning a project?

A28.8 Of course, every project and organization has its own unique characteristics, but if you worked for me and your project were in big trouble, you should expect to do only one major replanning. Although no one wants a project to miss its original date or commitments, it can happen to even seasoned project managers. We all make mistakes, and things can happen that are outside our direct control. I have a lot of tolerance for a person making mistakes—but not if he makes the same mistake twice. When you are in trouble and must ask for more time, money, skilled team members, or whatever, plan to ask only once—so make your request count. If you're given a second chance, you are expected to do it right. Do not settle for a half-baked plan, and do not move forward with a new plan without fully understanding and addressing the problems that caused the original plan to fail.

Q28.9 I was taught long ago to never change a project's baseline plan—to keep it static so all work can continue to be measured against that plan. Do you agree?

Changing a project's baseline plan

A28.9 No. If you have ever been on a project that consistently misses its baseline dates, you know how frustrating it can be to the core project players. No matter how hard or smart they work, they know that they cannot catch up to the original dates. This causes members to not want to work overtime and zaps their creative juices—after all, nothing they do will pull them out of their spiraling nose-dive. To avoid this, the project members should pause from time to time to catch their breath and reevaluate the project plan. They should look at the progress they have made and identify lessons that can be applied going forward. This is the time to rebaseline. Whenever the project plan is rebaselined, it means that, by default, the project is now back on schedule at that particular point in time.

Frequency of rebaselining a project plan

Q28.10 How can I determine when a project should be rebaselined?

A28.10 A project plan should be reevaluated once every month or two. If this assessment causes major dates in the project plan to change, then you should also rebaseline the plan. Of course, if a project is only days or weeks in duration, then you cannot pause to reevaluate the project plan every one or two months—but for these shorter projects, there typically should not be a need to routinely reevaluate them.

Relationship between rebaselining and the project end date

Q28.11 But if you reevaluate a project every one or two months, doesn't that translate into moving the project end date?

A28.11 Not necessarily. In fact, it helps in *preventing* the project end date from slipping. The idea behind assessing the project plan every one or two months is to discover problems as soon as possible, make mid-project corrections in the project plan while the cost to the project is lowest, and emerge with a more realistic, thoughtful, and seasoned plan.

Rolling-wave commitment model

Q28.12 Is there a name for this technique of reassessing a project plan every one or two months and rebaselining as needed?

A28.12 Yes, it's called the *rolling-wave commitment model* and is depicted in Figure 28.1. Basically, here's how it works. When planning a new project—say, a project that appears to be about eight months in duration—you identify a major milestone every one or two months. Starting at the first (leftmost) "X" in Figure 28.1, the closest milestone (MM1) is the only milestone that you commit to, while the remaining milestones (MM2 through MM5) are viewed as target dates. Of course, this means that the project end date is also a target date. Your project plan should be as detailed as it needs to be to achieve the first major milestone; however, the granularity of the project plan decreases the fur-

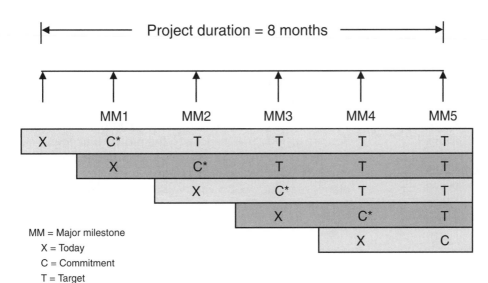

Figure 28.1. Rolling-wave commitment model

ther you move away from the first major milestone and the closer you get to the project end date.

Q 28.13   **Wait! Are you saying that you recommend project managers not commit to a project's end date if that date is more than two or three months away?**

A 28.13   Bingo! Think about it: How often do the project manager and team commit to the project end date before they even know what it is they are building or performing? Almost all of us have done this at one time or another. Knock it off! I have a far better approach, so stay with me here.

Returning to Figure 28.1, when the first major milestone is achieved on schedule—and it likely will be—it's time to pause and reevaluate the project plan. Now we have reached the second "X." Looking at the lessons from the past one to two months and adding more granularity to the project plan for the major milestones ahead of you, you update the project plan. You now commit to the next

Avoid committing to project end dates that are more than two or three months away

major milestone (MM2), which is one or two months away, and you reassess the targeted major milestones beyond (MM3 through MM5). This process is repeated until the last committed major milestone is the project end date.

Holding target milestone dates and preserving the project end date

Q28.14 This isn't going to fly with my project sponsor and client. You are giving carte blanche to the project manager to move major milestone dates—including the most important date, the delivery date—each time the project plan is reevaluated. Do you really believe that this approach can be sold up the management chain?

A28.14 The intent is to *not* change target dates—and, most importantly, to preserve the project end date. That's why you pause after you achieve each committed major milestone. You reassess the work ahead of you based on the lessons that you have already learned. If you have serious problems on a project, you want to expose them and work on them as soon as possible so that the damage can be minimized. This approach helps to preserve the targeted delivery date, not extend it.

Client acceptance of rolling-wave commitment model

Q28.15 But won't the client be uncomfortable with the possibility that the project end date could be delayed?

A28.15 What makes a client nervous is *not* knowing that the end date may move until it is upon them. The rolling-wave commitment model helps expose problems sooner and gives the client early warning so that the client can reevaluate its needs and make the best business choices.

Contingency buffer within first major milestone window

Q28.16 What else can you tell me about the rolling-wave commitment model?

A28.16 Whatever contingency buffer you have for your project, put a bit more in the one- or two-month period leading to the first major milestone. I want you and your team to successfully achieve the first major milestone. If you don't, you will lose credibility with the senior stakeholders (e.g., project sponsor, client, senior management)—credibility that you may not be able to regain for the remainder of the project. I want your team to start off the project with a big win on the first major milestone. This helps to build up confidence and self-esteem within the team.

Q28.17   **What is the likelihood that a project team will be able to repeatedly achieve its next major milestone?**

A28.17   Very high. When milestones are set every one or two months apart (versus every three or four months), people tend to be more comfortable with them. I expect the project team to do whatever is reasonable to achieve each major milestone. Some members of the project will probably have to work harder and smarter as they approach the major milestone date. Some overtime hours may also be required. The objective is to achieve the major milestone. If heavy overtime is required as the team nears the committed date, then the team needs to have a chance for rest and relaxation afterwards. A little-to-no overtime period at the start of the next major milestone cycle helps provide much-needed R&R.

Likelihood of achieving major milestones

Q28.18   **If you expect there may be some overtime required to achieve the next committed major milestone, would you immediately ask the project team to work some overtime to balance the overall overtime hours to be worked across each week of the one- to two-month period?**

A28.18   Typically, no. Although I am quite passionate about meeting commitments and getting the job done successfully, I am not a fan of heavy overtime. My experience runs counter to conventional wisdom. Conventional wisdom often supports directing project members to work overtime early in the project if you suspect that it will be required later in the project. My experience, however, shows that if team members work overtime early in a project, they will work even *more* overtime at the end. Why? Because management and the client see that the project team can take on even more work because it meets its commitments—though the commitments were met in the first place be-

Avoid working overtime early

cause of overtime. I favor little or no overtime at the start of each one- or two-month period before the next committed major milestone.

Applying model to project with a hard-stop end date

Q28.19 The rolling-wave commitment model appears to have merit for a project that can allow the end date to move, but it doesn't seem like a good approach for a contracted project where the delivery date is committed in writing. Do you agree?

A28.19 No, I do not agree. In fact, this model should *especially* be used for projects with a committed end date. The model allows you to discover and work problems earlier, thus helping to protect the end date. Here's a story that may help clarify my view.

An international company asked me to conduct a two-day workshop for 12 of their project managers and to conduct a half-day workshop the following morning for the senior executives, including the president, several senior VPs, and other VPs. During the half-day workshop, I was to present a summary of the main points I'd shared with the 12 project managers.

I led the two-day workshop for 12 alert, inquisitive project managers. Then I conducted the summary workshop for the senior management team. About an hour and a half into the summary workshop, the executives were saying among themselves, "This guy is really good. We should have had him here years ago." That is, until I told them that I taught their 12 project managers to stop committing to end dates that are more than two or three months away. Some of the executives were furious. Here is a portion of the dialogue between me and an overly heated senior VP.

Senior VP: *It's terrible that you taught our PMs not to commit to end dates. Are you aware that most of our business is conducted via contracts?*

Neal: *Yes, I am.*

Senior VP: *Are you aware that contracts are legal documents and what goes in them must be achieved?*

Neal: *I am.*

Senior VP: *Are you aware that we place committed end dates in those contracts?*

Neal: *I am.*

Senior VP: (Looks at me with contempt—and gloats a bit.)

Neal: *I need your help with something. Would you please identify five projects that actually completed on their original dates as documented in their contracts?*

Senior VP: (Remains quiet, but is red-faced and fidgety.)

Neal: *I'll wait. I am in no hurry. I am being paid by the hour.* (Pauses for a moment.) *I thought you said that contracts are legal documents? I thought that I heard you say that you place committed end dates in those documents and those dates must be met? Yet you are not meeting those dates—any of them! It appears that you are speaking out of two sides of your mouth. You say one thing, but practice another. You are the problem. I know you don't mean to be, but the culture that you have cultivated here has caused the problem. When I walk your hallways and encounter project managers, I ask them if they will meet their committed end dates. They always say, "I have to." I reply, "I know you have to, but will you?" They don't want to answer. They have been conditioned to believe that committed end dates cannot be missed, so they are fearful of bringing up any bad news that might indicate a slippage in the projects. What happens is that for 90 percent of the project duration, they report that they are on schedule. And for the remaining 90 percent of time, they say they need one more month . . . then one more month . . . then one more month, and so on. Your culture here encourages your project managers to lie—to withhold the truth. You encourage them to sweep problems* *under the rug. I have been teaching your PMs that we want to know our problems so that we can address them as quickly and as responsibly as the business requires. I am here to help you, the other executives, and all the project stakeholders to look good and develop a culture that supports the consistent success of the business. The rolling-wave commitment model can help you achieve this goal.*

Client acceptance of model

Q_{28.20} Is it typical for your clients to have trouble buying into the rolling-wave commitment model?

A_{28.20} Many of my clients were uncomfortable when we first began to discuss the rolling-wave commitment model because of my admonition "Do not commit to end dates that are more than two or three months away." However, most clients have embraced this methodology with great results. A few clients have adopted the model with only one twist: They do not want their project members to refer to the project end date as a "target"—although they are okay with all other major milestones being labeled as targets.

Q_{28.21} How do clients in general feel about the rolling-wave commitment model?

A_{28.21} After clients understand the concept, they typically prefer the rolling-wave commitment model. They see that the model gives them a window into potential or real problems much earlier so that they can be involved in deciding the best business solutions. Many clients have said that they have for years lived with the fear of being told at the proverbial "eleventh hour" that the delivery date will not be met. They see that this model reduces surprises and increases the camaraderie among all project stakeholders.

Using PM tools

Q_{28.22} As a project manager, should I personally construct the project schedule plan using project management tools?

A_{28.22} No, not in most cases. If you do the math, you will find that in most cases, it is far more cost-efficient and productive for an organization to hire one or more "project analyst" types to support PMs. Not only are project analysts far less expensive to hire than project managers, but project analysts will learn to be far more efficient with PM tools because doing so is one of their specialties. However, the PM must still approve all items that are added, deleted, or changed in a project schedule plan. The project analyst's job is to support the PM in any manner necessary to help the PM be successful.

Q_{28.23} **When defining the duration of activities for a project plan, how much time should I allow for each one?**

A_{28.23} In most cases, activities (also called "tasks") should last one week or less. This is because projects typically should be tracked weekly. Of course, depending on the activity, some could last a day or less. For example, for a project in which a company's data records are converted to a different format over a weekend, the duration of an activity could be measured in hours or minutes.

Duration of activities

Q_{28.24} **It can be really difficult to plan some activities to last a week or less. Is it okay if some activities are two weeks or more in duration?**

A_{28.24} Do your best to define activities as lasting one week or less when laying out a plan to achieve the next major milestone. It may be all right for some activities to last two weeks, but work to make that the exception rather than the rule. Of course, those activities that are more than one major milestone away from where the project stands today are not expected to be defined so granularly; therefore, many of those activities can be defined as more than a week in duration.

Remember, the rolling-wave commitment model helps here: You are not expected to be able to define activities to one week's duration or less unless those activities reside in the portion of the schedule plan that is leading up to the committed major milestone.

Creating a written plan

Q28.25 Should I create a written plan for work I have committed to, even though I am not required to do so?

A28.25 Yes. The plan gives you something to pace yourself against. Without a plan, it is nearly impossible to know if you are on schedule. It also helps ensure that your plan has been carefully thought through. You shouldn't plan well because you are told to; you should do so because it is the best business approach.

Completing activities on time

Q28.26 How important is it that project activities or tasks are completed on time?

A28.26 Somewhat important. In the rolling-wave commitment model, the focus is on major milestones. This is the best method to manage projects. If you can achieve the milestones, you have a great likelihood of achieving the project end date. There may be dozens—sometimes hundreds—of activities that must be completed to achieve a major milestone. Although I certainly would like activities to be completed on time, I am not obsessed with *every* activity being completed on time. I am determined, however, that major milestones complete on time.

If an activity may be late, determine if its lateness will cause any damage. Plans should be in place to limit this collateral damage so that it does not delay the corresponding major milestone date.

Defining completion criteria for activities

Q28.27 Is it overkill to define the acceptance (completion) criteria for every activity, task, or deliverable?

A_{28.27} In most cases, it is not overkill. If the activity is on the critical path and is of special importance or high risk, then setting the criteria that define its completeness is a very smart thing to do. However, if you are on a very small project that has just two or three people and is only weeks long, then it might be overkill to do so. But be careful here. If it is possible that expectations for an activity could be confused or misinterpreted, it would be prudent to define the acceptance criteria for the activity.

Q_{28.28} What's more important to control on a project: schedules or budget?

Importance of schedules versus budgets

A_{28.28} Depends on your perspective. Most commercial-related projects weight schedules as more important because of the competitive environment. Most government-related projects weight budgets as more important because of how they are funded and the need to more closely account for the disbursement of those funds. I believe that both are important and both should be sufficiently managed.

Management and PMs for most commercial-related projects I have seen claim that they manage to a budget, but they don't. Many organizations believe that if you add up how much money you spend each month and compare that to your planned budget for that month, you are managing to a budget. This is only reporting status. If you own your own company, have only one project, and have a limited budget, you know firsthand the importance of managing to a budget.

Here's another example that's close to home for all of us: the need to manage to a budget in your personal life. Most of us have limited income and must manage our personal spending against that budget. We must deliberately make choices in controlling expenses and investments so that we can maintain both short-term and long-term financial integrity.

Completing a project early and under budget

Q28.29 Should I always strive to finish a project early and under budget?

A28.29 Not necessarily. First and foremost, you should strive to finish on time and within budget. The project should have been planned with an aggressive but achievable schedule and budget. Beating that schedule and budget should not be an expectation or a likely outcome. If it is, then the schedule and budget were likely not aggressive enough.

Conventional wisdom often says that project managers should always strive to beat their schedules and budgets, but I question the business model that supports such a goal. A great deal of energy and focus are directed to mitigating obstacles and driving a project to meet its commitments. If project managers add another layer of complexity—to *beat* schedules and budgets—then that complexity can add significant risk to the project and even threaten achievement of the originally stated schedules and budgets, or delivering with acceptable quality.

Incentives to beat schedules and budgets

Q28.30 Then you are not in favor of incentives to beat schedules and budgets?

A28.30 That is the only exception. If incentives, such as monetary bonuses for the team, are in play, then I expect project managers to stretch themselves and their teams. I still believe that such stretching can add risk to the project, but if senior stakeholders offer bonuses, that is a signal that *they* accept the additional risk. If senior stakeholders stand to gain great benefit from improved schedules and budgets, they should seriously consider offering such incentives. They can be a great win-win-win for the client, senior stakeholders, and project members.

Q 28.31 Is a project's final deliverable "finished" when it is delivered to the client or when it is accepted by the client?

A 28.31 A project's final deliverable is considered complete and accomplished when it has met the acceptance criteria that were established and agreed to well before the delivery—preferably when the project was originally being planned. Many projects do not have well-defined acceptance criteria, which is a major mistake that can cause great long-term hardship to both the client and the deliverer. Of course, acceptance by the client of the final deliverable likely will not constitute completion of the *project*. There may be many more activities defined in the project plan that must be completed, such as training, support, and project closeout.

Q 28.32 As a project manager, how should I obtain the needed people resources for my project?

A 28.32 The process can vary widely depending on the culture within an organization or company, but I favor project managers obtaining people resources from resource managers. For example, as projects are being planned, project managers request subject-matter experts (SMEs) from the appropriate resource managers. These SMEs then participate with the project manager in the initial planning of the project. The SMEs, in turn, work closely with their resource managers to acquire the needed project members with the appropriate skills.

Q 28.33 What if a resource manager won't help? She says she has no one available to assign to my project.

A 28.33 If you have an approved and funded project, then the resource manager is obligated to obtain the needed skills. If you believe that she will not cooperate or is dragging her feet, then you must escalate so that higher-ups are aware of the problem. Ultimately, it's your project, and you will be held accountable for its success—*don't ever forget that!*

Applying a contingency buffer

Q28.34 Should a project plan have a contingency buffer built in?

A28.34 Almost always. The contingency buffer—also referred to as *contingency* or *buffer*—is a designated period that is built into a plan to serve as extra time to help absorb delays that might occur unexpectedly. The buffer helps plan for the unexpected—and the unexpected will occur. Very small projects that will take just hours or days and constitute an urgent need might not have any buffer built into them because of the criticality and urgency of the project, but for almost all other projects, the buffer is essential to help ensure the project's success.

Revealing contingency buffer

Q28.35 As a project member, must I tell others how much buffer I have in my portion of the project plan?

A28.35 Only if you're asked. But if you are asked—and I would be surprised if your project manager, project sponsor, client, or resource manager did not ask—always be truthful so that additional buffer isn't inadvertently added to your buffer, and also so that a better assessment of the risk can be determined.

Relationship between activities and contingency buffer

Q28.36 Should buffer be added only to activities that are on the critical path?

A28.36 It depends on the planning model you endorse, such as critical chain. In most cases, I recommend that you build a buffer into *every* activity in a plan, rather than adding on separate pooled buffers for the project as a whole.

Critical chain scheduling

Q28.37 How do you feel about critical chain scheduling?

A28.37 Eliyahu Goldratt's critical chain model can be quite effective. The reason I typically do not endorse it is that most organizations and companies are not project-man-agement-mature enough to effectively benefit from the model. For example, if a project has a weak project plan, weak tracking, and overall weak leadership, critical chain concepts will be lost in the chaos. However, critical chain, or some variation, could be considered on projects that are quite mature in their adherence to project management best practices and are run by a strong, seasoned leader.

Q28.38 Does contingency buffer apply only to schedules or also to budgets?

A28.38 Both. A project should have buffer built into both the schedule and the budget.

Applying contingency buffer to both schedules and budgets

Q28.39 How much schedule buffer should a project include?

A28.39 This cannot be easily answered, because the correct amount can depend on so many factors, such as the complexity of the project, whether members work locally or remotely, the state of technology being used, the maturity and skills of the project members, and the skill of the project man-ager. However, as a general rule, I like to see somewhere between 15 to 25 percent buffer added, more typically 25 percent.

Size of contingency buffer

Q28.40 But won't a 25 percent buffer move the project end date out 25 percent?

A28.40 Yes, but without an appropriate buffer to plan for the un-expected, the project schedule and budget commitments will likely be too high risk, which is not a good way to start a project.

Q28.41 Is buffer also added to compensate for scope creep that likely will occur?

A28.41 The simple answer is "no, that's what change control is all about." Arguably, buffer can cover very minor scope changes, but I wouldn't plan to use buffer that way.

Relationship of scope creep and contingency buffer

CHAPTER 29

Project Tracking

66A plan is like a living organism; it changes from the moment it was approved. It must be routinely tracked and nurtured for it to fulfill its intended objective.99

Staying in control

Q29.1 Why do we track projects?

A29.1 Simply put: Project tracking is all about *staying in control*. Project planning is about *getting in control*, but no sooner is the plan complete and approved than it begins to unravel before us. Project tracking has been compared to herding cats. The plan must be routinely tracked so that those involved understand and can compensate for the ongoing dynamics and changes occurring throughout the project.

Ineffectively run project tracking meetings

Q29.2 What should I do if my project manager is not very skilled at conducting effective project tracking meetings?

A29.2 If your domain of responsibility includes looking out for the project—not just your portion of the project—discreetly suggest to the PM changes that can help project tracking meetings run more effectively. You might also volunteer to take on some of the meeting duties to support the PM. In other words, you should constructively look for ways to help the PM and the project be more successful.

Q29.3 What if my domain of responsibility is defined more narrowly; that is, my performance is measured only as it relates to my portion of the project?

A29.3   Then, technically, you have no duty to help the PM conduct more effectively run project tracking meetings. It's important for resource managers to carefully define their employees' domains of responsibility because each project member's understanding of his obligations can affect his behavior in relation to the project.

For a moment, however, let's look at this from a different perspective. If you owned the company, what would you want an employee who has ideas on how to improve project tracking meetings to do? You would hope that the employee would get involved in a constructive way to help make the project successful.

Your willingness to go the extra mile can not only benefit the project and project team, but can also strengthen your value to your organization and company.

Q29.4   But if I help the project manager look good, isn't there a chance I won't get any credit?

Getting credit for helping the PM

A29.4   Don't expect to receive kudos for every little thing you do on a project—or in this world. I would hope that the PM would show appreciation and give you due credit. Moreover, the team would likely be aware of your contributions to the project. If you want to ensure that your efforts are recognized, you need to keep your boss informed of your actions through routine status reports and one-on-one discussions. Your boss should know about your extra contributions and let you know that you are appreciated.

Remember that many times we should do things because *they are the right thing to do*, not because we're hoping to get something out of it. Over time, you will earn the reputation that you are trying to cultivate.

Q29.5   Should I have to attend every weekly project tracking meeting run by the project manager, even if I have no new status to report?

Attending the project tracking meeting

A_{29.5} You should discuss this with your PM. The PM may mandate your presence at project tracking meetings because you might need to know what is going on and how it might affect you, or you might have information that others need to hear. If neither of these apply, and your status report is very short (or nonexistent) each week, perhaps the PM will ask you to stop by at a certain time to briefly state your status and give others a chance to ask you questions. Again, the PM makes the call. Your job is to work with the PM and suggest what you think is the appropriate level of participation to give him some options to consider.

Ensuring a method for logging project-related problems

Q_{29.6} What should I do if there is no method in place on my project for logging project-related problems?

A_{29.6} If you need to log a problem, then it is your responsibility to ensure that the problem is logged, assigned, and tracked to closure. Not having a proper logging procedure affects your domain of responsibility, so you must work with the PM to ensure an appropriate mechanism is adopted. If you personally do not need to log any problems, you still may want to talk to the PM about developing a logging system. Remember, if you owned the company, you would probably hope that your employees would make constructive suggestions to ensure the project's success (see Q&As 29.2 and 29.3).

Conducting routine project tracking meetings

Q_{29.7} Should tracking meetings be held each week, every two weeks, or monthly?

A_{29.7} For most projects, project tracking meetings should be held each week. If you wait longer than a week between meetings, you lose valuable time that could be spent identifying and working on problems. For very small projects—those that may be only days or weeks long—you should, of course, consider meeting more frequently.

Q29.8 As a project manager, I have weekly project tracking meetings, but I would also like to have brief meetings each morning to make sure the team is appropriately focused each day. Is this a good or bad idea?

A29.8 Although daily meetings are not mandatory, I believe having them is generally a good idea as long as the meetings are short—preferably 20 minutes or less—and effectively run. As PM, it's your call. Do your best to pick a time when project members are available.

Q29.9 Does it matter which day of the week is reserved for project tracking meetings?

A29.9 Yes. They should be held on Tuesdays or Wednesdays. Avoid Mondays and Fridays for many reasons, the most important being that holidays are often observed on those days and project members may take long weekends. You want to avoid having mandatory meetings on days that team members are likely to be out.

I like to reserve the day immediately after the project tracking meeting for work and escalation meetings to tie up loose ends—for example, to close drifting issues. These work and escalation meetings will fall on Wednesdays or Thursdays—whichever is the day after the project tracking meeting. (To avoid holding work and escalation meetings on Fridays, project tracking meetings should not be held on Thursdays.)

Q29.10 What exactly do you mean by reserving the day immediately after the project tracking meeting for work and escalation meetings?

A29.10 I often call this day "PM's day" (substitute the name of the PM for "PM"). When a project member makes a commitment to resolve an issue before a weekly project tracking meeting, but that issue is still unresolved by the time of the meeting, the PM schedules a meeting the next day to re- solve or help resolve the issue. By scheduling this follow-up meeting, the PM is saying that the project member had the first crack at resolving the issue before the weekly project tracking meeting. If the project member was unable or unwilling to resolve the issue, the PM does not allow the missed commitment to continue drifting. Instead, the PM gets involved to facilitate resolution of the issue, signaling to all members that they are accountable for meeting their commitments on time.

Q_{29.11} When does the project manager schedule these work and escalation meetings?

A_{29.11} Every attempt should be made to schedule them at the end of the project tracking meeting.

Q_{29.12} What if I am asked to attend one of these meetings, but my calendar is full?

A_{29.12} Change your calendar to accommodate the meeting. That's why the day after the project tracking meeting is called the "PM's day"—so that project members leave their calendars for the day as open as possible to resolve drifting issues.

Urgency of resolving problems that have drifted

Q_{29.13} What's the big deal if the issue is worked on the day after the project tracking meeting or a few days later?

A_{29.13} First of all, the issue should already have been closed. In addition, the PM cannot waste any more valuable project time and must limit any collateral damage that could harm other parts of the project. The issue has drifted too long already and cannot be allowed to drift any longer. The team needs to resolve these issues and move on.

Q₂₉.₁₄ When do action items become part of project plans?

A₂₉.₁₄ An action item is a project problem that is logged, assigned to an owner to resolve, and tracked until it is closed. When a project plan is being reevaluated after a major milestone has been achieved (see Q&A 28.10 and several subsequent Q&As in Chapter 28, "Project Plans, Schedules, and Budgets"), any action items still open and requiring weeks to resolve should be considered for inclusion in the revised project plan as activities that must be worked on and tracked. These will then be tracked along with all the other activities that make up the project plan.

Relationship between action items and project plans

Q₂₉.₁₅ As a project manager, must I listen to the full status of each member during the project tracking meeting?

A₂₉.₁₅ Typically, no. You want project tracking meetings to be as short as reasonably possible. Focus mostly on status reports from those members who have activities that are coming due or who have specific issues that need attention.

For example, if you have six attendees, you may choose to hear from only two or three of them—those who are in the critical path or are in important or urgent situations. The status reports from other attendees are important, but you can read them after the meeting. After reading the reports, if you have any questions or concerns, you can meet individually with project members.

Most project tracking meetings that I have witnessed last too long and waste a lot of project members' valuable time. As PM, you are still accountable for catching up on all team members' status—but do so outside the tracking meeting. Not only does this approach save time, but it also sends the message that the team should focus on the most important issues in project tracking meetings.

Selecting status to be presented

Addressing open action items

Q29.16 As a project manager, should I make sure that every open action item is discussed in each tracking meeting?

A29.16 No. This can be a big waste of time. Let's say you typically have 30 open action items. I suggest you determine the most important ones to discuss—maybe the top five—and review the status of the other 25 action items outside of the meeting. Preferably, the project members who own the 25 action items can update their status in a community intranet database. Addressing only the most pressing action items in your tracking meeting can save valuable time, and it makes you more effective in conducting project tracking meetings and managing the project.

Ground rules for project tracking meetings

Q29.17 Do you have any ground rules for project tracking meetings?

A29.17 Yes, a few short ones:

- **Come on time.** It is essential that everyone comes to the meetings on time and does not leave early—except in justifiable cases.
- **Come prepared.** Be ready to discuss your latest status and to work with others in the meeting as needed.
- **If an activity may be late or is already late, then address:**
  - Why it is late or potentially late
  - Areas of the project that will be affected
  - A recovery plan
  - Whether you need help.
- **Resolve time-consuming problems outside of the meeting.** I believe that project tracking meetings are not working meetings, but if a problem can be resolved within two minutes, then go for it. It can be far more expedient to resolve some issues now than to wait until after the meeting.
- **Raise your hand if the meeting seems to be going off track.** This technique gets all meeting members involved in helping meetings stay focused.

Q29.18 I have noticed as a general rule that project managers who conduct effective project tracking meetings tend to have more successful projects. I've also observed the opposite: Project managers who run consistently ineffective meetings tend to have less successful projects. Do your experiences match mine?

Relationship between well-run meetings and well-run projects

A29.18 Yes. The discipline exhibited by the PM and project members in this meeting is directly related to the discipline that can be expected from them throughout the project. If the PM doesn't insist that members come to meetings on time and prepared, if members are repeatedly late on their deliverables yet have no recovery plans, and if they are not forthcoming about their problems and whether they need help, I see a project headed for failure. An experienced, successful PM can sit through one project tracking meeting, study its exhibits and observe the actions of the PM and project members, and walk away with a reasonable sense of whether the project is under control or is on the path of crash-and-burn.

Q29.19 Should I ever hold back information from my boss, the project sponsor, or the client?

Selecting information to report upward

A29.19 Yes, but be careful here. I expect you to demonstrate integrity. Don't ever lie or mislead. But sometimes you should validate data before broadcasting that "the sky is falling." Perform due diligence—but do it quickly. Do not hang on for long to what might be important and timely news. If the news leaks out to senior stakeholders before you have informed them, your credibility can be hurt. On the other hand, if you inform them too quickly and later discover that the news is not as significant as you first thought, this too can affect your credibility. Keep in mind that once you claim that the sky is falling, be prepared to be "helped" far more than you want to be.

Finding fault versus solving the problem

Q 29.20 When there is a problem, how important is it to identify the person who caused it?

A 29.20 The first order of business is to solve the problem. It's all about business, not emotion or pinning the blame on someone. The second order of business is to ensure that the problem will not happen again. (Many projects and organizations are not mature enough to stop problems from recurring.) By the time the problem has been identified, everyone likely knows who caused it. We all make mistakes. Let's learn from them and move on.

"Trusting" commitments from others

Q 29.21 Is it okay to trust that others will do what they say?

A 29.21 No, not in most cases. Most people working on projects will not intentionally lie, but most of us are eternal optimists. We mean well, but when faced with a problem we can paint ourselves into a corner and inadvertently cause problems for others. If you have a dependency on someone for something, it is *up to you* to ensure that you have an appropriate plan for tracking the progress of the dependency. (Chapter 9, "Accountability, Dependencies, and Commitments," offers additional related advice.)

Asking questions and the perception of looking stupid

Q 29.22 As a project manager, I am concerned that I will look stupid if I ask my project members too many questions. Is this something I should be concerned about?

A 29.22 If you must ask the questions to ensure that things are progressing as they should, then ask them. Don't stay quiet and assume everything is going according to plan. When the project is over and your team is going over lessons learned, a key question will be what you could or should have done sooner or differently to improve the outcome. The answer will likely be that you should have probed more—not less—to understand issues. As I have said be-fore, it's *your* project and *you* will be held accountable for its success. Do what you believe must be done to ensure a successful project. All stakeholders are depending on you.

CHAPTER 30

Scope Change Control

*66 Controlled scope changes are essential
to building the 'right' product 'right.' 99*

Q30.1 I have seen many projects suffer from unbridled scope creep. What can be done about this?

A30.1 Every project requires an effective change-control process for managing scope changes. The project manager is accountable for having such a process in place and ensuring that it is enforced. The process can be informal for very small projects or formal for large ones.

A change-control process is relatively simple to define and implement. Every change request should be processed through the change-control process and sized for its effect on the project in areas such as schedule, staffing, costs, quality, and customer need. Before a change request is accepted, its impact should be understood and appropriately addressed. There is no valid excuse for not having an effective change-control process.

Q30.2 What if the client requests a scope change, and as the project manager, I determine that we could "eat it" at no charge and still make all of our commitments? Should I charge for the change or perform it gratis?

A30.2 Be careful. It is not unusual for small changes to add up and sink the planned commitments. Nor is it unusual for what was perceived to be a small change to have a far greater impact than originally expected. If you truly can absorb the change, then the goodwill that can come from performing it at no charge may strengthen the relation-ship between your organization and the client. Therefore, it may be a good investment to perform the change free of charge, but be careful of setting a bad precedent. Make sure you fully understand the contract terms and condi-tions to avoid unintended consequences from making a free change. In most cases, I suggest you work with the project sponsor and legal counsel, if appropriate, before making the decision. For very minor changes, I think the project sponsor should give you some leeway to make the call yourself.

Q_{30.3} As a project manager, how can I control scope creep caused by my own team "sneaking" extra features into the product?

A_{30.3} It is your job to manage this situation. Everyone on your team must understand your ground rules and expectations for their conduct—and it's imperative that those ground rules are enforced. The rules should require team mem-bers to submit proposed scope changes through the des-ignated change-control process. If you have team leaders, charge them with enforcing this policy. Also, inform the project members' resource managers of your ground rules to elicit their support.

Where appropriate, establish "gates" that can catch changes during design reviews, product inspections, and submission of code fixes for software. If you discover a clear violation, then consider a penalty for the guilty party. This is business, and team members must remember that they are all in it together.

Scope creep caused by project members

Q_{30.4} Would you agree that scope creep is a bad thing?

A_{30.4} Typically, no. No one is smart enough to identify all the re-quirements and predict the full scope of a project the first

The need for scope creep

time. Scope changes during a certain part of the project can be welcome. They ensure that the right product is being developed and delivered. This ongoing fine-tuning is essential for the success of most projects.

The problem occurs if the project's requirements (defined problems to be solved) or the resulting scope and specifications (defined solutions to those problems) are seriously incomplete or poorly written. Poor documentation can cause product changes so overwhelming that they damage the project. Even an effective change-control process cannot manage this nightmare without serious harm to schedules and budget.

Project sponsor directs team to "eat" significant scope changes

Q_{30.5} As a project manager, what should I do if the project sponsor tells me and my team to absorb a large change request from the client that will cause great hardship for the project members and could severely harm the project's commitments?

A_{30.5} Discuss with the project sponsor in a professional manner how her decision will affect the project and your team. You may find that she recklessly overcommitted to the client, or the opposite: A great opportunity for the organization has just emerged, and a lot is riding on your making these changes. Clearly explain the negative effects of the request to the sponsor so that she can reevaluate her decision. Don't just say, "It will be hard to make those changes." Be specific about the costs to the project, its members, and the project commitments. The project sponsor must fully understand the impact of her decision.

If the sponsor still directs you to implement the changes, then that's what you must do. I suggest you also inform your boss of the situation. Bring your team together, and do your very best to rally them to the cause. Do whatever is reasonably possible to perform the request and to make the project sponsor look good. You may want to ask the project sponsor for something special for your team if it can successfully pull the change request off. Don't *expect* to get anything from fulfilling the request—but my experience shows that you will benefit from executing the request in more ways than you might expect.

Quality

“*In the business world, 'quality' and 'perfection'
are not necessarily synonymous.*”

**Achieving
perfection**

Q31.1   Should I strive to do things perfectly the first time?

A31.1   Typically, no. It is nearly impossible to do things "perfectly" the first time; however, you should do things "right" the first time. Doing things right the first time can prevent problems and save you from having to redo work later. You might have to spend a bit more time on the work up front, but investing extra time can save far more time, energy, and expense later.

**Doing things
"right"**

Q31.2   Where do you draw the line between "perfection" and doing things "right"?

A31.2   I consider "perfection" to mean doing things perfectly, that is, without flaws, errors, or mistakes that will require attention later. This level of achievement—if it is achievable at all—can be exceedingly costly in terms of time and money. But doing things "right" the first time yields a *sufficient* return on your investment of time and money. You want to perform your duties well, but not so well that the extra expense does not yield a sufficient return on that investment.

Q31.3   Can you give me an example that contrasts doing things "perfectly" with doing things "right"?

A31.3   An example can be found in defining the requirements for a new product. Ensuring that the requirements are 100 percent thorough, accurate, and understandable by the client and the party building the product will probably require an exceedingly large investment of time and money. Moreover, even though the goal was perfectly defined requirements, it should be expected that the requirements will change while the project is underway. This scope creep should be seen as positive as long as it is introduced to a project through an effective change-control process. After all, no one—I mean *no one*—can nail the requirements down perfectly the first time; some change must be expected.

Based on this simple example, working toward perfect requirements typically costs too much—perhaps double the time and costs. Developing the requirements "right" the first time, while understanding that some changes will be introduced throughout the project as the product and stakeholders evolve and mature, can be the most effective approach.

Q_{31.4} **How can I tell if I have chosen to do things "right" or "perfectly"?**

A_{31.4} I believe that you will know the difference, especially if you are working around others. Many people aren't shy about confronting a peer or subordinate who seems to be spending too much time or money performing an activity.

I am more concerned that you will err on the opposite side—that is, instead of trying to do things "right," you won't do them well enough. Making poor choices, taking shortcuts, and not doing work of an acceptable level of quality the first time are major problems. They lead to having to redo work, which drains time and money from a project.

Q_{31.5} Earlier you said that typically, you should not strive to do things perfectly. When is perfection the right thing to strive for?

When perfection is "right"

A31.5 Perfection is essential if lives are at stake—for example, if you are developing a software product that controls a person's heart valve, building a manned aircraft or a bridge that people will traverse, or performing brain surgery. You get the idea.

Understanding the level of quality to be achieved

Q31.6 How can a person determine what level of quality is expected of his work on a project?

A31.6 Most activities should have completion criteria that must be met before the task can be considered completed. These completion criteria help define the level of quality considered sufficient. In many cases, the individual is supposed to follow defined processes intended to help yield the expected level of quality.

Q31.7 If I am not sure of the level of quality I am to achieve, who can help me?

A31.7 The person or group (hereafter referred to as "person") for whom you are producing the deliverable or service is the primary person to work with to ensure that the deliverable will be of an acceptable level of quality. If the level of quality required is not apparent, work with this person until a mutual understanding and agreement has been reached. The person you work with may not be the final client. You might work with another project member who works with your deliverable and then passes it along to the next project member, and so on, until a final product has been built or service has been performed. Depending on who you are and the role you play, you can also turn to your team leader, boss, or project manager for guidance.

Being responsible for quality

Q31.8 Do you believe that each of us is responsible for the level of quality we produce?

A_{31.8} Absolutely yes! Moreover, I believe you also have some accountability for the quality of the deliverables you receive from others.

Q_{31.9} **Whoa! I should not be held accountable for the quality of someone else's work. That's outside my domain of responsibility. Why do you say that I am accountable?**

A_{31.9} How can you make commitments for work that is dependent on the quality of a colleague's work unless you also play some role in ensuring that the colleague is following an acceptable quality process? If the colleague delivers low-quality work to you, you will have a harder time meeting your commitments. Therefore, you have the duty to ensure that deliverables on which you are dependent are delivered with an acceptable level of quality.

Q_{31.10} **Can you give me a specific example of how I can do this?**

A_{31.10} Yes. Let's say that you are a software tester. You believe that your primary responsibility is to ensure that products delivered into production conform to requirements. You determine that your testing (before the delivery of a product into production) will take ten weeks, based on the number of test cases to execute, the expected quality of the deliverable into your test phase (such as the number of defects likely to be present and their severity), and the turnaround time required to fix defects, among other factors. If you have not stayed abreast of the quality processes being followed by the developers and do not know whether the product is of satisfactory quality, you cannot know if the ten-week test period you've planned will be sufficient. Why? Because the quality of the product could be far worse than you expected, requiring a longer testing period.

As a tester, you have the duty to understand and approve the quality processes committed to by the developers and to ensure that the agreed-to quality processes are being followed.

Q_{31.11} But what can I do if the person producing the deliverable does not want me "mucking around" to ensure that his work is of acceptable quality?

A_{31.11} Remember the saying: *If it is to be, it is up to me.* Heed this creed, and your contributions on projects will improve significantly. Why do you think many companies routinely "qualify" vendors? To ensure that they are following acceptable quality processes. Why should you be any different? If the quality of a deliverable can negatively affect your subsequent commitments on a project, then it's time to start taking some accountability for deliverables that can affect your domain of responsibility.

Q_{31.12} How can I do this?

A_{31.12} When a project plan is being developed, you have the opportunity to identify your dependencies and discuss the quality processes that will be followed to produce the deliverable. If you feel that the processes are weak, then play an active role in making sure they are sufficiently defined and followed. As the project progresses, remain alert in routine project tracking meetings to ensure that the appropriate processes are being followed and appropriate metrics are being reported. If at any time you need help, work with your team leader, project manager, or boss.

Determining if all problems should be fixed

Q_{31.13} Before a product is completed, should all of its problems be fixed before it is delivered to the client?

A_{31.13} Typically no, but it depends on the problem. Fixing all problems can be too costly, too time-consuming, or both. My experience shows that clients typically want the product as soon as possible. If it has a few blemishes that can be worked around and that do not prohibit the product's major features from functioning satisfactorily, the client wants it—*now*!

Q31.14 How can a project manager determine which problems should be fixed before delivering the product to the client?

A31.14 As an example, here are four questions that a project manager of a software development product can ask when the product is in the final phases of testing. In most cases, these questions should be defined in the project's test plan(s) approved by the client (or equivalent). The project manager should use her best business judgment when answering them.

The questions begin, "If I do not correct this defect, then . . . "

1. **What is the impact on the client?** That is, will this problem cause significant or unreasonable harm to the client?

2. **What is the effect on my company's reputation?** Will I want this problem highlighted in industry media?

3. **How will it affect the product's profit and loss statement?** Should the problem be fixed now at a cost of about $50, or fixed after the product is in production for $5,000 or more? Will the many small fixes made after the product is in production negatively affect the potential profitability of the product?

4. **What is the impact to me, my reputation, and my career?** Will this problem make me look bad and harm my reputation going forward?

When you ask these four questions, you likely will identify some problems that must be corrected before the product is made available, as well as problems that can be corrected later. Of course, when appropriate, work closely with the project sponsor and client to ensure that you are indeed making the best business decisions.

CHAPTER 32

Post-Project Reviews

"Learning is not compulsory; neither is survival."

—W. Edwards Deming, American statistician
and quality control expert

Importance of post-project reviews

Q_{32.1} Are post-project reviews a good thing, or are they overrated?

A_{32.1} Post-project reviews are a *great* thing and are highly *under-rated!* Earlier in the book (Q&A 10.14), I identified three actions that I would mandate if I were to take over your organization; the first action was to ensure that post-project reviews are conducted on all projects meeting certain criteria. There is nothing better that an organization can do to continuously improve itself and become more competitive than to perform routine post-project reviews and apply those lessons going forward.

Definition of post-project review

Q_{32.2} What is your definition of a post-project review?

A_{32.2} A *post-project review* is the review of a completed project by all or a selected group of project members who represent all the major organizations that participated in the project. The group identifies what went right, what went wrong, and optionally, how improvement can be made on future projects. The objective is to learn from past project experiences so that future projects can benefit.

Q_{32.3} Post-project reviews are common in the project management world, but projects and organizations are not always successful in performing them. What are some of the things that are typically done wrong during post-project reviews?

A_{32.3} Plenty of things are done wrong. Here's a short starter list of the *right* way to do things:

- ***Post-project reviews must be a mandated part of an organization's project management methodology.*** Post-project reviews must become part of the culture being developed within an organization. The philosophy should be that the organization is never "good enough" and that all members must continuously look for ways to improve how the business of projects is conducted.
- ***Resource managers should not attend the post-project review.*** Their presence often causes others in the meeting to "clam up" and not be as forthcoming in helping to identify areas in which they could have performed better.
- ***The project manager should not conduct the post-project review.*** Instead, an outside project manager—preferably one who is a trained facilitator—is typically a better choice to run the meeting.
- ***Do not focus exclusively or primarily on those things that went wrong—pay as much attention to the things that went right.*** Let's not just fix the problems—let's take note of the good things and ensure that they are not overlooked on future projects.
- ***Do not solve the identified problems during the post-project review.*** Trying to solve problems now guarantees that the meeting will become rushed and will be far less effective.
- ***Do not attempt to solve most of the problems identified.*** After the review, focus primarily on the top three problems and the top three actions that were performed well.
- ***Formally report the post-project review results to senior management.*** Allow the review team to get face time with senior management and to show man-

agement that the team cares about moving the business forward.

- ***Do not overlook the importance of applying the lessons learned to future projects.*** Performing a post-project review is important, but applying the lessons learned to future projects is far more important.

Resource manager as project manager

Q32.4 Wow! According to your list, my organization does many things wrong when we conduct post-project reviews. You say that resource managers should not attend post-project reviews, but what if the resource manager is also the project manager?

A32.4 As I discuss elsewhere in the book (Q&A 1.24), a person should not be—in most cases—both a resource manager and a project manager. This is but one reason mixing the roles should be avoided. But in your case, if the resource manager is also the project manager, I would prefer that she participate in the meeting because she brings value as the project manager.

Attendance of resource manager

Q32.5 As a resource manager (but not a project manager), I feel the need to participate in post-project reviews to better understand how my employees performed. What do you think?

A32.5 Technically, resource managers have the right to attend any business meeting, but this is the only time I ask that you back off. Your absence will almost surely help the free flow of ideas. You will have access to the post-project review results and the final report after the meeting, so you will likely get the information about your employees that you're looking for. The difference is that the written results will not report any emotions that may have surfaced during the review.

PM conducting post-project review

Q32.6 In my organization, the project manager often conducts his own post-project reviews. Why is this to be avoided?

A32.6 Many project managers have difficulty separating their role as project manager from the neutral role of post-project review facilitator. A project manager often believes that nearly all problems are his fault, either directly or indirectly. Furthermore, the project manager tends to be too close to the problems, is perhaps a bit biased, and can become judgmental. Also, project managers facilitating their own post-project reviews often tend to defend their own actions. Facilitators are not judges; their opinions are outside the scope of their duties as facilitators. An outside facilitator is far more likely to be objective in conducting the meeting.

Q32.7   **Would you prefer that the project manager not participate in the review?**

PM participation in review

A32.7   No. The project manager should participate throughout the review and will likely be the most valuable participant. The PM is the only person who sees the entire project and has interfaced with most, if not all, of the project members.

Q32.8   **Why is it a bad idea to have the project team also solve the problems that they identify during the review while they're gathered together?**

Solving problems during the review

A32.8   The project being reviewed (or the portion of the project thereof) is over. The project members are now working on new duties—and may already be behind in their work. The review should take as little of their time as possible. Also, project members may suggest the first solutions that come to mind if they're expected to solve problems during the review. This is not a time to propose half-baked solutions to problems that could cause serious harm to future projects. An organization is far wiser to assign individuals or teams to solve these problems after the post-project review—when they can be more thoughtfully studied.

Q32.9   **The post-project reviews that I have attended usually identify some 20 to 50 problems that need to be worked on. Why do you say to focus primarily on the top three problems and the top three actions that were performed well?**

Addressing the top three problems and the top three noteworthy items

A₃₂.₉ Most organizations make a big, big blunder. With good intentions, they attempt to assign and solve most, if not all, of the problems that are identified. The result is that countless folks are assigned problems to solve, but almost none of the problems are ever really solved and closed. There is little enforcement and follow-up, and the many problems assigned seem to lose their importance and urgency when compared with the everyday challenges of ongoing projects. In short, we attempt to boil the ocean and then . . . give up.

When an organization focuses on solving just its top three problems, it is far easier to stay focused and effectively address them. If an organization would fix only the top three problems identified from each project's post-project review, that organization would make giant leaps forward in applying lessons learned.

Participation of clients

Q₃₂.₁₀ Should the client participate in the post-project review?

A₃₂.₁₀ Yes, if the client is internal to your company. If it's an external client, perhaps yes, if you have a good working relationship. If you have a tenuous relationship with your external client, no. External clients can be tricky because you do not want to allow them to hear you admit to making mistakes on a project—this information could be pivotal if a client initiates litigation.

Always obtain advice and counsel from the project sponsor and possibly your organization's legal counsel before including an external client in the post-project review. On several occasions, I have recommended that project teams not conduct a post-project review at all. These were cases in which their clients were considering litigation, and if a post-project review were performed, its report could be subpoenaed to support their clients' cases.

Q_{32.11} If an internal client caused big problems for the project, should I include the client in the review?

A_{32.11} If the client is included in the review, it's very possible that he may feel as if he is under attack, and the review could turn into a disaster. If you suspect this is a possibility, conduct a review without the client. Afterwards, conduct a mini-review with the client, where the environment can be more easily controlled and less threatening. (By the way, the facilitator is fully responsible for ensuring that a review does not turn ugly.)

Q_{32.12} Should vendors and contractors participate in post-project reviews?

Vendor and contractor participation

A_{32.12} Typically yes, if you and your organization have long-term and good working relationships with them.

Q_{32.13} How important is the facilitator in ensuring a successful post-project review?

Importance of facilitator

A_{32.13} The facilitator is critical. He must have strong leadership skills to drive the meeting from start to finish. Also, the facilitator must have strong people skills—soft skills—so that he can create and enforce a non-threatening, participatory, constructive environment that feels safe for all participants.

Q_{32.14} Briefly, how do you conduct a post-project review?

Conducting a post-project review

A_{32.14} I have conducted these reviews in many ways. Here is the process I typically employ:

- *Make sure everyone on small projects—and representative members from large projects—is invited to attend.*

- *Attempt to make the event enjoyable for all; cater in lunch if possible.*
- *Introduce the objective of the post-project review, list ground rules to be followed, and explain how the review will be conducted overall.*
- *Set up two flip charts, one for "praise," the other for "improvement."* Assign a scribe to list brainstormed items on the flip charts. (The scribe should not be a member of the project.) As the charts are filled, attach them to the meeting room walls so everyone can see them. The scribe should only add items to these charts after the facilitator has told him to do so.
- *Create a high-level chart that represents the processes followed on the project.* Use this chart to take everyone down memory lane, beginning with the early processes and ending with the last project processes. This chart will be a catalyst for generating ideas for the praise and improvement lists.
- *After completing the brainstorming, select the top three items from the praise list.* Do the same with the improvement list.
- *After the meeting, prepare a relatively brief report that can be archived for others' reference.* Present the results to management; assign people to work the top problems.

(This topic is treated in more detail in *Neal Whitten's No-Nonsense Advice for Successful Projects*, Chapter 35, "Conducting a Post-Project Review.")

Duration of post-project review

Q32.15 How long do you expect a post-project review to last?

A32.15 Anywhere from two hours to one day, but never more than a day. Remember, the primary focus is on finding the top three items to praise and to improve. Small teams of two or three members, on projects lasting two to three months, may be able to complete the review in about two hours.

Q32.16 I am a project manager on a two-year project. Should I wait until the end to perform a post-project review—or perform mini-reviews along the way?

A32.16 It is a good idea to conduct post-project reviews at least every six months or so on long-running projects. These reviews could be called post-phase reviews. This approach enables you to identify lessons learned while they are still relatively fresh in the minds of the project members and allows you to benefit from some of the lessons as you move on to the next phase of the project. Under the rolling-wave commitment model discussed in Chapter 28, "Project Plans, Schedules, and Budgets," performing a mini-post-milestone review every month or two can benefit your project as plans for upcoming major milestones are reevaluated.

Q32.17 In my organization, we often perform post-project reviews, but seldom do a good job of applying the lessons learned. Any ideas to help ensure that follow-on projects apply these lessons?

A32.17 Here are some ideas, several of which have been mentioned earlier in this chapter:

1. ***Do not solve the identified problems during the post-project review.*** Team members will not feel motivated to solve them. They will feel rushed, and the solutions will not be the best.

2. ***After the post-project review, choose selected members across the organization to address the top three problems to fix and the top three actions that were performed well***—hereafter called the *top six items*. The objective is to identify how to institutionalize improvements to processes and your organization's culture so future projects can benefit.

3. ***Resource managers should look over all the remaining lessons learned beyond the top six items*** and determine which of the items, if any, should be addressed within their own domains. Resource managers are responsible for improving the productivity, quality, and work culture of their domains (typically called departments).

4. ***Assign action items on new projects to address the relevant top items from recent post-project reviews*** if those items have not yet been institutionalized across the organization.

5. ***Create a three-member new-project review board*** to ensure that future projects benefit from the lessons learned on past projects.

Resource managers reviewing all lessons learned

Q32.18 As a resource manager, what duty do I have to help implement the lessons that were *not* designated as the top six items?

A32.18 As a resource manager, you represent the foundation of the organization and company. Project managers come and go as each project starts and finishes, but you are a permanent fixture on the organizational scene and should always try to improve the status quo. Your employees should learn from their most recent projects and apply those lessons to future projects. For projects in which your employees participated, you must review all the lessons learned from each post-project review and search for those that can be applied within your domain of responsibility. Your employees' productivity, the quality of their work, and your department's culture should continue to improve from project to project.

Assigning lessons-learned action items on new projects

Q32.19 As a project manager starting a new project, what duty do I have to work on the top six items from recent post-project reviews that have not yet been institutionalized across the organization?

A_{32.19} The top-three most harmful problems and the top-three most helpful actions from recent past projects have been identified. Now your job is to open action items on your project that appropriately address this important data. Do not wait for the organization to address these problems; address them now at the start of your project.

Q_{32.20} **As a follow-up to the last question, should these problems be addressed only for my project, or is it my duty to address them across the whole organization?**

A_{32.20} You are to address these items only as they relate to your domain of responsibility. If that domain is only your project, then your duty stops there. Typically, more time and energy are needed to solve problems outside the scope of your project—time and energy you likely do not have. Of course, if you do have the bandwidth to address these items on a broader scale, doing so will not only benefit your organization, but can also help your career. But be careful that you do not expand outside your domain of responsibility at the expense of performing well within your domain.

Q_{32.21} **What do you mean by creating a three-member new-project review board to help follow-on projects apply lessons from past projects?**

Three-member new-project review board

A_{32.21} Picture this: Three project managers—PM1, PM2, and PM3—form a new-project review board. You are a project manager—PM4—who is starting a new project. As part of your organization's project management methodology, you must go before the new-project review board and convince them that you have studied the most recent post-project reviews of projects with some relevance to yours and have learned lessons from those projects. That is, the major problems from those projects will not occur on your watch, or if they do, they will be lesser in magnitude. If the new-project review board is not convinced that you have done your homework or that you have not sufficiently applied those lessons, then the board will not allow you to move on to the next phase of your project. Instead, you must convince the board that you are learning and satisfactorily applying those lessons going forward.

Q32.22 Is the new-project review board made up of permanent members?

A32.22 No, members should be rotated periodically, say every three months or so. This allows project managers both on and off the board to benefit from each other's knowledge and lets the organization mature more rapidly in project management-related areas.

Make it happen!

Q32.23 I am a project manager. Any last words of advice on post-project reviews?

A32.23 Do them! Don't make the excuse that they are not mandatory in your organization. You don't need someone to force you to do post-project reviews. An organization is not likely to show significant or routine improvement if it does not pause occasionally to reflect on its performance. We must study our weaknesses and blemishes if we want to become the best. Be a leader. Make it happen!

CHAPTER 33

Surveys of Client Satisfaction

❝The client's satisfaction with your product or service is a far better measure of your effectiveness and success than your own biased assessment.❞

Q₃₃.₁ As a project manager, should I survey my clients on how well my project and I are meeting their expectations?

Conducting client surveys

A₃₃.₁ Yes. If you do not routinely survey your clients for feedback, then you cannot really know what they think about your performance and whether or not you are meeting their expectations. My experience shows that most PMs who do not use surveys believe that their clients are 75 percent to 95 percent satisfied. But in most cases, the satisfaction rating after a first survey is conducted is almost always below 50 percent.

Q₃₃.₂ Why is the client's satisfaction rating typically so low?

A₃₃.₂ Just because your client smiles at you in the morning over a cup of coffee, asks about your weekend, or returns your phone calls does not mean that she respects your project performance and results. When you say to the client, "I'll try," or "We'll see what we can do," your client hears you making a commitment, even if you do not realize that you are doing so. If your deliverables have quality defects, even "minor" ones, your client will be disappointed. Satisfying clients is about managing expectations. If you fulfill your commitments and deliver work of the expected quality, your clients are likely to be satisfied.

Administering the survey

Q_{33.3} Should the project manager develop and administer the survey?

A_{33.3} Not necessarily. The PM should ensure the survey is performed, but a project management organization (PMO), another group, or the primary client liaison from the project (e.g., the business analyst) could manage it. Surveys administered to external clients should be reviewed and approved by the project sponsor and possibly by a legal advisor. Surveys should be included in an organization's project management methodology.

Frequency of surveys

Q_{33.4} How frequently should surveys be conducted?

A_{33.4} Generally, surveys should be conducted at the end of a project or at the end of a major phase of a long-running project. As a rule of thumb, conducting a survey every three to six months should be sufficient. Conducting surveys too often dilutes their effectiveness as a communication tool and can lead to their being viewed as a nuisance. But if they are conducted too infrequently, they have little benefit to project performance.

Length of survey

Q_{33.5} How long should a survey be?

A_{33.5} Short—preferably no more than 10 questions. The format can be multiple choice, with answer choices on a graduated scale, such as "very satisfied," "satisfied," "neutral," "dissatisfied," or "very dissatisfied." There should be enough space for the client to write additional comments in response to each question. The survey should not exceed one double-sided page, but it would be most efficient if it were administered electronically.

Q_{33.6} What kinds of questions should be asked?

A_{33.6} The questions should relate to the client's satisfaction with your ability to meet commitments, communicate in a timely, accurate manner, and manage scope changes, as well as the client's satisfaction with project schedules, costs, and the quality of deliverables. You may also want to give the client the opportunity to respond to open questions, such as "What did you like least?" and "Any other comments?"

Survey questions

Q_{33.7} How should the survey results be used?

A_{33.7} Survey results should be used to measure an organization's performance improvements. The first survey sets the baseline. The organization then takes action to improve subsequent survey results, and adjusts accordingly if the next survey does not indicate improvement in certain areas. Many professionally mature organizations also use survey results as a measure of a project manager's long-term improvement and effectiveness.

Using survey results

Q_{33.8} I am not a project manager. Should I consider surveying my clients?

A_{33.8} Yes. All project members and employees have clients. We all create deliverables or perform services for someone. Clients can be either internal to the project, organization, or company; or external to the company. Your client can be in the next office, down the hallway, across the street, or halfway around the world. We all need to know how well we are performing—and strive to continuously improve our performance.

Surveying project members

Q_{33.9} Can you give me an example of how a project member can survey other project members?

A_{33.9} The following example pertains to any project comprising multiple members. In a software or IT shop, the development team on a project can survey its internal clients on the quality of the team's performance. The survey can be sent to the PM, the business analyst, the test team, the technical writing team, the training team, and others. The survey can be administered when each major milestone is completed, such as the completion of the product specifications document, the design, the coding, and the testing.

Infrequent use of surveys

Q_{33.10} If project members conducting periodic internal surveys is such a great idea, why is it rarely done?

A_{33.10} Actually, one type of survey is fairly commonly done on projects. It's often called a post-project review. Think about it: During the review, the project team typically gathers together to evaluate what went right and what could have been done better. During this review process, it becomes apparent how well project members performed their activities and tasks.

Q_{33.11} Yes, but that's at the end of a project. Why is it not common to conduct surveys specific to a team or person throughout the project?

A_{33.11} There are many reasons. Project members may not even consider doing surveys, or may believe that there is too little time. Or there may be so many problems already identified that they do not want to try to uncover more. But I believe two really big reasons are the fear of being criticized and the burden of having to add more work to one's already full plate.

Interestingly, my experience is that the few people who bother to conduct surveys with the objective of improving their performance are also people who are among the best performers and have the greatest potential in their careers.

Q33.12 Is it appropriate to automatically survey a client each time I perform a service?

Automatic surveys

A33.12 Maybe. It depends on the frequency and type of service. Perhaps it is if you are providing an infrequent service. It is not appropriate if you are providing a routine or daily service. Surveys can become bothersome and lose their impact if you expect your client to complete one with every frequent and routine transaction. However, you might want to consider allowing your client to have ongoing access to a survey so that the client can give feedback when necessary.

Q33.13 Does it make sense for a project manager to occasionally survey the members of a project on how well he is performing?

PM surveying opinions of project members

A33.13 This can be most helpful. However, it takes courage, boldness, and a great deal of professional maturity to voluntarily submit one's performance to criticism by one's team members. Although most project members will not abuse the survey, professional immaturity could rear its ugly head.

I challenge any PM to periodically offer such a survey to your project members. If you do—and you learn from and improve your performance based on the survey results—you are the type of PM who will have a great career.

Q33.14 Any closing thoughts about surveys?

Surveys can be most helpful

A33.14 Yes. If you are a PM who really cares about your customers, your performance, and the performance of your project members, be bold enough to conduct surveys. Surveys can help you help your customer. They are a win-win! Moreover, if you owned the company, would you want your employees to complete these surveys to help improve the business? If your answer is "yes"—and it will be—then make it so.

PART FOUR

Introducing These Topics and Discussions in Your Organization

"Let's not talk about it—let's walk it!"

Q₁ This book certainly covers a broad range of topics that affect project members and employees. I wish that my organization would openly discuss and address these types of issues. If it did, I believe that my organization would be far more effective in building our products and performing our services. Moreover, there would likely be improvement in key areas such as leadership, accountability, personal initiative, productivity, professional maturity, employee morale, costs, schedule commitments, customer satisfaction—and so much more. Do you have any ideas on how to start discussions on these topics in my organization?

Methods to promote discussions

A₁ There are a number of methods that can help you initiate discussions about these topics and issues and derive solutions. Notable methods include:

- Study groups
- Culture-training classes
- Performance-expectation workshops.

Let's discuss these methods and then address the need for obtaining management support.

STUDY GROUPS

Q₂ What do you mean by study groups?

Definition of *study group*

A₂   A *study group* is a group of people who routinely get together to discuss organizational and project management
issues and solutions. The group can be made up of members of a project, members of a department headed by a
resource manager, or members from across an organization. Here are some general guidelines that can be used to
get you started:

- **The group can be made up of three to ten people.**
  You want the group to be small enough so that all attendees feel they can easily participate in the discussions.
- **The group plans to meet at routine intervals,** anywhere from once a week to once a month. I recommend
  weekly meetings if the team is relatively new at working
  together or if there are a lot of issues prohibiting the
  team from working well together.
- **The duration of a meeting is typically one to two
  hours.** If possible, consider having lunch catered to help
  extend the length of the meeting. This also might increase the likelihood that the members will attend.
- **Each meeting can focus on a general topic,** such as
  accountability, dependency, and commitments; awards
  and recognition; ethics and integrity; leadership styles,
  attributes, and behaviors; or personal development, job,
  and career. If the topics for discussion are identified beforehand, then the members can be more prepared to
  participate by bringing their own questions and problems for discussion. However, selecting the topics at random at some meetings can be a refreshing change.
- **Typically, the meeting is facilitated by a resource
  manager, project manager, or team leader**—someone who understands behaviors that can help promote
  a successful and effective business culture.

**Choosing a
facilitator**

Q₃   I wouldn't think that it is a good idea to have a resource
manager facilitate these meetings. The presence of
management could inhibit the free flow of ideas and
discussions. Do you agree?

A₃   If members are gathered from a department or from across an organization, then a resource manager (RM) is a good candidate to facilitate the study group. The RM will likely have instant credibility because she understands the culture that the group should be striving to achieve. If the members all come from a single team or project, then the corresponding team leader or project manager could facilitate the study group. Here again, an RM could still be a great choice as a facilitator.

As for your concern that a manager's presence may cause some members of the group to withdraw—yes, this could happen. However, an effective facilitator can win over most participants so that they all understand that candor and openness are truly in everyone's best interest and that they are all in this together.

Q₄   Should a report be produced after each meeting?

A₄   Not necessarily. It depends on the level of formality you want the meetings to have. However, I suggest that a list be made of the topics, issues, and solutions discussed so that the team can better remember the lessons learned and have a handy "cheat sheet" to refer to.

Creating a repository for later reference

Q₅   Should this book be an integral part of the meetings?

A₅   In the beginning, this book should prove quite helpful. (After all, it contains this section on how to start a study group.) It also lists common topics and issues and their corresponding solutions, which can help you get discussions started. However, your group might want to discuss some topics in more depth and tailor them to your environment, as well as add new topics.

Using this book as a starting point

CULTURE-TRAINING CLASSES

Q₆   What are culture-training classes?

A₆   Culture-training classes are described in Chapter 27, "Project Culture." A culture-training class typically relates to a specific project. It can be a great forum to discuss the topics and issues in this book that are especially interesting to the members of a project. However, culture-training classes can also benefit all the members of an organization. I have worked with organizations that have made these classes mandatory for all members of the organization. Culture-training classes can be a great method to help define, establish, and nurture the desired culture across an organization.

PERFORMANCE-EXPECTATION WORKSHOPS

Definition of performance-expectation workshops

Q₇   You also mentioned performance-expectation workshops. Can you elaborate?

A₇   A *performance-expectation (PX) workshop* is typically a one-day workshop with 10 to 20 participants. Before the workshop, each participant lists two or three important organizational issues in the form of questions. Each participant submits his questions to the workshop facilitator, who compiles them in a single list and eliminates duplicates (some rewording of the questions is done if necessary). The questions are then shared at the one-day workshop, and the best solution is derived for each question.

Sample problems to discuss

Q₈   Can you list some sample items that often appear on the final list?

A₈   The items can vary significantly from company to company, organization to organization, and project to project depending on the attributes of the participants in the group—such as professional maturity, experience, culture, and comfort with working with one another. Moreover, many items that would appear on the group list might be specific to the nature of the work performed by the group.

Here are some common topics that any group could come up with:

- How to say "no" when "no" is the right answer
- How best to identify and manage priorities throughout the day, especially conflicting priorities
- How to run more effective meetings
- What are the behaviors that leaders expect from their members?
- How to stay positive in a negative environment
- How to make projects more effective by applying lessons learned from past projects
- How to hold someone accountable for his commitments
- How to escalate issues to closure
- How to avoid being "too soft"
- How to manage conflict
- How to give positive reinforcement
- How to deal with an uncooperative stakeholder
- How to deal with too many meetings
- How to get work done without being a tyrant
- How to determine one's domain of responsibility
- What are the duties of a project manager or resource manager?
- How to motivate project members
- What is the best style of leadership: consensus, democratic rule, or other?

Q₉ Why are PX workshops only one day long?

Length of workshop

A₉ Many members of a project or organization find it difficult to take time away from daily responsibilities for training, but most can manage to get away from the job for one day. Also, these workshops are rather intense for all the attendees; everyone participates fully by sharing views and questioning other participants' solutions. Finally, these workshops are kept to one day because many topics and issues requiring considerable thought and introspection will be discussed, and participants might feel overloaded if more time was given for discussion. For most members, one day is long enough!

| **Number of workshop participants** | **Q**10 | Why do you recommend 10 to 20 members participate in PX workshops? Why not hold a workshop for the five-member team of a small project, or for 30 participants from across an organization? |

A10 If more than 20 people attend, it will be difficult for each person to fully participate in the discussions. If fewer than 10 people attend, then fewer ideas for creatively tackling problems are shared. A workshop for five members of the same team is feasible, but it may not need to be a full day long.

| **Obtaining a mix of participants** | **Q**11 | Should the workshop attendees include both management and non-management? |

A11 Yes. Non-management is the primary audience; these workshops are intended to teach the behaviors expected of them. Management should be included in the workshops so that the solutions discussed have their blessing and support. Also, management should attend so that they better understand the needs of the group and can help satisfy those needs. Each workshop should have a mixture of attendees from all levels of the project or organization. Management can learn a lot from these workshops, too.

| **Number of problems to address** | **Q**12 | How many problems should be addressed in a PX workshop? |

A12 If about 10 members attend, then each can identify three problems they would like to have addressed by the group. If about 20 attend, then each can identify two problems. The goal is to start with a base of some 30 problems. After duplicate problems are removed, expect 20 to 25 unique problems to remain on the list. The objective is to address most of these problems.

Q₁₃ Why did you say that some of the problems attendees mention may be reworded?

Editing
the list of
problems

A₁₃ The goal is to describe each problem in as few words as possible—allowing anywhere from one sentence (this is preferable) to a small paragraph. Because everyone's writing skills and styles are different, editing of the submitted problems can help them be understood more readily by the group.

Q₁₄ How much time should be given to the participants to prepare the questions?

Homework
before the
workshop

A₁₄ A few days to a week should be adequate in most organizations. Then allow a week or so to collect them, make a master list, and perform the appropriate editing. The edited list is made available to each participant a day or two before the workshop so that they can identify the items that they have the most interest in discussing. If preferred, the edited list can be presented to the participants at the start of the workshop.

Q₁₅ Any pointers on how the workshop should be conducted?

Conducting
the workshop

A₁₅ This is typically how I proceed as the workshop facilitator: Everyone briefly introduces themselves (if not all participants have met) and shares what they hope to get out of the workshop. These "expectations" help to focus the team on the objective of the workshop.

The facilitator then lays out the ground rules of the workshop. Nearly any question or problem is fair game. Attacking people is never permitted, but attacking problems is healthy and necessary. The participants are told that the correct solution to a particular problem may make clear that they are not performing as effectively as they need to or should, but they should not take this personally—it's business.

For the workshop to be most effective, we must be candid and truthful in as few words as possible. Such candor can occasionally hurt one's pride or feelings, but we must get past this. The objective is to raise the level of professional maturity and overall effectiveness of the group. These workshops can be defining moments for participants, positively affecting their future behaviors and career.

Discussing a problem

Q16 Do you recommend a particular approach to discussing the questions?

A16 Yes. I choose someone (a problem identifier) to select the first question for discussion. Then I immediately choose someone else, a problem solver, who is asked to solve the problem. The problem identifier describes the problem as he sees it. His perspective is important because some items listed likely can be interpreted in more than one way. This technique focuses on a specific view of the problem.

The problem solver states what she believes is the proper approach to resolve the problem. It can help for the problem solver to think like the owner of a company: What would an owner expect an employee in this situation to do? When you think from the owner's perspective, solutions are far more apparent. Other participants can add their own ideas for a solution. After the group has discussed the problem, I offer my views on the solutions discussed. I then identify the best solution—whether it was already mentioned, a solution I came up with, or some combination thereof. After one last opportunity for discussion, we move on to the next problem.

Selecting the next players

Q17 Is there a special technique for identifying the next person to be the problem identifier or problem solver?

A17 Yes. The first problem identifier selects the next problem identifier. Likewise, the problem solver selects the next problem solver. This random-generating process continues throughout the duration of the workshop and is another way to empower the participants. It also helps keep participants alert.

I display a list of workshop participants' names. When someone is selected as a problem identifier, I place an "I" next to the name; for a problem solver, I place an "S" next to the name. This simple technique helps ensure that no one is overlooked and that everyone has an opportunity to play.

Q18   Can new problems be added to the list once the workshop has started?

A18   Absolutely. I want all the participants to discuss issues and problems that are of special interest to them. The problem identifier can add a new problem or select an existing problem from the edited list.

Adding new problems spontaneously

Q19   What if the participants feel they cannot fully address and solve some problems that come up? How can the head of the organization weigh in on addressing these problems?

A19   I suggest the head of the organization attend the last hour of the PX workshop. At this time, the participants can ask the questions that have been queuing up throughout the workshop. The reserved hour is a great opportunity for the organization's head and the participants to communicate honestly with one another.

Participation of the head of the organization

Q20   Does the workshop end when a pre-specified number of problems have been discussed, or when the allotted time has elapsed?

A20   Typically, the workshop ends at the time it was originally planned to end. It would be rare for a group to exhaust the list of problems to discuss.

Ending the workshop

Q21   Are minutes recorded for the workshop?

A21   Yes. A scribe should be available to capture the best solutions or answers to each of the problems discussed. The scribe does not participate in the discussion and focuses fully on recording the information. After the workshop,

Recording minutes

the notes are compiled as a document in a Q&A format and approved by management to ensure that the solutions and answers represent the actions and behaviors that management endorses for the organization. The document of Q&As is revised as more workshops are performed. This way, a single document exists that can help shape the behaviors for a project, department, or organization.

Q$_{22}$ Should everyone in the organization receive a copy of the minutes?

A$_{22}$ At a minimum, everyone who participated in the workshop should get a copy of the minutes for later reference. It can be helpful for all members of a project or organization to receive a copy so that they are fully aware of the "culture" being promoted. However, this places a special burden on the scribe to ensure that both the questions and the solutions are easily understood and that a reader will not take the messages out of context. For this reason, management should carefully review the solutions to ensure that they illustrate the culture management wants to create and nurture.

Frequency of attendance

Q$_{23}$ Should a person attend more than one PX workshop?

A$_{23}$ All members of an organization should have the opportunity to participate in at least one performance-expectation workshop per year, whether it is related to a project, department, or company. Some organizations may have their members attend several workshops over the course of a year.

The frequency of attendance depends on the professional maturity of the group in question, the level of development of the desired culture in the group, the number of new members added to the group, and the effectiveness of the original workshops in covering the key issues and problems. My experience has been that most organizations need their members to participate in more than one workshop in the first year as the desired culture is being established.

Q24   Do you find that some topics are more difficult than others for participants to openly discuss—especially if management is present?

Creating a comfortable discussion environment

A24   Yes. There may be some topics that are more sensitive, but it is healthy for a group to explore these topics so that individuals can work more effectively with one another. Broaching tough topics can also help each member of the group achieve his best work and work toward achieving his personal potential within the project or organization. At the start of a workshop, it is important that each member is made to feel at ease and comfortable expressing his thoughts honestly, without fearing retribution.

Q25   Is it really reasonable to expect that 20 or 25 problems or issues can be solved in only one day?

Limiting time spent per problem

A25   Not necessarily. The objective is to articulate the behavior or solution expected for each problem discussed. However, you might be pleasantly surprised with the great progress and benefit that can come from a workshop. If a problem is relatively complex and has several steps that must be followed to derive a solution, then the group might only identify the high-level steps rather than work each step to closure. This is an empowering technique that shows the path to resolving the topic or issue, but gives the detail work to a person or small group of people after the workshop is over.

Q26   I really like the idea of PX workshops, but I am concerned that some people will not want to participate. Any ideas?

Obtaining full participation of attendees

A26   The first workshop can be made up of folks who have volunteered to participate. With volunteers, you are far more likely to have great workshop participation—and to collect suggestions for improving the effectiveness of future workshops. If you have participants who are not comfortable, then you must reach out to create an environment of openness and safety and make it easy for them to express themselves.

If you have participants who do not want to cooperate, too bad for them. They may need the workshop more than most. Reach out to them and welcome their participation. In my experience, attendees who were the most reluctant to participate often gained the most from workshops. Sometimes leadership is all about strongly nudging others to do things they need to do, but are reluctant to try on their own.

Commonsense "training tool"

Q27 It seems that the topics, issues, and problems discussed in a PX workshop are mostly about common sense—just as this book is. Do you really believe that most projects, departments, and organizations really need such a "training tool"?

A27 Absolutely yes! The members of a project or organization cannot be expected to perform in accordance with a specific, preferred culture unless that culture is well defined. We all come from different backgrounds and have different experiences, and some of those experiences have left emotional scars that we carry around for years—scars that we allow to affect our behaviors.

Even if many of the solutions or answers seem to be common sense, my experience is that most participants are unsure of the behaviors expected of them by their project leadership and management. People will perform at their best when they understand what is expected of them. This workshop helps to define those expectations.

Don't overlook the need to teach people who are just entering the workforce, as well as experienced new hires who have no knowledge of what your culture is about. And as I said earlier, project leadership and management will also learn a lot from these workshops.

This book can help

Q28 Should this book be an integral part of PX workshops?

A₂₈   Ideally, if every workshop participant reviewed the content of this book before participating in a workshop, they would likely be far more prepared to constructively participate in the discussions. So yes, the book can be a great help, but with or without the book, these workshops can be highly effective in raising the professional maturity of a group, creating the desired culture, and improving other key areas such as leadership, accountability, personal initiative, productivity, employee morale, costs, schedule commitments, and customer satisfaction.

Q₂₉   **Any other tips to consider when planning and implementing these workshops?**

Tips for planning and implementing a workshop

A₂₉   Here are more tips that can help:

- *Consider recruiting a handful of volunteers to plan and host these sessions.* The volunteer team can solicit volunteer participants for the first workshop and determine the mix of folks in each successive workshop to ensure the best cross-project or cross-organization representation.
- *Consider holding the workshops away from the routine workplace* so that attendees can remain more focused on the workshop.
- *Consider mid-morning and mid-afternoon snacks and catering lunch.* A catered lunch will not only help keep everyone around, it is a way for management to show they appreciate their employees by making this a special day.
- *Use two flipcharts (or equivalent media) with marker pens*—one for working issues and the other for parking ideas that the group will revisit later.
- *Seat attendees at tables arranged in a "U" configuration* so that group members are in the best position for eye contact and discussion with one another. The facilitator stands at the open end of the "U."

**Attendees
should feel
like they have
been helped**

Q₃₀ These workshops appear to be rather "personal" in terms of the demands they place on each participant. Has a PX workshop ever turned sour?

A₃₀ I have never seen a PX workshop that failed or came close to failure. However, there are times when some participants may be uncomfortable because they must face the truth or deliver the truth to someone else. It's essential to have a highly qualified facilitator to mitigate discomfort. Everyone should feel as if they have been helped by having attended the workshop.

**Attributes
of effective
workshop
facilitator**

Q₃₁ Are there any special attributes to look for in identifying a workshop facilitator?

A₃₁ The facilitator should be an experienced, successful resource manager or project manager with a strong working background in coaching/mentoring people and leading teams. He should have a good handle on the culture that the project or team must strive for. And the facilitator should also have strong soft skills in order to teach others professionally and constructively. Although this person could be contracted on a short-term basis from outside the company, it is best to develop these skills from within your company for the long term.

**Changing
the mix of
participants**

Q₃₂ Are these workshops only for mixed audiences of managers and non-managers?

A₃₂ No. The same kind of workshop can be held for just project managers or resource managers. Whenever like-skilled individuals gather, it benefits the entire group to discuss common issues.

MANAGEMENT SUPPORT

**Seek
management
support**

Q₃₃ Do I need management's support to implement one or more of the methods identified (study groups, culture-training classes, and performance-expectation workshops) or a related idea?

A₃₃ An individual can do a lot, but more can be accomplished by soliciting support from and working collaboratively with management. Some of the ideas, such as study groups, do not necessarily require management support—although I would recommend getting it. Other ideas, such as PX workshops, should be supported by management before they are adopted across an organization.

Q₃₄ What does management support buy me?

Benefits of management support

A₃₄ Plenty. Examples of what management support can offer include:

- *Legitimacy.* If your group, class, or workshop is a sanctioned and supported activity, members of the organization may be more likely to participate.
- *Collaboration.* Sharing ideas with management helps ensure that the results of your workshop support the organization's business objectives and strategy.
- *Funding.* Funds may be required to help support the initiative, either in a small way, such as providing meals at special meetings, or in larger ways, such as funding for contract instructors and obtaining rooms off-site.
- *Increased effectiveness.* Having to sell the idea and periodically report progress helps you fine-tune your proposal, delivery, and objectives.
- *Recognition.* Management sees firsthand your personal initiative and the contributions you are making to the overall success of the organization.

Q₃₅ Who should I work with to obtain the recommended support?

Work first with your manager

A₃₅ The first management interaction is typically with your boss. Make sure your idea passes muster with him. Once it has his support, take your idea to the next level of management, and so on, until you have reached the level of management required to get sufficient support for your idea.

Shared accountability

Q₃₆ If an organization has a weak work culture, failing to elicit the best performance from its members, is this management's fault?

A₃₆ Partially. The problem is jointly owned between management and all others—including *you*. Management is in a power position; they can choose the priorities that drive the activities and focus across the organization. They also have the power to disburse funds as they see fit to get the greatest return on investment. However, management cannot personally solve the many, many problems that come across their desks. They are in need of folks like you to propose and sell ideas to them—ideas that you are willing to own and personally drive to successful conclusions. Management, of course, wants the organization to consistently improve in those areas that matter most to the business, but they may not always know what to do or how it should be done. They welcome your ideas . . . *and your follow-through*.

Moving your organization from good to great

Q₃₇ Any last thoughts on obtaining management support?

A₃₇ The topics discussed in this book are at the core of what makes an organization the best it can be. As I have said earlier, if the members of an organization know what their leaders expect from them—and a productive, effective work environment that encourages business success as well as personal success is created and nurtured—the organization is destined for greatness. Many organizations are weak in creating and institutionalizing a deliberate culture that will set them up for continued success. Remember, although there is a lot that an individual can do, more can be accomplished by soliciting support from management. By working closely with management, you can play a bigger role, if you choose to, in moving your organization from good to great.

PART FIVE

Closing Thoughts

"Every one of us alone has the power to direct the course of our lives by choosing what actions we will or won't take. While sometimes it's easier to believe you don't have a choice, the reality is that you always have a choice to behave differently."

—Francine Ward, motivational speaker and life coach

I would like to leave you with a thought. It has to do with your behavior and your ability to choose to be and behave however you imagine and dream you can. *It's about your moment.*

The universe is a vast, vast expanse of, well, space and things. It is so large that the earth, in comparison, is virtually nothing. Earth, compared to the universe, is not even a speck of sand on a big beach. Of all the possible permutations, what are the odds that Earth would even exist in this endless universe? But it does!

Let's now look a little closer to home. What are the odds that you would be here today? I don't necessarily mean reading this book—I mean alive? The odds of your conception alone—the unique genetic combination that makes you *you*—were less than one in a million. Unlikely odds, but you are here!

But let's go back just one generation. What are the odds that both your parents would have been conceived? The answer is "less than one in a million" multiplied by "less than one in a million." This is "less than one in a million million," or "less than one in 10^{12}." Just factoring together your parents and you, the odds of your existence here today are less than one in 10^{18}—and we only went back one generation! In other words, if you truly want to see a miracle, look in a mirror. You already have overcome far worse odds than any lotto on this planet!

Where am I going with this? We all have our personal beliefs about what happens beyond this life, but one thing we cannot refute: We are here now—and we do represent a miracle. You have at least one shot throughout all of the expanse of the universe and the eternity of time by being here today. Why would you want to believe that you cannot make a difference on your projects and in your organizations (or with your family, community, or even world)?

Earlier I said, "It's not about the ability of those around you to lead; it's about your ability to lead, despite what is happening around you." Why would you want to go through your job—your life—being too soft, fearing failure, being afraid to assert yourself, being ineffective, taking abuse from others, playing the victim, not pursuing your dreams, not believing in yourself—not demonstrating the courage to make things happen? You have this one shot that you have been handed. Why blow it? Again, as Henry Ford said, "Whether you think you can or you think you can't, either way you are right."

Living your dream is a whole lot more exciting than just dreaming your life. This is your moment. It is yours to seize! Life is an adventure. Dare to partake! Now go make a *bigger* difference!

Index

mentor, 39, 108, 189–197, 227, 249

mergers and acquisitions, 243–245

methodologies and processes, 253–256

micromanaging, 42, 103, 110, 112, 134–135

milestones. *See* major milestones

mission statement, 39

mistakes, 62, 111, 125, 127, 159, 192, 231, 273, 296

monkeys, 4

morale, 13–14, 28, 103, 215, 262

motivating others, 113, 182

N

natural weaknesses, 24

"need" vs. "want," 68–70

negative attitude. *See* attitude

new-project review board, 106, 316–318

Nin, Anais, 131

"no," saying, 68–69, 136

nurturer

of people (resource manager), 23, 140

of projects (project manager), 3, 140

of products and services (project sponsor), 45

Nyberg, Lars, 67

O

"open door" policy, 170–171

overtime, working, 184–188

P

PA. *See* project analyst

Penn, William, 198

people resources, obtaining, 285

perfection vs. quality. *See* quality

performance evaluations/reviews, 6, 10–13, 32–33, 39, 50, 93, 166, 168

performance expectations workshop, 328–337

performing questionable work, 202–204

Perry, Jack, 192

persistence, 130

personal development, 218–233

personally, taking things, 55, 132, 159, 163

Plato, 269

"please," saying, 158

PM. *See* project manager

PM's day. *See* project manager's day

PM tools, using. *See* project management tools, using

PMBOK® Guide, 249–251

PMI®. *See* Project Management Institute®

PMO. *See* project management organization

PMP® certification, 249–250

poor performer, dealing with, 30–31, 114–115

post-milestone review, 315

post-phase review, 315

post-project review, 308–318

priorities, managing. *See* managing priorities

processes. *See* methodologies and processes

procrastination, 115

professional immaturity

abusing use of surveys, 323

allowing a problem to fester, 174

complaining, 151